THE STRUGGLE FOR TIBET

THE STRUGGLE
FOR TIBET

WANG LIXIONG and TSERING SHAKYA

VERSO

London • New York

First published by Verso 2009
© in the collection Verso 2009
© in individual contributions the contributors 2009
All rights reserved

The moral rights of the authors and translators have been asserted

1 3 5 7 9 10 8 6 4 2

Verso
UK: 6 Meard Street, London W1F 0EG
USA: 20 Jay Street, Suite 1010, Brooklyn, NY 11201
www.versobooks.com

Verso is the imprint of New Left Books

ISBN-13: 978-1-84467-043-7

British Library Cataloguing in Publication Data
A catalogue record for this book is available from the British Library

Library of Congress Cataloging-in-Publication Data
A catalog record for this book is available from the Library of Congress

Typeset by Hewer Text UK Ltd, Edinburgh
Printed in the USA by Maple Vail

Contents

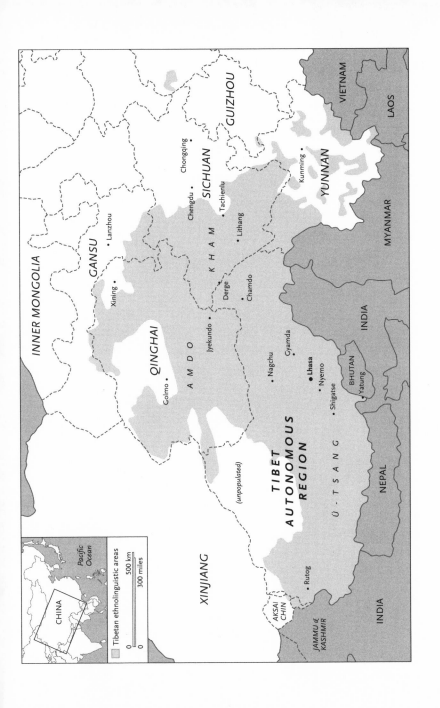

Introduction

The three characters in this book are two writers and a place—Wang Lixiong, Tsering Shakya and Tibet. All three them are outsiders, edge-dwellers. Their lives revolve around or represent those places that Theodore Roosevelt, borrowing from Tennyson, called the 'lonely lands', areas and worlds that to others seem remote, deserted, peripheral or antithetical to their own. For Roosevelt, the term glorified the work of frontiersmen and ranchers in America; he used the same term to justify his principal pleasure: killing animals in their hundreds in the plains of Africa. It took generations of writers, scholars and activists, from Henry Nash Smith onwards, to teach Americans to question assumptions about images which depict places as empty and as available for the taking, and to show the historical impact of such pretty phraseology. The three characters in this book debate, with a kind of fierce tenacity, the use of similar designations for Tibetan history. Initially they challenge each other on these issues, but increasingly they speak back to the centre and its certainties, its confidence in its assumptions and its aggressive pursuit of its objectives. In doing so, they speak about all situations where a powerful centre dominates the voices of those it perceives as outsiders.

Much commentary on Tibet, from the best to the most trivial, has focused on exposing the exoticization of that place by foreigners who have been enthralled or appalled by its religiosity, its mountains or its lack of access. Such practices have long been shown, even before the seminal work of Edward Said, to be a dressing up of the Other for consumption by an acquisitive and more powerful Self. The critics of exoticization did a great deal to show the shabby links of such practices with empire, missionaries and aggressive trade, but their writing was addressed to and about their home audiences. This is not the task of the two writers in this volume. As Shakya once pointed out, the problems of foreign misrepresentation are self-evident to Tibetans, who have no trouble distinguishing others' fantasies from their reality.[1] The issue for Wang and Shakya is Tibet, what happened there, who its inhabitants are, and what they think of what they have experienced.

That perspective has been lacking in the modern discussion about Tibet. In part, this is because it has been a conversation dominated by people external to Tibet—primarily exiles, Chinese, and Westerners. The voices of Tibetans inside Tibet are heard only in snatches and fragments. Even if the Chinese authorities allowed these voices to be fully articulated, which they rarely do, one wonders if they would be listened to. In that absence, Wang and Shakya, in their different ways, struggle to describe the Tibet that is not heard, the all-but-silent character in this triad. In this, they face the difficult intellectual tasks: to present someone else's views and history without appropriating the right to represent them.

Tibet: A half-heard voice

There was a brief period when Tibet was not a largely silent character in the West, one ripe for explanation and

---

1   See, for example, Tsering Shakya, 'Who are the Prisoners?', *Journal of the American Academy of Religion*, vol. 69, no. 1, 2001, pp. 183–9.

representation by exiles, travellers, novelists and invaders. When it was effectively independent, it spoke quite volubly. Or at least one woman did. The first English-language book by a Tibetan, *We Tibetans* (1926), was by a woman from Kham (eastern Tibet), Rinchen Lhamo. Shortly after arriving in London at the beginning of the last century (she had married a British consul stationed in Chongching), she made a forceful declaration of intellectual autonomy:

> I suppose our distant country holds little of interest for your public except for what of the strange can be written about it, and so you get a strange picture of us. The most absurd and the most scandalous things are said about us, and . . . your writers often contradict each other.[2]

Her plea fell on deaf ears, for the exoticization trend was already well established by this time. At the British Empire Exhibition held at Wembley Stadium in London in 1924, a group of Tibetans had been presented to the public dressed as lamas doing a 'devil dance', and the following year a group of what the programme described as '*real* lamas' had been brought to London to perform at a cinema before each showing of a film about Mount Everest, which in turn showed a Tibetan eating lice.[3] The Tibetan government lodged a formal complaint to the British government, no less voluble than Rinchen Lhamo's, but

---

2   Rinchen Lhamo King and Louis Magrath King, *We Tibetans: An Intimate Picture, by a Woman of Tibet, of an Interesting and Distinctive People, in which it is Shown how They Live, Their Beliefs, Their Outlook, Their Work and Play, and How They Regard Themselves and Others*, London 1926, p. 95. Cited in Tashi Tsering, *How the Tibetans Have Regarded Themselves Through the Ages*, Dharamsala 1996, p. 3.

3   Peter H. Hansen, 'The Dancing Lamas of Everest: Cinema, Orientalism, and Anglo-Tibetan Relations in the 1920s', *The American Historical Review*, vol. 101, no. 3, 1996, pp. 712–747.

it was dismissed. 'The weird and fantastic music will convey to the people in England a feeling of the mysticism and romance of Tibet', the programme declared. Since then, much of the foreign literature about Tibet, even that written by Tibetans in English, has been more about the strange or the scandalous, the pitiful or the victimized, than about Tibet's own history.

In the last hundred years, that history has been a story of violence, brutality and forced change. The twentieth century began with a British army invading Tibet from the south on a pretext in 1903, mowing down with machine-gunfire some 3,000 Tibetans armed with matchlock guns, and forcing the Tibetan government to a humiliating surrender. This invasion, politely called an 'expedition' by London, succeeded in turning Tibet into a major security concern for Beijing. In 1910, the Manchu Emperors in Beijing dispatched an army to Lhasa to turn Tibet into a Chinese province, lest it again be used by London or Delhi as a back door from which to threaten China.

A year later, the Xinhai revolution led to the fall of the imperial dynasty in Beijing, and the Manchu troops were soon driven out of Tibet by the Tibetan army. The thirteenth Dalai Lama, whose predecessors or their regents had ruled Tibet since 1642 from the Potala Palace in Lhasa, issued a proclamation that Tibet was no longer under Chinese rule, if it ever had been: the relationship between Tibet and China 'had not been based on the subordination of one to the other', he declared.[4] Tibet remained effectively independent for some thirty years, during which it hosted diplomatic missions from Nepal, Sikkim, Britain and later India, though it never succeeded in obtaining formal recognition of its independence from any major powers. The

---

4   'Proclamation Issued by H.H. the 13th Dalai Lama on the Eighth Day of the First Month of the Water-Ox Year (1913)', in International Committee of Lawyers for Tibet, *Legal Materials on Tibet*, Berkeley 1997, p. 106.

nationalist government in China did not give up its claim to Tibet, but, preoccupied by resistance to the Japanese invasion and, later, civil war with the Communists, could do little to enforce it.

That changed in 1949 with the rise of Mao Zedong and the Chinese Communist Party (CCP) and their founding of the People's Republic. This freed the People's Liberation Army (PLA) to complete the task that the Manchus had begun. In October 1950, the PLA crossed into Tibet and within a week defeated the small Tibetan army. The following year the Tibetan government signed a document of surrender known as the 'Seventeen-Point Agreement', accepting for the first time that Tibet was part of China. Once the Tibetan leaders had acquiesced to being a part of 'the big family of nationalities of the People's Republic', Mao had no need to impose direct rule on Tibet, declaring instead that the Dalai Lama could continue to run the government and that religion and society should function as before. At the same time, a shadowy Party command unit known as the Tibet Work Committee was set up in Lhasa to oversee all affairs, run by Chinese generals and backed by a large military presence, while roads were being built, cadres recruited and translations of Maoist texts prepared.

No social changes were imposed in Lhasa at that time, but in eastern Tibet aggressive social reforms, land distribution and the destruction of monasteries began in 1955. Resistance armies were formed by local merchants and running battles ensued with the PLA. Refugees from the conflict fled in their thousands to Lhasa, leading to the watershed events of March 1959, when tens of thousands of Tibetans surrounded the Dalai Lama's palace to prevent him visiting the Chinese military camp, where they feared he would be abducted. The battles that followed in Lhasa are now seen by many or most Tibetans as a popular uprising in defence of the nation against a foreign occupier, and by Chinese officials as an armed rebellion instigated by the Tibetan upper classes with the secret support of the hostile foreign forces—meaning the Americans and the CIA. In any event, the 1959 uprising failed and led the Dalai Lama and 80,000 followers to flee across the Himalayas to India, where they still remain, with an exile government established in the small hill station of Dharamsala in the northwestern Indian state of Himachal Pradesh.

At this point, the place called Tibet becomes lost as a distinctive voice and player in its own history. The region was isolated from the outside world, indigenous leadership was suppressed, and all media rigidly managed from Beijing— features which in substance have changed rather little in fifty years. What we know of subsequent popular opinion or of the new Tibetan leaders comes on the one hand from official announcements by or through the Chinese state, and on the other, piecemeal accounts gathered by outsiders—reports by refugees, messages smuggled to exile relatives, veiled writings, individual outbursts, interpretations of unrest or occasional encounters with visitors. Tibet becomes a muffled, incoherent voice and in its place a battle takes place to represent it, continuing till today.

The early work of Wang Lixiong and Tsering Shakya emerged out of that battle, and traces of it can be seen in the initial debate between them. But they rapidly became the leading figures among those who try, by understanding the intricacies of representational conflict, to navigate beyond it. Their objective has been the attempt to piece together the likely profile of that fragmented voice, to construct soundly-based and finely-tuned generalizations about Tibetan opinion and experience. To do this, they have tried to set the commonly expressed disputes over

Tibetan history and politics within what each one sees as the proper context—as defined by Tibetans rather than outsiders.

Those disputes consist of a series of passionately held disagreements between the main parties in the conflict. In these disputes the facts used by either side are generally correct, in the sense that something of the sort occurred. But their significance and nature are bitterly contested, as are the words used to describe each event or fact. The most prominent element of the conventional dispute is that of political status. The Chinese side sees Tibet as having been for centuries an integral part of China. Since at least the 1970s, Beijing has dated this incorporation to the thirteenth century, when Tibet became a part of the Mongol empire. From the early eighteenth century, imperial Ambans or Commissioners had been stationed by Beijing in Lhasa; their task, according to this view, was to oversee the Tibetan government on behalf of the Emperor. Beijing's actions in 1950 were thus those of a central government which was simply regularizing its authority over what it termed 'the Tibetan local government'. From a Tibetan perspective, Tibet's relations had been with the Mongol or the Manchu Emperors, not with China as a state or with their successor regimes, and it had therefore become fully independent in 1913. The Ambans in this account had indeed been representatives of the Emperor but had not been superior to the Tibetan government. The events of 1950 were therefore an invasion.

There is a similar disagreement over the question of Tibetan territory. Just over 50% of what is now some 5.7 million Tibetans live in the eastern part of the Tibetan plateau, in the mountainous parts of western Sichuan, northern Yunnan, southern and western Qinghai and southern Gansu—areas usually known in Tibetan as Kham and Amdo. The population in those areas was almost exclusively Tibetan in the 1950s. To a contemporary Tibetan, all these regions constitute Tibet, as evidenced by the fact that all these areas fought together in the various anti-Chinese resistance movements of the 1950s, in which thousands of Tibetans from all areas died. But, though the Tibetan army had briefly recovered some of these eastern domains in the early twentieth century, most of these areas had not been ruled by the Dalai Lama's government for decades, if not centuries. So in Chinese usage, both official and popular, the word Tibet, or *Xizang* in Chinese, refers only to the domains ruled directly by the Dalai Lama's government in 1949, namely the western and central parts of the Tibetan plateau. Only that Tibet had been covered by the terms of the Seventeen-Point Agreement of 1951.

The immediate consequences of the flight of the Dalai Lama in 1959 are similarly contested. According to the Chinese narrative, the rebellion was routed by the PLA and, to the relief of the common people of Tibet, the perpetrators and their supporters were 'eliminated' or 'suppressed', to use the official jargon of the time. The suppression of the rebels was accompanied by 'democratic reform', meaning that slavery, serfdom and debt-bondage were annulled and land distributed to the peasants amid great celebration. There was no attack on religion or customs at this time, and in 1965, according to this account, the Tibetan people (a phrase which at that time referred in Tibet to the farmers and nomads) were made 'masters of their own affairs' by the establishment of what was called 'nationality regional autonomy' in Tibet, henceforth to be known as the Tibet Autonomous Region or TAR, with a Tibetan as its governor.

According to the Tibetan or exile view, the 1959 uprising was followed immediately by an orgy of persecution, mass arrests and killings. Forced collectivization and the establishment of communes began within a year or two, taking back the individual land-holdings that had been given to the peasants in 1959. Attacks on religion and on monasteries also began at around this time. At least four years before the Cultural Revolution began, most monasteries had been closed down and most monks had been forcibly defrocked. Persecution of former lamas and officials was widespread from at least 1964; the nine-week struggle session that autumn against the Panchen Lama, the most important figure to have remained in Tibet after 1959, was the most striking and appalling example of already rampant persecution. This situation continued more or less unabated until the end of the Cultural Revolution and the death of Mao in 1976.

Another fundamental cleavage of views concerns the events of the late 1960s and 1970s. Underlying this is the question of whether those events are still the responsibility of the present leadership. The official Chinese explanation is that what was called retrospectively 'the Cultural Revolution' took place from 1966–76, during which time there were many savage, unjustified attacks on religion, learning, culture and people who were not members of the revolutionary classes. These illegal and regrettable events occurred throughout China, were later declared to have been an error, and were a result of a coup by 'ultra-leftists', for which the members of the 'Gang of Four' were duly sentenced and punished in 1981. These events were not aimed particularly at Tibetans, since people in every area in China suffered to a similar degree. They were carried out by people of all nationalities, including Tibetans, against certain social classes, not against any ethnic group. The subsequent leadership in effect apologized to the nation, and a specific apology was made to Tibetans in 1980. Followers of this view speak as if a new Party and a new Chinese government emerged in 1979 or 1980, with no responsibility for the previous era.

A general Tibetan, if not Western, version can be characterized as maintaining that, whatever its nature within China, in Tibet the Cultural Revolution was an attempt led by Chinese political activists to eliminate Tibetan culture and religion. In this view, it was thus seen as a form of ethnocide. It began in its essential features soon after 1959, and in some respects, elements of it have recurred repeatedly since that time or have never completely ceased. In this view, the CCP that was responsible for the persecutions of the 1950s was in its main features the same as the one that carried out the Cultural Revolution and the one that is still in power, albeit under a rubric of modernization rather than socialist revolution.

In the post-Mao era, the arguments accumulate but become more detailed. By 1979, Deng Xiaoping and later Hu Yaobang had succeeded in routing the immediate followers of Mao, the 'Gang of Four', and had introduced the household responsibility system throughout China, allowing something like a private economy again. They also believed in the celebration of cultural difference among the non-Chinese nationalities, and so envisaged China as a 'multi-national state' (the word 'national' in this case means nationality or ethnicity), in which certain religions, to some extent, could be freely practised. Buddhism was one of these permitted religions. Additionally, they opened the country up to foreign trade and cultural interaction, and in areas like Tibet they invested vast amounts of money in the form of subsidies or infrastructural development.

No one disputes the visible evidence of modernization in Tibetan towns, as in other areas of China, and the striking increase in wealth, especially in the urban areas. But there is bitter antagonism over the intentions behind these policies, or over their effects. One side sees the investment as a kind of cultural levelling, eroding Tibetan language and culture; the other sees it as beneficial modernization that is an overall advantage to Tibetans. The increase in Chinese migration to Tibetan areas is seen by one side as reducing Tibetans to a dispossessed minority and by the other as helping boost the market economy and prosperity by encouraging competition. In extreme cases, Tibetan exiles use the term 'cultural genocide' to describe what from another perspective is said to be no more than the normal changes that take place to traditional practices under conditions of modernization. Similarly, the Chinese government claims that its autonomy system gives Tibetans control over local affairs, while others say that this is a fiction applicable only to the local government, if that, and then only through puppet appointees, when in fact it is ethnic Chinese officials in the local Party apparatus who run Tibet. When there are Tibetan protests against Chinese rule, the Chinese government and its supporters typically depict them as instigations by exiles and 'hostile foreign forces', while others see them as expressing the fundamental opposition of the Tibetan people to Chinese rule.

A similar dispute surrounds recent Chinese policies in Tibet, which, perhaps as a response to the fall of the Soviet Union, attributed by Chinese analysts to its laxity with nationalities, had become much more aggressive in the 1990s. Major policy changes had been imposed at a meeting in 1994, called the Third National Forum on Work in Tibet, which had ended the 1980s dispensation whereby Tibetans were free to worship the Dalai Lama. It also banned his photographs, forced monks and nuns to denounce him in writing, fixed the number of monks and nuns in each monastery, encouraged retired Chinese soldiers to settle in Tibet, ended plans for Tibetan-language education in TAR middle schools, and led to rules forbidding Tibetan students and Tibetans in government jobs from any religious practice. To China, these moves were seen as acceptable steps that were necessary to staunch the growth of Tibetan nationalism. But to others they were seen as a fundamental attack on Tibetan culture and religion.

Such differences can be listed indefinitely, down to the level of the individual word. The word 'country', for example, antagonizes Chinese if used of Tibet, who see this as a claim for the independence of what they term a 'region' or an 'area'. Similar tensions surround words like 'invasion' or 'occupation', let alone saying 'Tibet and China' instead of 'Tibet in China'. As I have mentioned, Tibet (*Xizang*) refers to the western half of the Tibetan plateau in Chinese usage, but sometimes the entire plateau when used by others. Political terminology inevitably has many problems. The word 'propaganda' (*xuanchuan*) means manipulative information to Westerners, but to older Chinese people simply describes distributed information, without any negative connotations. A 'cadre' (*ganbu*) means to Westerners an official in a Communist Party, but in China it describes any employee of the state, whatever job they do. Conversely, 'the government' (*zhengfu*) sounds to Westerners like the supreme entity that runs a country, but in China it describes only the administrative officers who carry out the instructions of the Party leaders and committees positioned within each office and department. Chinese people use the relatively new term 'Han' to refer to the ethnic Chinese, and nowadays see the standard English use of the term 'Chinese' for that function as a deliberate insinuation that Tibetans, Mongols, Uyghurs and other nationalities within China are not Chinese too. That term, 'nationality', was used by China to translate the Chinese word *minzu* until the 1990s and continues to be used that way by foreigners, but is now no longer permitted among Chinese officials, who instead have to use the term 'ethnic' or 'ethnicity', apparently to avoid any implication that a nationality might be entitled to a state. In religion, many words lead to misunderstandings. The word 'lama' is used in Chinese to refer to any Tibetan Buddhist monk, whereas in Tibetan and in Western usage it refers only to a highly revered teacher. The term 'Living Buddha' (*huofo*) is common in Chinese as a translation for the Tibetan term *trulku* or *tulku* (written as *sprul sku* in Tibetan), which means a reincarnated lama and has nothing specifically to do with living Buddhas, a concept that is not found in Tibetan Buddhism. Westerners use the titles of Tibetan lamas, but Chinese government officials only use their given names, or their titles in truncated form, such as 'Dalai' instead of 'Dalai Lama'. Mutual incomprehension and sensitivity is rife at every level of discussion of the Tibet issue.

Attempts at talks

Surprisingly, some points of agreement can be made out, though they are rarely emphasized. All parties to the China-Tibet dispute more or less agree that the Cultural Revolution was a disaster on a massive scale, but differ on whether it has been correctly explained, sufficiently amended for, or even stopped. There is broad consensus that Tibet is not simply another Chinese province and has special characteristics—during the 1980s, that was the term, *tese*, used by Chinese leaders to describe Tibetan and other nationality entities—and so is entitled to a different, devolved form of administration compared to the inland provinces of China. No one except extreme leftists disputes the benefit of Deng Xiaoping's policies in the early 1980s, when economic liberalization, opening up and some tolerance of religion were introduced. There is also broad agreement that there was or is something magnificent and valuable about Tibetan culture, and by the 1990s many Chinese, particularly from affluent sectors of society, had come to see the Tibetan landscape as a spiritual resource, and even to turn to Tibetan religion and Tibetan lamas as a source of spiritual 'purity'. Both sides talk about 'preserving' Tibetan culture and environment, as though these were museum specimens, though they differ sharply in how this should be done and who has the right to do it. And all agree that economic improvement in society, plus increases in social welfare, infrastructure and modernization, are a benefit, though not at any cost.

The consensus over these issues was broad enough in the early 1980s for contacts to resume between Beijing and the exiles for the first time since 1959. Deng Xiaoping met with the Dalai Lama's older brother, Gyalo Thondup, in March 1979 and promised concessions, provided the exiles agreed not to ask for independence. This condition was accepted, and three exile fact-finding delegations were allowed to visit Tibet in 1979 and 1980, discovering extraordinary depths of poverty in Tibet and widespread devotion to the Dalai Lama. In 1982 and 1984 two rounds of 'exploratory talks' took place between the Chinese and the exiles. Their content has never been publicized, but they broke down by 1985, with China declaring that it would only consider discussion of the Dalai Lama's personal terms of return, and not any changes to its policies in Tibet.

Two years later, the exile leadership 'was left with only one option' as it saw it, which was 'to appeal directly for the assistance of the international community'. In September 1987, at the Capitol in Washington, DC, the Dalai Lama gave his first political speech abroad, seeking Western support. In this speech and at the European Parliament in Strasbourg the following year, he presented the issue in terms of human rights abuses and environmental damage. He did not call for independence and asked China in return to make all the Tibetan regions a 'self-governing democratic political entity'. In the face of strong resistance from Beijing, he later withdrew this request and asked instead for 'genuine autonomy' or 'meaningful autonomy', adding under further pressure in 2008 that this should be allowed by the Chinese constitution. This approach attracted support from several major Western governments.

Some fifteen years later, in 2002, after much international pressure, talks finally began again. Eight rounds of discussions took place between the two sides, but reached stalemate in October 2008, when each side publicly accused the other of insincerity. The exiles said that Beijing had no intention of making any progress on talks and was waiting only for the Dalai Lama to die, believing that the movement will then collapse. The Chinese side insisted that the exiles were lying, secretly plotting independence, planning ethnic cleansing and demanding to separate a quarter of China through their plan for a single autonomous region covering the entire Tibetan plateau. The twenty-five years of attempted talks had passed without success; indeed, relations had sharply deteriorated.

Essentially those talks had taken place between two outside bodies, Chinese and exile, under foreign pressure, concerning a mute entity called Tibet that took no part in these discussions. Beijing never suggested bringing local Tibetan representatives to the table with the exiles, and, except for once, did not allow the exile delegates to bring with them any Tibetan refugee who had been brought up within China. But in many ways, the absent partner remained the most forceful presence in these discussions: during two periods in the post-Mao period, Tibetans inside Tibet took to the streets in significant numbers to protest against Chinese rule, and were perhaps the reason that Beijing agreed to talks.

The first wave of protests occurred in Lhasa between 1987 and 1989, when there were four major rallies against Chinese rule, each involving over a thousand laypeople. Between 75 and 150 Tibetans were shot dead by paramilitary troops during these protests, two of which ended in rioting. In March 1989 the army was sent in to impose martial law on Lhasa, remaining on the streets for thirteen months. Some 200 smaller protests were staged by monks and nuns in this period and during the following six years. A second phase of protest erupted in March–April 2008, when some 150 protests took place in or near Lhasa and in rural towns and villages of eastern Tibet, including parts of Qinghai, Gansu and Sichuan. At least four of these incidents involved serious rioting. Chinese official reports say nineteen people were killed by protesters in the riot in Lhasa on 14 March 2008, and have said at different times, without giving details, that up to eight protesters died. Exile organizations say that between one and two hundred protesters were killed by security forces or died from abuse in custody. As before, the response by the government was militarization, this time by paramilitary troops rather than the army, in towns across the entire Tibetan plateau rather than just Lhasa. The troops remained on the streets of Lhasa and other areas for at least fifteen months and were still there at the time of writing.

In this sense, a Tibet of some sort had made its voice heard. But what had it said? Some people claimed that the 2008 protests had shown that Tibetans wanted independence, since many protesters waved the Tibetan national flag, which is strictly illegal in China. Numerous protesters carried pictures of the Dalai Lama, leading some to argue that this showed support for his proposals of compromise. Other observers speculated that the protests were about the excessive Chinese policies of the 1990s, which had been applied increasingly to eastern Tibetan areas as well as to the TAR. On the other hand, Chinese officials and their supporters insisted that the protests were violent and coordinated, and therefore showed deliberate instigation by the Dalai Lama and his followers.

The question of class and benefit

The protests raised a fundamental question, beyond the symbolic disputes over Tibetan independence and the ideological arguments over representation: whether the Tibetan farmers and the nomads, some 85 per cent of the population, had benefited from Chinese rule. China's principal strategy in 1959 had been to win over the Tibetan peasantry with land distribution. That support was squandered through such policies as rushed collectivization, impoverishment and the Cultural Revolution. But in 1980, Beijing dismantled the communes and again distributed land to individual rural households, liberalized the economy and allowed people to practise religion. It also invested huge sums in infrastructure, roads and services in Tibet. Do rural Tibetans see the modernization and the market economy as net advantages, given that some religious practice is now allowed? Or did the Party's heavy-handed attacks on Tibetan nationalism and on the Dalai Lama since the 1990s lose any goodwill it might have acquired from those gifts?

Such questions have received little serious discussion. For decades, Tibet has been treated by intellectuals and policy analysts as something of a sideshow, an arcane conflict between incompatible ideologues, as if it were a political orphan among adult concerns. Much of this disdain can be attributed to discomfort about the popular exoticization of Tibet, its new age devotees, its Cold War antecedents and history of earlier contacts with the CIA, as well as an increasing reluctance to criticize

China or antagonize Beijing. The victimization narrative of the exiles has added, in yet another way, to this marginalization effect. At a deeper level, it reflects a nervousness, particularly on the Left, about religion and populist political movements, and a reluctance to consider those phenomena as worthy of serious political consideration. At the opposite end of the spectrum are commentators who see China as an extreme authoritarian force and regard any pragmatic explanations of its Tibet policies as specious.

But any such diffidence in policy circles has been overtaken by events. The 2008 protests in Tibet were so widespread, both laterally in location and vertically in class, that they triggered a re-militarization by China of the Tibetan plateau, which sits between the three established nuclear powers of Asia. The Tibet issue emerged as one of strategic significance to the region, and not only because it raised doubts about the CCP's claims to legitimacy and nationwide support. In addition, in spring 2009 China claimed great power status, increasing the importance of being able to demonstrate domestic stability and legitimacy. It began a zero tolerance policy towards meetings by foreign leaders with the Dalai Lama, cancelling an EU summit in December 2008 because of a planned meeting with the French president. In March 2009, its foreign minister announced that the issues of Tibet and Taiwan were of 'equal sensitivity' to China.

If anyone was surprised to find the lonely lands near the top of China's list of strategic concerns and attracting international attention, it would not have been Tsering Shakya or Wang Lixiong. They had long predicted, from different vantage points, the seriousness for China of the Tibetan question—as Wang had written in 2002:

> Tibet is more prosperous now than ever before in its history. However, this has not gained the PRC the allegiance of the Tibetans, more and more of whom have become attached to the Dalai Lama . . . In the words of one retired official: 'The current stabilization is only on the surface. One day people will riot in much greater numbers than in the late eighties.'

Both gained their status as interpreters of these events by trying to make sense of the muted Tibet, to find plausible, concrete explanations for Tibetan actions and beliefs. This effort is situated within a view of China which implies that Tibet is not merely an idiosyncratic element among China's many problems but a core issue which shows the workings of the large state and thus has direct implications for its viability as a state. In other words, the Chinese state cannot resolve its key contradictions and become sustainable until it resolves its problems in Tibet.

Wang Lixiong

The Chinese intelligentsia has suffered from a difficult reputation, being divided, factionalized and frequently compromised. The leading Chinese journalist Liu Binyan blamed China's writers and intellectuals for the failure of reform efforts after 1989, describing them as 'a craven intellectual elite that has made a bargain with the regime: political support in exchange for personal privilege. No group has gained as much from the bargain as the literary intellectuals have.'[5]

The writer and essayist Wang Lixiong has increasingly distanced himself from that group. He became famous for the novel *Yellow Peril* (*Huanghuo*, 1991), a futuristic fantasy about

5 Binyan Liu and Eugene Perry Link, *Two kinds of Truth: Stories and Reportage from China*, Bloomington 2006, p. 17.

an autocratic China that descends into chaos and world war. But since the success of *Yellow Peril*, he has not worked as a fiction writer or returned to the lucrative world of film or commercial writing, where he first began. Unlike most of his peers, he has no position among the Party clientele, no linkage to a work unit or an official publication, and no position in any institution: he is an outsider among Chinese intellectuals. His links to organizations or movements have been brief or cautious. He cofounded China's first acknowledged NGO, Friends of Nature (*Ziran ʒhi you*), in 1994, ten years after he had first drawn attention to environmental issues in China by travelling 800 miles down the Yellow River on a raft made from the inner tubes of truck tyres. But the government forced the members of Friends of Nature to evict him in 2003, reportedly because of his work on Tibet and Xinjiang.[6] His only concession to the state was his membership with the Chinese Writers' Association, a government body which he had joined in 1988. He resigned from the association in 2001, issuing a sensational denunciation of literary-government collaboration:

> It is no longer acquiescence which is demanded, but the annihilation of the whole personality, of all conscience and of all individual pride, in order to make crouching dogs of us. To continue to belong to this organization is not an honour, it is on the contrary the shame of any writer worthy of the name.

This is the language of morality, not politics, and it may be this that has kept Wang out of prison, apart from a month in 1999 when he was detained in Xinjiang: his criticisms of

6   Elizabeth Economy, 'Environmental Enforcement in China', in Kristen A. Day, ed., *China's Environment and The Challenge of Sustainable Development*, New York 2005, p. 115.

the state have been trenchant and incisive, but they were not ideological attacks on the right of the Party to exist so much as tightly focused analyses of its incompetencies, blindness and contradictions. The Sinologist Rémi Quesnel has detected in Wang's writing the ideal of the *zhinang*, the adviser who puts his knowledge at the disposal of a ruler, rather than that of a revolutionary who wishes to overthrow the state.[7] This is not a sign of accomodationism, but a sign that Wang had discarded or not inherited the presumption, so embedded in the Xinhai and May Fourth intellectual movements of 1911 and 1919, that public reform is inseparable from overthrowing existing structures, a view that had led to Leninism, violence and autocracy. Wang's focus has been on constructive efforts at political change, centring on his proposal for a gradualist democratic system, described in what he has called his major work, *Distribution of Power—An Electoral System by Stages* (*Rongjie quanli—Zhuceng dixuan zhi*), published in 1998. He has continued to develop this idea, not by creating organizations or claiming a leadership position, but through peer-group discussion on websites (such as http://wlx.sowiki.net) and through information-sharing networks on the internet within China.

Wang was born in the city of Changchun in Jilin province (in former Manchuria) in 1953. His father, Wang Shaolin, died while in custody during the Cultural Revolution; until then, he had worked in a car factory, where his subordinates are said to have included the future Chinese President Jiang Zemin (some speculate that this connection may be another reason the younger Wang has so far evaded long-term detention). Wang Lixiong's mother had been a writer at the Changchun Film Studio, but he was able to get education as a *gongnongbindaxuesheng*—a

---

7 Rémi Quesnel, 'Wang Lixiong, an Atypical Intellectual', *China Perspectives*, no. 50, 2003, available at *chinaperspectives.revues.org*.

worker-peasant-soldier-university student—at Jilin Industry University (later consolidated into Jilin University) during the Cultural Revolution. From 1977 until 1980, he worked as a mechanic in car factories in Jilin and Wuhan. But even from 1975, he was developing his ideas about stage-democracy and at the same time writing short stories, the first of which was published in the dissident journal *Today* (*Jintian*) in 1978. Two years later he left the factory to become a writer.

It was his journey along the Yellow River that had first brought him into contact with the peoples beyond the Chinese heartlands. His subsequent writing about Tibet and Xinjiang, the western peripheries of China's polity, led him to be seen, even among Chinese nationalists, as the most thoughtful and most respected of all Chinese analysts of those lands. In 1998, after frequent journeys to Tibetan areas, he published *Sky Burial: The Destiny of Tibet* (*Tianzang: Xizang de mingyun*), and in 2001, *Xinjiang zhuiji* (*Memories of Xinjiang*), an account of a failed attempt to carry out unofficial research about the situation of the Uyghur people in Xinjiang and a description of the month he spent in jail there. Numerous other articles and books appeared, published mainly outside China or in Hong Kong. These impressed reviewers with their lack of ideological fervour and their depth of research: they were based on exhaustive critical reading. But even more so, they drew on extraordinarily extensive discussions with local people. If the mechanic in Wang could view the system dispassionately and identify the parts that needed radical reassembly, the writer in him listened to the voices of people rarely heard from, and sought to understand the historical and social origins of their thoughts.

There were other Chinese who had lived longer in Tibet and had written about its people, but the types of work they had produced had ranged from the sexploitation novellas of Ma Jian to the critical but stridently anti-exile screeds of Xu Mingxu. As the intellectual historian Wang Chaohua wrote in 2003, 'for the most part . . . Chinese intellectuals have so far locked out the nationalities question from their concerns, as if it had no bearing on China's future.'[8] In any case, their priority had not been empathetic listening. Wang had another advantage: he was open to change and criticism. His early writings on Tibet were received rapturously by many Chinese intellectuals, especially those in the diaspora, who saw in them a way of solving the Tibet problem and responding to Western criticism without damaging China and its claims.

But the Tibetan intelligentsia inside China was more suspicious. Communicating privately rather than in print, they detected in his writing an underlying residual essentialism, akin to the ethnic Chinese tradition of discussing a troublesome *xiongdi minzu* or 'brotherly nationality'. Roughly speaking, they challenged the tradition of positivistic interpretation— collecting a series of well-documented facts without criticism of the selection and construction of those facts—and invoked larger questions of cultural politics. Perhaps in light of such critiques, Wang's thinking changed rapidly in the following years, developing far beyond what he had written in *Sky Burial* or the controversial article for *New Left Review* (2002, but written in 1998) in response to which Tsering Shakya was to outline the cultural politics response. Wang's subsequent papers, 'Religion in Tibet' (2003) and 'Two Imperialisms' (2004), were based on intensely personal experiences—the sentencing to death of a little-known Tibetan lama who by chance he had come to know

---

8   Wang Chaohua, ed., 'Introduction', *One China, Many Paths*, London and New York, 2003, p. 43. See also Steven L. Venturino, 'Inquiring After Theory in China', *Boundary 2*, vol. 33, no. 2, 2006, pp. 91–113.

years earlier in Sichuan, and the bureaucratic ostracization of his wife after her publications about Tibetan life. They revealed an increasingly subtle and more reflective approach, which sought to understand the contextual framework of participants' knowledge as well as to critique self-reflexively his own intellectual tradition, as implied in the cultural politics approach.

This led in the latter paper to a specific elucidation, in the Chinese context, of the concept of cultural imperialism, a critical and unique insertion of this question into Chinese discussion of its dealings with the non-Chinese within its borders. With these articles, Wang moved into new intellectual territory, beyond his peer group, no longer looking at the non-Chinese border areas as specimens to be analyzed from the perspective of the centre, but looking back from them toward the centre as well. This development in Wang's thinking has also led some Chinese critics to accuse him of losing objectivity and turning to the Right. For those of that opinion, his work in 'Independence after the March Incident' (2008) would have been even more shocking, for it presented a scathing critique of the Party bureaucracy responsible for handling nationalities and religion in China. It deemed the CCP incapable of solving the Tibetan issue.

These changes in his thinking occurred around the time he met and married the Tibetan poet Woeser (Weise in Chinese), who emerged as the leading public dissident among Tibetans inside China in 2003 with the banning of her book, *Notes from Tibet* (*Xizang Biji*). The bond between the two writers is palpable. Once, sitting with them in a dingy cafeteria in the Tibetan town of Jyeku, in between their visits to a Tibetan lama who had set up a local library, a temple dedicated to the Tang Dynasty princess Wencheng, and a visionary Tibetan nun said to be over a century old, I asked Wang what was his favourite food. 'What I like is what she likes', he replied, laughing, leaving me to wonder if it was a metaphor not just for their relationship but for the empathetic approach in his writing too.

But it would be wrong to reduce the changes in Wang's thinking to his encounter with Woeser. Even before they met, he had described the effects of the month he spent in a prison cell in Urumqi with some Uyghur dissidents in 1999, during which he attempted suicide after feeling he had compromised himself in the interrogations:

> Thinking over what happened to me in Xinjiang, time and distance allow me now to transcend the initial feelings and suffering, and I am beginning to realize the depth of what I gained from it. This led me to reflect deep inside in the course of this struggle for dignity, which made possible the rejection of dependence on the government to become consciousness; I was able to experience the feelings of the national minorities by putting myself in their place, and sweep away once and for all the last vestiges of nationalism which remained in me; I understood by personal experience the weakness of human nature, and I have since become all the more tolerant of fear and submissiveness and I abhor autocratic tyranny twice as much. Having walked the frontier between life and death makes it possible for me to adapt to any situation; the courage I begged heaven to give me then, has since penetrated my soul, silently, like the rain which makes the earth fruitful. I do not believe that I will never again show weakness, but I will certainly be less subject to fear, I will be stronger, I will go out to meet the evil whose arrogance threatens our world, with a more courageous attitude.[9]

The passage echoes the debate at the time among Chinese intellectuals over 'humanistic spirit' (*renwen jingshen*).[10] That

---

9 Cited in Quesnel, paragraph 37.
10 See Gloria Davies, *Worrying About China: The Language of Chinese Critical Inquiry*, Cambridge, MA 2007, pp. 87ff.

sensibility and openness to an ideal centred on human sympathy underlies Wang's Xinjiang writing, and indicates an ongoing commitment in his work to a morally-based view of politics and conflict resolution, one founded on listening to outsiders—even on becoming one oneself.

Tsering Shakya

Shakya and Wang were born two thousand miles apart, one in Lhasa and the other in Changchun, two cities in what was by then effectively the same country. Wang was born four years after Mao came to power in China and two years after the first soldiers of the PLA reached Lhasa. Shakya was born eight years after the troops arrived, three months after the Tibetan uprising of 1959 ended the initial Sino-Tibetan pact.

Like Wang, Shakya stands somewhat apart from his peer group. Many of his exile generation were born in India after the 1959 exodus, but he was brought up for some years inside Tibet, where his father was a translator for the Nepalese consulate in Lhasa. That quasi-diplomatic status meant that the family was not subjected directly to the ideological demands and obligations that then surrounded them; Shakya recalls, for example, his mother sheltering dozens of the city's dogs in the diplomatic compound after the administration had ordered that they be wiped out in the Cultural Revolution. In 1967, the family was allowed, because of its special status, to move to Nepal, and Shakya was sent to study for five years in an exile Tibetan school in Mussoorie, Northern India. At the age of thirteen, he was moved further to the edges of the dominant exile community, being sent to a small boarding school in England. Rarer still for a Tibetan exile, he went on in 1978 to take an undergraduate degree at a British university, the School of Oriental and African Studies at the University of London.

After graduating he sought funding for a further degree to carry out research about the country in which he had been born. But the elite British institutions and academics of the early 1980s had no interest in supporting an Asian immigrant who wanted to study his own society, seeing him as by definition biased. In any case, in reaction to the Cold War polemics of the time, Western intellectuals regarded Tibet as an example of socialist liberation, and critical study of that approach was seen as the domain of right-wing imperialists and feudal-religious apologists. For some eight years denied access to higher studies, Shakya worked as an adviser on race relations for local NGOs and the local council, then run by the Labour Party in more left-leaning days, in Ealing, a borough of west London. Just as Wang gained his first work experience in a factory, Shakya spent his formative years working with Asian migrants and local politicians on the streets of London—experience that would give him a substantive basis when thinking about race and politics concerning his own community in years to come.

It would be twenty years before Shakya would finally be readmitted to SOAS to pursue a doctorate. By the time it happened, in 1998, he had already become through his own efforts a major scholar in the field. The funding was from a private donor who admired his work, and was not through the Chinese department that would normally have been expected to have received him. Even as an undergraduate he had realized that the most immediate gap in the Tibetan issue was the lack of serious academic study in the West, and especially the lack of a definitive modern history. He had begun publishing scholarly articles as an independent scholar in 1983. Those early publications had been in his capacity as an anthropologist, based on independent research among Tibetans and others in Ladakh. But he soon set out to fill the larger gap he had identified—the absence of a textbook on Tibetan history since the arrival of the Chinese there in 1950. He trained himself to become a historian through many years as a private scholar combing the records at the India Office Library and conducting oral interviews with leading Tibetan exiles in India, long before such practices became popular. In time, he became the leading Tibetan exile historian in the West. In 1990, he co-organized with me the first conference on modern Tibetan studies, and the following year was invited to teach part-time in Refugee Studies at Oxford University. In 1999, still without formal affiliation or graduate training, his major work, *The Dragon in the Land of Snows: A History of Tibet Since 1947* (Pimlico, 1999), was published by a trade publisher. It was described by the *New York Times* as 'the definitive history of modern Tibet' and widely acclaimed by scholars of both Tibetan and Chinese studies.

Even more than Wang, Shakya had done this as an outsider, without any professional support, affiliation or endorsement: no institution or state structure supported his work. For much of this time, he was supported by his wife, who worked as a nurse in a London hospital. At one time, he was about to take up work as a postman, until an independent Tibet-related research project, Tibet Information Network, which I was running at the time, was able to raise funds to retain him as its Research Director while he finished the book that, in effect, gained recognition for the study of modern Tibetan history as an important subject in Western academia.

In those early years, there were those in the exile community who saw him as a threat, since he operated as a free thinker, not bound to any particular authority except the tenets of social science as he understood them. I remember in the late 1980s an official of the exile government, speaking personally, telling me not to associate with this unreliable person whose family was linked to Nepal and was not truly Tibetan. Those prejudices were swept away as Shakya became a highly respected intellectual in the West. That status was cemented in 2005 when he was given the Canada Research Chair in Religion and Contemporary Society in Asia at the University of British Columbia.

Shakya's doctoral research had been on contemporary Tibetan literature within Tibet. This field brought him into ever deeper contact with writers and thinkers inside Tibet, and at the same time familiarized him with the conceptual vocabulary of post-colonial studies. This enabled him to discuss colonialism as a historical phenomenon within social praxis and thinking in Tibet, rather than being trapped in narrow arguments about Tibet's political status. He had thus begun as an anthropologist, published as a historian and earned his doctorate as a literary scholar. Like Wang, his thinking had evolved, in his case through different areas of the social sciences as he sought for intellectual tools with which to analyse and describe the conditions in the country that he had left some forty years before. And like Wang, Shakya prioritized research and connections with Tibetans inside China from his earliest days, and familiarized himself with Chinese and Tibetan scholars inside Tibet, travelling there whenever allowed. He was thus one of those responsible for the critical shift in Western thinking about Tibet that followed the opening up of the area in the early 1980s, the turn of attention to Tibetans inside Tibet and the study of the Chinese society and system within which they lived.

Within the exile Tibetan community, he remained something of an anomaly. That community had demonstrated excellence after 1959 by producing outstanding exponents of religious studies, and creating major institutions to train successors in

monastic philosophy and Buddhist practices. It also had a very
high success rate with basic education in Tibetan schools in the
lay community. But post-graduate, secular education had been
more difficult for its small community, some 130,000 strong
by the 1990s, and emphasis on higher degrees in Western
scholarship or on professional education had not been great,
to say the least. The main scholars in the modern sense were
the late Dawa Norbu, an important figure in studies of Third
World nationalism and a professor of international relations
at Jawarhalal Nehru University in Delhi, Samten Karmay,
a leading figure in Tibetology and the study of religion
based at the University of Paris, and Loden Sherab Dagyab
in Bonn, an expert on Tibetan art and religion. The highly
respected historian, Tashi Tsering, worked independently from
Dharamsala and rarely published in English. The popular writer
Jamyang Norbu produced historical essays, but his strengths
were the polemical essay and imaginative fiction. Younger
exile scholars of exceptional ability have now emerged—exile
women educated in the West, with extensive experience inside
Tibet, notably the literary expert Yangdon Dhondup, Tashi
Rabgey and Losang Rabgey—but their writing careers are still
at a relatively early stage.

There continues to be exceptional and voluminous
intellectual production inside Tibet, particularly among the
Tibetan intelligentsia in Amdo, which far outstrips work
produced outside Tibet, whether in academic studies or in
creative writing and polemics. But little of this has appeared in a
Western language, and all of it is limited by censorship or self-
censorship, or confined to traditional conceptual approaches
taught in provincial Chinese schools. The exile situation is
likely to improve dramatically as more of the highly educated
Tibetans trained inside China resettle in India or in the West,

such as the leading literary critic Pema Bhum, formerly based at China's Northwest Nationalities University, bringing high standards of scholarship and intellectual rigour. But most of these scholars write in Tibetan or Chinese rather than a Western language, and the cross-fertilization of ideas and capacities with exile writers takes time to come to fruition.

Shakya was thus not unique as a Tibetan scholar with Western training, but he was exceptional in applying the techniques of Western social sciences rigorously to contemporary Tibetan politics and society. In 2002, at the suggestion of the Chinese intellectual historian Wang Chaohua, *New Left Review* published a translation of Wang Lixiong's essay, 'Reflections on Tibet'. Looking for a scholar to respond to Wang in print, it was natural for the journal to turn to the pre-eminent interpreter in a Western language of contemporary Tibetan history. The *NLR* dialogue is the basis for this book, and for something of a new chapter in intellectual discussion of the Tibet issue, since it was probably the first time a major intellectual journal in the West had published a serious political discussion about the Tibetan situation.

It was not *NLR*'s decision to dedicate space to two vantage points instead of one that was exceptional or significant— what changed the shape of the issue was the decision to recruit those essays from intellectuals, figures whose knowledge was not merely scientistic or detailed, but situated, through years of reading and debate, within a broad intellectual context. By asking Shakya and Wang to be the two proponents, the journal was not only putting to one side decades of leftist diffidence about the Tibet issue, but also helping to establish that issue as having intellectual significance in a wider world. It showed that it was part of much larger discussions—about China, about politics, about colonialism and Western scholarship, beyond the interests of those immediately affected or intrigued by the particular situation.

In this, the *NLR* was ahead of its time, because within four years, stimulated by the resurgence of protest in Tibet in 2008 and the clashes aroused by China's decision to take the Olympic Torch relay around the world, serious intellectual debate about Tibet emerged in China. From varying perspectives, some Chinese intellectuals began to take up the issue, following the lead of Wang Lixiong. They included scholars and commentators like Wang Hui, Xu Zhiyong, Chang Ping, Zhang Boshu and the writers of *Gongmeng* (the Open Constitution Institute) as well as Wang Chaohua herself.[11] Just as Chinese thinkers had begun in the 1990s to challenge normative assumptions in China about social evolution (derived from the work of Lewis Henry Morgan), a debate began to emerge around the intellectual framing in Chinese thought of discussions about Tibet. That process was triggered by respect for the writings of Wang Lixiong, so that when he organized the public petition to the government in March 2008 calling on it to rethink its policy responses to the protests then taking place in Tibet, it was signed by over 300 scholars and intellectuals in China. The process is in its early days, but is reminiscent of the achievement of Henry Nash Smith and others in deconstructing the mythologies of the founding fathers of American expansionism: the relegation of the notion of the lonely lands to history, and the gradual explication of the political damage resulting from such images.

By choosing two scholars whose intellectual credibility is based on their understanding of the ideas circulating among Tibetans within Tibet, the *NLR* became part of the attempt to

11 I owe much of this to Wang Chaohua's presentation at The Art and Politics of East Asia Workshop, 'Competing Nationalisms: Tibet, China, and the West', University of Chicago, 21 November 2008.

listen to Tibetans who live there, seeing them as best informed about the conditions there. That shift, one that can also be detected in the Dalai Lama's thinking since the late 1980s, has been taking place in the Tibet debate slowly over 20 years, though hamstrung by Chinese limitations on contact with insiders and on their publications. It coincides with a much larger trend in global studies, which increasingly looks to so-called peripheries to learn how large powers think and act, and how their pasts and futures should be understood, rather than relying on the displays of political and social vibrancy at their centres. It is this rehabilitation of the outsider, the bringing of the overlooked to the centre of debate, that marks the work of Wang and Shakya (themselves exterior to their own groups) and gives us an opportunity through their research to hear something of the views of the Tibet that lies at the heart of this issue.

Robert Barnett
Columbia University
June 2009

Initial Exchange

1

Reflections on Tibet

Wang Lixiong

In the current debate on Tibet the two opposing sides see almost everything in black and white—differing only as to which is which. But there is one issue that both Chinese authorities and Tibetan nationalists consistently strive to blur or, better still, avoid altogether.[1] At the height of the Cultural Revolution hundreds of thousands of Tibetans turned upon the temples they had treasured for centuries and tore them to pieces, rejected their religion and became zealous followers of the Great Han occupier, Mao Zedong. To the Chinese Communist Party, the episode is part of a social catastrophe—one that it initiated but has long since disowned and which, it hopes, the rest of the world will soon forget. For the Tibetan participants, the memory of that onslaught is a bitter humiliation, one they would rather not talk about, or which they try to exorcize with the excuse that they only did it 'under pressure from the Han'. Foreign critics simply refuse to accept that the episode ever took place, unable to imagine that the Tibetans could willingly and consciously have done such a thing. But careful analysis and a deeper reflection on what was involved in that trauma may shed light on some of the cultural questions at stake on the troubled High Plateau.

1   This chapter first appeared in *New Left Review* 2: 14, March–April 2002, and was translated by Liu Xiaohong and A. Tom Grunfeld.

First, however, a survey of the broader historical background is required. For many centuries Tibet was an integral political entity, governed by the local religious leaders and feudal lords. Under the Qing dynasty, China exercised its jurisdiction over the region through the submission of this elite and did not interfere directly in local affairs. Between 1727 and 1911, the principal symbol of Chinese sovereignty over Tibet was the office of the Residential Commissioner, known as the Amban. The imperial presence in Lhasa, however, consisted 'solely of the commissioner himself and a few logistical and military personnel.'[2] These, together with a handful of civilian staff members, were responsible for carrying out all the daily administrative routines. Speaking no Tibetan they had to rely on interpreters and spent most of their time in Lhasa, making only a few inspection tours a year outside the city.[3] It is inconceivable that such a tiny apparatus would be able to exercise effective control over Tibet, an area of more than a million square kilometres. By and large, the Residential Commissioner could only serve as what I shall call a 'connector', mediating between the Qing authorities and the local rulers, the Dalai Lama and the Kashag.[4] Under this system, Tibetan peasants submitted solely to Tibetan masters—they 'only knew the Dalai, not the Court'. On certain occasions—when the Qing army had helped repel aggressors, for instance—the Tibetan elite would be full of praise for the Commissioner's advice. For the rest of the time, it would

2　*Lianyu zhuzang zougao* [Tibetan Memoranda to the Emperor by Lian Yu], Lhasa 1979, p. 89. There were indeed a few Qing garrisons stationed in Tibet, but their function was purely military.

3　Lian Yu, the last residential commissioner, noted plaintively in his memorandum: 'There are one or two people in this humble servant's office who could speak Tibetan; so far we have not met any Tibetans who could speak Chinese.'

4　The Kashag, composed of four high-rank officials, was the highest executive body in Tibet.

be unrealistic to expect that a few alien officials—linguistically handicapped, militarily weak, socially and politically isolated—would be obeyed by the local rulers, who held all the region's power and resources in their hands.

Consequently, as the Qianlong Emperor admitted, 'Tibetan local affairs were left to the wilful actions of the Dalai Lama and the *shapes* [Kashag officials]. The Commissioners were not only unable to take charge, they were also kept uninformed. This reduced the post of the Residential Commissioner in Tibet to name only.'[5] In response, the Qing court issued in 1793 an imperial decree, the Twenty-Nine Articles on the Reconstruction of Tibetan Domestic Affairs, which consolidated the Commissioner's authority over administrative, military and religious appointments, foreign affairs, finance, taxation and the criminal justice system.[6] These measures have given rise to the claim that the power of the Residential Commissioners subsequently 'exceeded that of the governors in other provinces'.[7] Nevertheless, when the Imperial Commissioner Zhang Yintang visited Tibet a century later, he was greatly distressed to hear the Dalai Lama ridiculing the Qing representatives as 'tea-brewing commissioners'. (Tea-brewing is a kind of Tibetan Buddhist alms-giving ceremony—one of the Commissioner's duties was to distribute this largesse to the monasteries on the Emperor's behalf; the insinuation was that he did nothing else.)[8] The Commissioner of the late Qing period, Lian Yu, also

---

5 *Utzang tongzhi* [Tibet General Gazette], vol. 9, p. 315.

6 The full text is given in *Xizang tongshi: songshi baochuan* [Tibetan History: A Chain of Precious Stones], Lhasa 1996, pp. 779–86.

7 Ding Shicun, *Qingdai zhuzang dachen kao* [A Study of the Qing Residential Commissioners to Tibet], n.d.

8 *Qingji chouzang zoudu* [The Qing Court Correspondence on Tibetan Affairs], book 3: *Zhang Yintang zoudu* [Zhang Yintang's Memoranda to the Throne], vol. 2, p. 17.

complained that 'the Dalai Lama arrogated undue importance to himself and wanted to manipulate everything.' If Tibetan officials appeared to be respectful and deferential, with an 'outward display of honesty and simple-mindedness', he found their actual behaviour was nothing less than 'secret resistance', and 'very often they left orders unattended to for months on the pretext of waiting for the Dalai Lama's return or for decisions yet to be made, simply ignoring urgent requests for answers.'[9]

To some extent, however, this state of affairs was acceptable to both sides. In terms of state power, the Qing court retained the ability to occupy Tibet, but did not need to do so; and the connector system had the merit of being extremely cheap. The crux of the framework of ancient oriental diplomacy lay in the order of 'rites': as long as the lamas were submissive and posed no threat, they would be tolerated. Despite the Commissioners' complaints and the Emperor's occasional displeasure, it was only the threat that Tibet might break away from its orbit that caused serious concern at Court, and entailed some form of 'rectification'. This occurred only a few times during the entire 185 years of Qing rule; for the most part, Residential Commissioners were stationed in Tibet to maintain the Emperor's symbolic mandate rather than to govern in fact.

Shadows of modernization

The overthrow of the Qing Empire by the Chinese revolution of 1911 created a quite new situation. Just before, in one of its last acts of authority, the dynasty had dispatched an army to occupy Lhasa. But with the collapse of the imperial order, followed by four decades of turmoil in China itself, Tibet for the first time

9   [Tibetan Memoranda to the Emperor by Lian Yu], pp. 47–8, 16.

in centuries enjoyed virtually complete de facto independence. The Residential Commissioner and his entourage were expelled in 1912 and the thirteenth Dalai Lama consolidated his position as a national leader, expanding and modernizing the Tibetan Army along British or Japanese lines and setting up banks, mines and a postal service. Trade was promoted and students sent to study in the West. Young officers began to imitate the fashions of their polo-playing counterparts under the British Raj and the military band was taught to play 'God Save the King'. But the price of the reforms was deemed too high by the monastic elite. The new officers saw the religious orders as the cause of Tibetan backwardness: not prayers but guns would make the country strong. While the Dalai Lama understood the importance of the Army in securing his secular power and resisting the potential Chinese threat, he could not tolerate any direct challenge to his authority; when the military leadership began to target his own position for reform, instigating a series of private meetings designed to pressure him to relinquish political power, he moved against them, putting a halt to Tibet's modernization. The Army went into decline after the officers were purged, meeting defeat at the hands of a regional warlord in Kham—the section of eastern Tibet that extends into Sichuan province—in 1931. After this, the Dalai Lama tilted back towards Beijing.

China, meanwhile, had been waging a ceaseless propaganda campaign within the international arena for its right to sovereignty over Tibet. This was tacitly granted by the West—the country would be a large and populous ally during World War II—which nevertheless continued to treat Tibet as, in practical terms, an independent state. The Tibetan elite, meanwhile, continued to vacillate: since they already had de facto self-rule, it was simpler to blockade themselves on their plateau, ringed with snowy mountains, than to get into arguments with China. As the thirteenth Dalai Lama told Charles Bell:

> Some countries may wish to send representatives to Tibet; the travellers of other nations may wish to penetrate our country. These representatives and travellers may press inconvenient questions on myself and the Tibetan government. Our customs are often different from those of Europe and America, and we do not wish to change them. Perhaps Christian missionaries may come to Tibet, and in trying to spread Christianity may speak against our religion. We could not tolerate that.'[10]

Arguably, if the forms of oriental diplomacy could have been maintained, some new system of connectors might have been an acceptable solution to the problem of mediating between China and Tibet. Once the Western concept of state sovereignty had been extended to the East, however, every Chinese regime was compelled to adapt to it; any attempt to prolong a more ambiguous approach could only encourage local rulers to move towards independent sovereignty, sooner or later.

'One country, two systems'

Such was the situation when the Communist Party triumphed over the KMT in China, and founded the People's Republic in 1949. Mao made no move towards Tibet till the outbreak of the Korean War in 1950. Then a 40,000-strong contingent of the PLA crossed into territory under the control of the Kashag, with a show of force that quickly routed the Tibetan army ranged against it in Chamdo. But Mao was in no hurry to bring the

---

10   Sir Charles Bell, *Portrait of the Dalai Lama*, London 1946, p. 350.

revolution to Tibet. The intention of the CCP, on the contrary, was to 'manage' the country from afar through something very like the Qing model. Despite its revolutionary commitments, the CCP did not at first attempt any social reforms in Tibet. Sovereignty took precedence. As long as Tibet 'returned to the arms of the motherland's big family', Beijing was quite willing to tolerate the preservation of the 'feudal serf system' there. Although the number of Chinese military and civilian personnel stationed in Tibet after 1951 was vastly increased from the Qing era, political and social relationships were still mediated through de facto 'connectors'. Local affairs continued to be administered by the Tibetan authorities, and a 'one country, two systems' mechanism was set in place. The name given to this tactic was the United Front. What it meant in practice was an alliance between the Communists and the Tibetan ruling class, who would cooperate in the consolidation of Chinese sovereignty. The basis for this was the Seventeen-Point Agreement signed by Li Weihan and Ngawang Jigme Ngapo in May 1951, in which the Dalai Lama's government acknowledged that Tibet was part of China, gave post facto consent to the PLA's entry and to the eventual integration of the Tibetan Army into its ranks, and accepted the central government's authority to conduct its external affairs. In return, Beijing promised 'autonomy' for Tibet, leaving the social and religious system, the Dalai Lama's status and the local officials' positions unchanged, while restoring the Panchen Lama, driven into exile by the thirteenth Dalai.

The United Front line was followed not only in the areas under the administration of the Kashag government but also in Chamdo, where the PLA had established control. A People's Liberation Committee of the Chamdo Area was set up, with seven Tibetans among its nine vice-chairmen. Apart from one

CCP member, all of these were from local ruling families, as were the majority of the 35-member Committee. In the twelve subordinate *zong* or county-level Liberation Committees, there were 14 Han officials and 154 Tibetans, all from the elite. Chen Jingbo, director of the United Front Department of the CCP's Tibetan Working Committee at the time, reported:

> After the establishment of the Preparatory Committee for the Tibetan Autonomous Region in 1956, a large number of individuals from the local upper classes were appointed to various posts under the Committee. At the time, there were about 6,000 people that belonged to middle and upper classes (including major clan chiefs) in the whole region (among them, 205 were fourth-rank officials, 2,300 below fifth rank and 2,500 from religious circles). 2,163 of these were already assigned to posts and the remaining 3,400 are scheduled to receive various appointments by 1960.[11]

The Dalai Lama and Panchen Lama were the paramount focus of the United Front. When in 1954 they were invited to attend the Assembly of the National People's Congress in Beijing, Zhang Jingwu, secretary of the CCP's Tibetan Working Committee and the central government's highest representative in Lhasa, was specifically instructed by the Central Committee to look after them on the trip, which he took the utmost pains to do.[12] On their arrival at Beijing railway

---

11　Chen Jingbo, 'Xizang tongyi gongzuo de licheng' [The Experience of the United-Front Work in Tibet], in *Xizang wenshiziliao xuanji: jinian Xizang heping jiefang sishizhounian zhuanji* [Selected Historical Accounts of Tibet: A Special Issue to Commemorate the 40th Anniversary of the Peaceful Liberation of Tibet], compiled by Xizang Zizhiqu Wenshiziliao Weiyuanhui, 1991, pp. 120–1.
12　Zhao Shenying, a reporter who entered Tibet with the 18th Army, describes their journey: 'In the section where there had been a landslide

station they were met by Zhou Enlai and Zhu De, while Deng Xiaoping personally checked their living quarters and Mao Zedong received and hosted several dinner parties for them.[13] The Dalai Lama, just nineteen, was made a vice-chairman of the Standing Committee of the National People's Congress and the Panchen Lama, even younger, nominated a Standing Committee member.

Beijing was, at this stage, perfectly willing to tolerate the Tibetan authorities' stalling tactics on the Seventeen-Point Agreement. As Mao explained in 1952:

> Although the establishment of the military and administrative committee and the reorganization of the Tibetan troops were stipulated in the Agreement, you had fears, and so I instructed the comrades working in Tibet to slow down their implementation. The Agreement must be carried out but, because of your fears, it has to be postponed. If you are scared this year, it can wait until

---

in Bolong, the road-construction corps arranged a company of soldiers standing in a row, holding red flags, all along the 400-metre slope. At one area where landslides could occur at any time, the soldiers stood shoulder to shoulder, creating a wall of bodies to protect the Dalai Lama. When the convoy passed through the stone-strewn section of the landslide, Zhang Jingwu, the 50-year-old general and central government representative to Tibet, tried to protect the young Dalai Lama by walking on the left side, near the mountain, and holding his arm. Zhang Jingwu's aide-de-camp, Li Tianzhu, also ran back and forth, helping to attend to the Dalai. Nervously and cautiously they passed along the rugged road, step by step.' Zhao Shenying, *Zhongyang zhuzang daibiao, Zhang Jingwu* [The Central Government Representative to Tibet, Zhang Jingwu], Lhasa 1995, p. 109.

13   Ji Youquan's *Xizang pingpan jishi* [Factual Record of Rebellion Suppression in Tibet], Lhasa 1993, records Deng Xiaoping's instruction to Xu Danlu, director of the liaison office of the Tibetan Working Committee: 'You will be held responsible if a fly gets into the houses of the Dalai and Panchen Lamas.'

next year. If you still have fears next year, it can wait until the year after that.[14]

Indeed, the reorganization of the Tibetan Army had not gone beyond the issue of new uniforms and conferring of PLA ranks by the time of the 1959 Rebellion, in which a considerable number of its troops and officers would play an active part.

Ethnography and culture

Historically, 'Greater Tibet' had rarely been under the control of the Kashag government, whose effective rule for the most part never extended beyond the current boundaries of the Tibetan Autonomous Region. The situation has persisted under the PRC. The latest available census figures, for 1990, show a majority of ethnic Tibetans (54.4 per cent) living in neighbouring provinces (see Table 1).

Table 1   Population distribution of ethnic Tibetans

Tibet Autonomous Region	2,096,000	45.6%
Sichuan	1,087,000	23.0%
Qinghai	912,000	19.9%
Gansu	367,000	8.0%
Yunnan	111,000	2.4%

1990 Census. Full results of the 2000 census have not yet been released.

These administrative divisions do not correspond to the actual social landscape. Lhasa is the indubitable political and

---

14   *Xinhua Yuebao* [Xinhua monthly], February 1952, p. 11.

religious centre of the whole Tibetan ecumene, but the region of Ü Tsang ('Central Tibet') in which it is situated—often mistaken for the ethnographic land as a whole—is certainly not on a higher cultural level than the regions outlying it. Amdo (covering much of Qinghai and Gansu) contains two out of the six most important Yellow Hat monasteries. Kham (covering western Sichuan and the north-west corner of Yunnan) contains a variety of religious schools, and its cultural riches are far beyond those of Ü Tsang, as can easily be seen by the traveller today. Traditionally, a greater number of high-rank lamas have come from Amdo and Kham than from Ü Tsang. If the people of Ü Tsang look down on the Khampas, the prejudices are mutual. The former regard the latter as 'uncivilized', the latter view the former as 'hypocritical'—similar stereotypes to those that divide southerners and northerners in other nations. Socially speaking, the people of Amdo are mainly nomads, those in Kham farmers. Authority in Amdo is tribal, but is more chiefly in Kham, where the local *chabu*—the Tibetan name means 'king'—customarily enjoyed quasi-regal powers. Such social structures were to facilitate collective resistance to the Chinese authorities; but even without this, the religious factor alone was tinder capable of arousing the whole population against Han domination.

Nevertheless, when it came to implement the United Front, the CCP in the fifties took a purely bureaucratic approach, as if provincial borders mattered more than the cultural integrity of the Tibetan population as a whole. While those living inside the Autonomous Region—essentially Ü Tsang—were to be exempted from PRC reforms, Tibetans in Han-majority provinces were not. Nationwide collectivization was launched in 1955, and by 1956 the 'high tide of socialist construction'—land redistribution, the creation of local CCP units, class-struggle organization and the battle against elites—was sweeping the Tibetan areas of Sichuan, Qinghai, Gansu and Yunnan. Work teams mobilized the masses, creating peasant unions; title deeds were burnt. With their traditional entitlements under threat, Tibetan landowners took the risk of initiating active revolts against the CCP. There was fierce fighting in Kham as the PLA stepped in to put down the rebellion. Refugees from the four provinces—some 60,000, between 1956 and 1958—fled to Ü Tsang. Epidemics spread a sense of panic among the uprooted population there.

Nevertheless, the initial reaction in Beijing was still to continue the United Front tactic within the TAR. When the Tibetan Working Committee, in 1956, made a move to step up social and economic reforms in the region, dispatching more than 2,000 Han cadres to Tibet for the purpose, Beijing swiftly reversed the decision and sent Zhang Jingwu—by then Director of the PRC President's General Office—to stabilize the situation, announcing that there would be no reforms for the next six years. In March 1957 the Central Committee's Secretariat decided to cut back significantly on the Party's work in the TAR, reducing local administrative personnel from 45,000 to 3,700, with Han streamlined by 92 per cent, while troop levels were brought down from 50,000 to 18,000, and the number of military bases reduced; all facts testifying to the central government's willingness to continue the connector-model United Front.[15] Zhou Enlai went so far as to assure the Dalai Lama that, if the region was still not

15   Xizang Zizhiqu Dangshiziliao Zhengji Weiyuanhui comp., *Xizang gemingshi* [History of the Tibetan Revolution], Lhasa 1991, p. 103; *Zhonggong Xizang dangshi dashiji* [Chronicle of Events in the History of the CCP in Tibet]; *Xizang gemingshi*, p. 106; Zhao, [Central Government Representative in Tibet], p. 126.

ready for reform, the waiting period could be extended for another fifty years.[16]

Tibetan Rebellion and the Dalai's flight

The situation in Tibet, however, was growing increasingly turbulent, and the contradictions of the 'one country, two systems' approach ever more stark. Even the most trivial changes constituted a threat to the Tibetan upper classes and could cause major disturbance within such a highly traditional society. Wage payments to Tibetans working on road-construction schemes were seen as an assault on the centuries-old *ulag* service system. Free schools impinged on the monastic monopoly of education. Training of cadres with serf backgrounds upset the existing social hierarchy. In 1957, a serf in Shannan was beaten up by his lord for failing to perform his *ulag* service— an unconditional duty, whose dereliction customarily received brutal punishment. In this instance, the victim was a CCP activist who had been assigned a cadre position at grass-roots level. The case became a touchstone for Party policy in Tibet. United Front tactics demanded non-interference, but this would both dishearten peasant activists and encourage elite attempts to prevent the masses cooperating with the CCP. On the other hand, to discipline the assailant would cause trouble with the authorities' feudal partners. Nevertheless, the CCP gave the instruction to relieve all Tibetan cadres of their *ulag* duties.[17]

Ultimately the United Front tactic could be no more than an expedient measure. Support for the Communists would always come from the poorest layers, but the United Front was unable

16 Dalai Lama, *Freedom in Exile*, New York 1990, p. 119.
17 A. Tom Grunfeld, *The Making of Modern Tibet*, Armonk, NY 1996, pp. 129–30.

to provide these with any clear prospect. As one commentator put it:

> The mass of Tibetans was steadfastly tied to the status quo without the slightest knowledge of, or experience of, any other way of life. Confused by the new ways offered by the Han, fearful of the Han who simultaneously urged 'liberation' of the serfs from the feudal masters while creating alliances with these masters, they did not join their 'liberators' in large numbers.[18]

At the same time, despite all the compromises and conciliatory gestures, the United Front would never win the good faith of the Tibetan elite, who saw it rather as a game of cat and mouse in which, sooner or later, the mouse would inevitably be killed. Gradually, Beijing realized that the United Front—one of its three 'big magic weapons'—not only failed to guarantee the lamas' loyalty but would not garner the support of the masses, either—the biggest magic weapon of all. If Tibetan peasants could not be won away from their traditional deference, they would inevitably side with their local rulers in any uprising against the CCP, and Beijing would never be able to ensure lasting sovereignty over the region.

There was ample evidence for this in the 1959 Tibetan Rebellion. The PLA initially demanded that the Kashag government punish the Khampa 'bandits' who had fled to Ü Tsang in 1956 and 57; in 1958 its own troops entered the TAR, travelling in 60-truck convoys through the hostile countryside. Lhasa itself, surrounded by refugee tents, provided no sanctuary: the tension in the city had grown explosive. The detonating spark was a rumour that the PLA was planning to

18   Grunfeld, *The Making of Modern Tibet*, p. 150.

abduct the Dalai Lama. Kashag officials and Khampa rebels united in the call for an uprising. For days on end, thousands of demonstrators surrounded the Dalai's Summer Palace, throwing up barricades against the troops and shouting 'Kick out the Han'. Fierce fighting ensued before the Red Flag was hoisted over the Potala. The Dalai fled to India. Beijing assumed direct control.

'Turn the body over'

The vast mass of lower-class Tibetans would have been genuine beneficiaries of Beijing's initial reforms, yet they rose against them. Why? Many perceived only one distinction: between themselves and the Han. The long history of deference to monastic authority and tribal leaders ensured that, when their masters raised the twin banners of religion and nationality, Tibetan workers and peasants would rally to them. The conclusion drawn in Beijing was that 'the fundamental improvement of national relations, in the final analysis, depends on the complete emancipation of the working classes within each nationality.'[19] Translated into plain language, this meant the abandonment of the United Front and a turn to class struggle, aimed directly at the overthrow of the local elite. Within every nationality, it was now argued, there would invariably be rich and poor, oppression and exploitation. The poor everywhere belonged to one family; the rich were all the same, as black as crows. Hoisting the class-struggle flag, the CCP proclaimed itself no longer a party of the Han but a leader and spokesman of

---

19 Xizang Zizhiqu Dangwei Xuanchuanbu comp., *Zhongyang he zhongyang lingdao tongzhi guanyu Xizang minzuwenti de bufen lunshu* [Some Expositions by the Central Committee and the Leaders of the Central Committee on the Nationality Issue of Tibet], n.d.

poor people everywhere. It now set out to win over the poverty-stricken Tibetans from their national and religious allegiance to the elite.

As soon as the fighting in Lhasa came to an end, work teams composed of tens of thousands of military personnel and civilian cadres were sent to every village and rural area to launch 'democratic reforms' and to determine 'class status' among Tibetans as a whole. The first step was to induce the Tibetan masses to 'vent their grievances' and 'find the roots of their misery', asking questions such as, 'Who is feeding whom?'. The work teams guided the discussions: 'Why did generations of peasants suffer, while the owners of serfs lived in luxury from birth, with the best food and clothes?'; 'Who was the Tibetan government protecting and serving?'; 'Suffering was not predestined'. The goal was to convince the fatalistic Tibetans of the existence—and the injustice—of class exploitation. The new concept of classes was vividly depicted as *fan shen*, 'flip the body over': it turned previous criteria upside down. Now the poorer one was, the higher one's social status. Work teams recruited a layer of activists from amongst the peasantry in order to expand their operations. This group became the backbone of the political regime at grass-roots level. The majority of them had never received any education, so there was much controversy when they were installed in leading positions. The work teams countered this with discussions around the questions of 'Who were the most educated in the old society?', 'Who understood the poor best?', and 'Would somebody help the poor in their *fan shen* if he had administrative experience but harboured evil intentions?'. Step by step, a loyal contingent of Party supporters was trained.[20]

---

20   *Xizang de minzhu gaige* [Democratic Reforms in Tibet], Lhasa 1995, pp. 310, 314–15.

Winning over the poor required tangible benefits, which could only come from a redistribution of wealth. This would have a double effect: not only earning the CCP the gratitude of the impoverished masses, but destroying the elite's capacity to initiate revolt. Monasteries had been used as military bases during the Rebellion—the monks taking up arms—and the PLA had bombed them as it re-established control.[21] Mao now raised the slogan, 'Lamas must go back home'. Monks and nuns were forcibly married, 97 per cent of monasteries were closed down, 93 per cent of their inmates—104,000 out of 110,000—dispersed, and monastic land was confiscated and redistributed among the poor. The property of all ruling-class participants in the Rebellion—some 73 per cent, or 462 out of the 634 noble households, according to the statistics of the time—was also seized and redistributed (those who had not rebelled being compensated when their land was nationalized).[22] The CCP found it harder, however, to win allies among the peasantry in Tibet than in China proper—work teams often found the level of class consciousness regrettably low. Many of the poorest herdsmen, for example, were apparently hired hands, but were reluctant to admit it, pretending instead to be the sons or daughters of the herd owners. Their response when the work teams tried to classify them as hired herdsmen—the highest rank in the new hierarchy—was resentful: 'Why are you trying to force me to admit I'm a hired hand?'[23]

---

21 Of the 2,676 monasteries in Tibet at the time—roughly 1 per 700 of the population—1,436 took part in the Rebellion.
22 [Democratic Reforms in Tibet], p. 26.
23 [Democratic Reforms in Tibet], p. 333.

A fear above all others

One of the unique characteristics of traditional Tibetan society was that, despite a considerable degree of social and economic polarization, there was hardly any history of actual class confrontation. Conflict was generally between upper-class factions, or between Tibetans and other ethnic groups. What explains such an unusual degree of deference and obedience? The answer surely lies in the deeply rooted religious traditions of Tibet. Even if aware of their suppressed and exploited status, the poor would resign themselves to their fate, seeing it as retribution for their previous lives. According to Buddhist doctrine, their hope of freedom from suffering lay entirely in the hereafter: only by resigning themselves to their present condition and enduring its misery might they hope to win the favours of the deities, and the chance of being born into a better afterlife. Any resistance was disobedience to the divine will and would be met with suitable punishment. This staunch belief moulded the Tibetans' attitude of passive submission. The benefits of reform in this world could never match the happiness of the afterlife; if they committed the crime of 'defying their superiors' or 'enriching themselves with dubious wealth', the dreadful punishment that awaited them would far outweigh any earthly gains. This was why so many felt uncertain about class struggle, and why they not only joined their masters in the Rebellion but also followed them into exile and continued to serve them there. It was thus impossible for the CCP to win over the peasantry without tackling the problem of religion.

This was no easy matter. It would have been quite unfeasible simply to convert the Tibetans into atheists. If the highly evolved doctrines of the lamaist tradition are almost impossibly abstruse, the faith of the masses is far more comprehensible. The roots of their intense religiosity lie in the terrors of their natural environment—the explanation, surely, for the extraordinary proliferation of deities and monsters within Tibetan Buddhism, differentiating it from Indian and Chinese variants. Fear is the key factor. To find oneself in the harsh surroundings of the Tibetan plateau is to experience the mercilessness of nature, the arduous task of survival, the loneliness of the heart. Settlements on any scale could not subsist in most of the region, resulting in tiny human colonies that have clung on in the face of the vast, raging forces of nature. Encountering, alone, this savage expanse of earth and sky inevitably produced a feeling of being overwhelmed by such preponderance, a terrifying sense of isolation and helplessness, repeated down the generations. Fear provoked awe, and awe gave rise to the totem of deities and monsters:

> The Tibetans were living in a state of apprehension and anxiety. Every perturbation, either physical or spiritual, every illness, every susceptible or dangerous situation, would drive them to search feverishly for its causes, and for preventative measures.[24]

But the search for solutions only reinforced the anxiety: the more thought and explanation was lavished upon it, the deeper it grew. Faced with a fear that they could neither escape nor conquer, Tibetans were in need of a larger fear, clearly defined and structured, one that exceeded all others and which, so long as one obeyed it totally, would keep at bay all the lesser fears, lifting the intolerable psychological burden.

Fear formed the core of the Tibetans' spiritual world. Only by propitiating their terror, by offering sacrifices to it

---

24   Tu Qi, et al., *Xizang he Menggu de zongjiao* [The Religions of Tibet and Mongolia], Tianjing 1989, p. 218.

in complicated ceremonies, by worshipping and obeying it, could one feel safe and free, reassured by its vast dominion and tremendous power. Such a fear already possessed, at a certain level, the nature of divinity; the origins of the vast number of ferocious and terrifying objects worshipped in Tibetan religion—including those of the Bon shamanism that predated the eighth-century introduction of Buddhism from India—can surely be traced back here.[25] In that frightful environment, humankind can scarcely persevere without some sense of divine guidance and support. From this perspective it might be argued that, even if all other religions were on their way to extinction, the Tibetan creed would probably be preserved to the very last day.

Tibetan Buddhism exacts an exorbitant price from its followers. The hope of a better life hereafter demands a punishing regime of forbearance, asceticism and sacrifice in the present. Tibetans also have to contribute a considerable part of their personal wealth to religious activity—building monasteries, providing for monks and nuns, performing ceremonies, making pilgrimages and so forth. Under the Dalai Lama's government,

---

25 Another peculiar feature of the Tibetan religion is that it is not only the demons that appear ferocious. The deities, too, are often green-faced, with long teeth and angry eyes, brandishing lethal weapons and trampling tortured bodies underfoot. In Chinese Buddhism, the Goddess of Mercy appears as a beautiful woman. In Tibet, she is often portrayed as a dark giant wearing a necklace of skulls, holding another skull in her hand and with one foot on a dead body. In the *Xizang wangchen ji* [Records of the Tibetan Princes and their Subjects] written by the fifth Dalai Lama, the first Tibetan king to proselytize Buddhism to his people had 'deeply sunk eyelids and emerald-coloured eyebrows; spiraled teeth filled his mouth and his arms were like wheels'. Clearly, within the Tibetan aesthetic such gods represent majesty, power, invincibility—the more trustworthy precisely because they rule the world, and uphold justice, through their terror.

92 per cent of the budget was devoted to religious expenditure.[26] Even today, according to some estimates, the Tibetans pay about a third of their annual income to the monasteries. This was money that would not be transformed into productive investment nor used to improve the people's lives. For over a thousand years, the sweat and toil of the Tibetans had gone to encrust the monasteries, while the governing monks formed an enormous parasitic social stratum. In the eighteenth century, according to Melvyn Goldstein's estimate, about 13 per cent of the population were monks—in other words, around 26 per cent of Tibetan males.[27] The Chinese scholar Li Anzhai, in his 1947 sample survey of the Gede area of Xikang, found that the proportion of monks reached as high as 33.25 per cent—the highest in the world.[28] This unproductive layer was a heavy burden on Tibetan society, intensifying the existing shortage of labour. In addition, the celibacy lamaism enjoined contributed to the depletion of the population, one of the major problems in the region. Tibetan scholars themselves have attributed the decline of the Tufan dynasty to the effects of the religious system.[29] In the ninth century Langdarma, last of the Tufan kings, tried to force the monks to resume the tasks of secular life in an effort to reverse the decline.

---

26   'Han Meng Zang duihua—minzu wenti zuotanhui' jiyao [Summary of 'Dialogue among the Han, Mongolians and Tibetans—A Forum on the Nationality Issues'], *Beijing Zhichun* [Beijing Spring], November 1997.

27   Melvyn Goldstein, *A History of Modern Tibet, 1913–51: The Demise of the Lamaist State*, p. 23.

28   Li Anzhai, *Li Anzhai zangxue lunwen xuan* [Selected Works on Tibetan Studies], Beijing 1992, p. 270. In Buddhist Thailand, the monks account for under 2 per cent of the total male population.

29   Rapa Tseren and Lobu Tseren, 'Zongjiao, lishi yu minzu jingshen' ['Religion, History and Spirit of Nationality'], in *Xizang qingnian lunwenxuan* [Selected Works by Tibetan Young Scholars], p. 232.

Rotation of the gods

The Tibetans' submission to a religion that apparently runs contrary to their material interests becomes perfectly comprehensible in the context of their worship of fear. Faced with a choice between a short spell of suffering in this world followed by a blissful hereafter, or an eternity of torture, the peasants inevitably remained in thrall to the monks who held the keys to heaven. But if it is impossible for Tibetans to live without a god, nevertheless their religion allowed for a reincarnation of the deity. What if a new god appeared who was not only more powerful and awe-inspiring than the old, but who also told Tibetans that this life was everything, that their suffering was injustice, and that they should seek happiness in the here and now? Would they still be willing to deny their own human needs?

As to who had more actual power between the Dalai Lama and Mao Zedong, there could scarcely be any doubt. At the Battle of Chamdo in 1950 the crack troops of the Tibetan Army were totally overwhelmed by the PLA; the Dalai Lama had to take refuge in Yatung. In 1959, with tens of thousands of rebels demonstrating in the streets of Lhasa, it took the PLA only 20 hours or so to prevail, and the Dalai fled into exile. The Tibetans were inevitably disturbed by the disparity. The divinity before whom they had prostrated themselves turned out to be less invincible than they thought. A god for them was, by definition, capable of defeating all with his overwhelming strength, of making clear demands and using stern, indisputable measures to reward and punish. This mentality permeated other aspects of Tibetan life, as evidenced in their submission to autocracy, their tolerance of suffering, their respect for winners and cruelty to enemies. In a thousand subtle ways the power of Mao Zedong corresponded to these needs; the same forms of worship could be extended towards him.

It is unlikely that Beijing understood the issue in terms of religion. The support of the 'emancipated serfs' was perceived rather as evidence of Marxism's universal validity. In reality, however, it was impossible to overthrow centuries of worship without playing the role of a new god who came trampling on the old one, proclaiming the dawn of a new era and instituting a new system of punishment and rewards. Mao Zedong fitted the part perfectly. His rule could satisfy both the religious and the human needs of the Tibetans peasants—for, however deeply the concept of the afterlife had been instilled in their minds, the natural instinct to 'seek gains and avoid losses' still remained. Once 'converted', they took Maoism to extremes, smashing the old world and declaring their loyalty to the new with all the zeal of their traditional faith. The period of 1960 to 1966—from the final suppression of the Rebellion to the start of the Cultural Revolution—saw a movement from 'awakening' to overall mobilization in the region. The predominant image of the time was of Mao waving his red-starred military cap from a distant, temple-like building; Tibetans were only too familiar with the strong religious flavour of such a sight, which had always evoked in them a powerful emotional response. They plunged into the frenzy of the Cultural Revolution fired up both by fideistic fervour and material interest. Yet even as they shouted 'atheist' slogans against the monasteries, the underlying pulse was still there; it was simply that Mao had replaced the Dalai Lama as the god in their minds.

In this psychology, the rotation of deities meant the recreation of the universe: the dominion of this more powerful ruler would endure forever, the old one would be eternally damned. It was entirely rational, then, from the viewpoint of traditional Tibetan culture, to switch sides, submit to the new order and tear down the remnants of the old. Looking back at this process of 'god creation' during the Mao era, one notices religious echoes almost everywhere: supreme ideology corresponding to faith; the ultimate goal of communism, to heaven; unconditional obedience to the teacher and leader, to worship of God; political studies, to preaching; reforming one's world outlook, to purifying one's consciousness; self-criticism, to confession; strict Party discipline and sacrifice for the cause, to asceticism. If the actual ceremonies of Mao worship were slightly different, their spiritual essence was close enough to lamaism to make it an easy switch. To hang Mao's picture in a cottage and bow to it daily, to recite his 'highest instructions' while clasping the Little Red Book, was not so far removed from the accustomed daily prayers and prostrations before the household image of the Dalai Lama.

As long as the need for a powerful deterrent force and for the corresponding placatory rituals was met, the actual religious content was far less important. The prayer-stone piles by the roadsides and on mountain passes were destroyed during the Cultural Revolution, and stone or cement billboards with Mao's quotations erected in their place: the peasants circled them when they passed by, just as they had with the prayer piles. In the traditional Ongkor festival at the start of the harvest season, they used to carry Buddhist images, chant scripts and sing Buddhist songs. During the Cultural Revolution, they carried Mao's picture, recited his quotations and sang 'The East is Red'. Historically, Chinese emperors had been seen in Tibet as the embodiment of the Bodhisattva Buddha, with a higher status than the Goddess of Mercy, incarnated in the Dalai Lama; many Tibetans now accorded Mao the same honour.

Clearly, Mao might be a better choice for the peasantry, the Communist heaven preferable to the 'paradise in the west' and revolutionary organizations a substitute for monasteries—as long as the new rituals satisfied the ceremonial demands of their religion. Beijing's harsh leftist policies were now principally targeted at the aristocracy; in a reversal of the previous relationship, in which the minority's privileges had been maintained by the majority's misery, it was the top 10 per cent that henceforward suffered most from the repression. The powerful new god was not only capable of inflicting the most brutal punishment on its enemies, it also took care of the impoverished masses, bestowing extraordinary favours on them: the abolition of the *ulag* and of taxation, airborne disaster relief, mobile medical treatment, the enrolment of peasant children at the universities. At the same time, the rules for differentiation were clear cut: everything depended on class. This philosophy of a fate predetermined by one's birthright was almost identical to Tibetan Buddhism's traditional account.

Destruction of the temples

The clearest manifestation of this rotation-of-the-gods in the minds of the Tibetan peasants was their active participation in levelling the very temples and monasteries they had once held most sacred. The Dalai camp and Western public opinion have always attributed this to Han Red Guards coming in from China proper, after the Cultural Revolution was launched in 1966. They have seen it as part of the CCP's 'systematic, methodical, calculated, planned and comprehensive destruction' of Tibetan religion.[30] The truth is that, because of poor transportation

30   Pierre-Antoine Donnet, *Tibet: Survival in Question*, London 1994, p. 81.

and the huge distances involved, only a limited number of Han Red Guards actually reached Tibet. Even if some of them did participate in pulling down the temples, their action could only have been symbolic. Hundreds of shrines were scattered in villages, pastures and on rugged mountainsides: no one would have been capable of destroying them without the participation of the local people. Furthermore, most of the Red Guards who did reach the TAR were Tibetan students, returning from universities elsewhere. The fact that they often retained their organizations' original names—Capital Red Guards, for instance—is one reason for the confusion over this. With the gradual return of these Tibetan Red Guards—who often combined their revolutionary work with visits to their families—the sparks of the Cultural Revolution spread across villages and pastures over the entire Tibetan plateau; followed by the rampage of destruction.

It is true that tension at the time was so high that no one dared voice any dissent; nevertheless, the rulers alone could not have created the sort of social atmosphere that then prevailed without the participation of the masses, who sometimes played a leading role. The authorities in Tibet often tried to restrain radical actions, with the PLA, for example, consistently supporting the more conservative factions against the rebels. Temples and monasteries survived best in the central cities and areas where the authorities could still exercise some control. In contrast, the Gandan Monastery, some sixty kilometres outside Lhasa and one of the three major centres of the Yellow Hat sect, was reduced to ruins.

To point out that it was largely the Tibetans themselves who destroyed the monasteries and temples is not to exonerate the Han; but it does raise broader questions, beyond the issue of responsibility. Why did the Tibetans, who for centuries had regarded religion as the centre of their lives, smash the Buddhist statues with their own hands? How did they dare pull down the temples and use the timbers for their own homes? Why did they ravage the religious artefacts so recklessly, and why were they not afraid of retribution when they denounced the deities at the tops of their voices and abused the lamas they had so long obeyed? Surely these actions are evidence that, once they realized they could control their own fate, the Tibetan peasantry, in an unequivocally liberating gesture, cast off the spectre of the afterlife that had hung over them for so long and forcefully asserted that they would rather be men in this life than souls in the next.

In 1969 an armed 'revolt' broke out against the introduction of People's Communes into Tibet, which had been spared them in the period of the Great Leap Forward; this eventually spread to over forty counties. The Dalai's camp saw this 'Second Tibetan Rebellion' as a continuation of the resistance of the fifties. In reality, the two were very different. During the earlier uprising, the peasants were fighting, in a sense, for the interests of the aristocracy. In 1969, they fought for their own. They did not want the pastures and livestock that had been redistributed among them from the old landowners to be appropriated by the People's Communes. At the time a few of these protests, provoked by the Cultural Revolution, were actually intensified into genuine 'revolts' by the authorities' repression.[31]

---

31 In a propaganda document complied by the Ali military subarea of the Tibetan military region in 1975, there was an article praising the achievement of 'rebellion suppression' by a military unit in the Gaize County. Some of the 'revolts' mentioned in the article included demands for *'sanzi yibao'* [more plots for self use, more free markets, more enterprises with sole responsibility for their own profit or loss, and fixing output quotas on a household basis]; protecting cadres who were removed from their positions; and setting up 'rebel organizations'. *Shijie wuji shangde yingxiong zhanshi* [The Heroic Soldiers on the Roof of the World], comp. by Zhongguo Renmin Jiefangjun Xizang Junqu Ali Junfenqu, 1975, pp. 112–21.

The turbulence was quickly quelled once they realized their mistake. In comparison with the factional rivalries and armed conflicts in other parts of China, Tibet at the time remained relatively stable. In short, Maoism appeared to have achieved an overall victory in the sixties and seventies: China's sovereignty over Tibet looked unprecedentedly effective and secure. The 'nationality question', later the cause of so much trouble, seemed scarcely worth consideration. Tibetans seemed on generally calm terms with the Han and the Dalai Lama almost forgotten, both in Tibet and in the West.

Costs of the Cultural Revolution

The reality was otherwise. The ideological success of Maoism in overturning lamaism was not matched by any comparable achievement in improving the material conditions of ordinary Tibetans. The ultra-leftist policies of the Cultural Revolution inflicted tremendous human and economic damage on Tibet, as everywhere in the PRC. Excesses on a massive scale had already been committed during the earlier campaigns for 'democratic reform' and the suppression of the 1959 Rebellion, many of which were discussed in the Panchen Lama's Seventy-Thousand Character Petition of 1962. The prevailing situation was, indeed, clearly mirrored in the Panchen Lama's fate. If any sense of the United Front approach had persisted within the CCP, he would not have been so mercilessly punished just for an internal petition. As it was, in 1964 he was classified as an enemy and removed from his posts, subjected to mass-struggle sessions and jailed for nearly ten years. Another important Tibetan religious figure, Geshe Sherab Gyatso, was sent back to his home town in Dunhua county, Qinghai province, where he was tortured to death. Political movements were launched across Tibet, one after another: the Three Educations, the Four Clean-ups, One Strike and Three Antis, Cleaning Ranks, Socialist Reforms, Double Strikes, Basic Lines Education, Purging Capitalist Factions, Criticizing Smaller Panchens. The 1980 Rehabilitation Conference held in the TAR after the Cultural Revolution revealed that, 'According to a rough estimate, more than one hundred thousand people in the region were either implicated or affected by unjust and wrong cases, which accounted for more than 10 per cent of the entire population.'[32]

During the entire period from the Tenth Plenary Session of the Central Committee in 1962, which reintroduced the class-struggle theme, to Hu Yaobang's inspection tour of Tibet in 1980, CCP policy had been based on the thesis that 'the nationality question is in essence a class question'. Anyone unfamiliar with the political jargon of the time would have a hard time understanding this. The nation itself was of no significance—'the workers have no motherland'; the essential distinction was that of class. There was thus no need to select leading cadres on a national or ethnic basis: as long as they were revolutionaries, they could lead the masses anywhere. To request leaders from one's own community would be to commit the error of 'narrow-minded nationalism'—tantamount to sabotaging the class camp. During the Cultural Revolution, the Revolutionary Committee—the highest political organ in Tibet—had a Han chairman and only four Tibetans among its thirteen vice-chairmen. In 1973, Tibetans made up only 35.2 per cent of Party Committee members; in

---

32 *Xizang zhongyao wenjian xuanbian* [Selected Important Documents of the Tibetan Autonomous Region], p. 121.

1975, they accounted for a mere 23 per cent of leading cadres at district level.[33]

For the peasantry, the introduction of the People's Communes—initiated in 1964, and covering 99 per cent of villages by 1975—meant an unprecedented degree of centralized control. If a Commune member wanted to get half a kilo of butter he had to report to his production team in advance and then work his way through a series of procedures involving team leaders, accountants and warehouse keepers. The remaining private elements of the economy were almost totally wiped out. Before 1966 there had been over 1,200 small retailers in Lhasa. By 1975, only 67 remained. In Jalung county 3,000 privately owned wool-looms and spinning-wheels were done away with in the name of 'cutting off the capitalist tails'.[34] The organization of the People's Communes killed off any enthusiasm for production; in conjunction with the political assaults of the Cultural Revolution this led to a stagnation of living standards, especially among the farmers and herdsmen. Although the suffering could be temporarily concealed by the high revolutionary energy of the time and by the introduction of other benefits, such as medical care and social promotion, according to the 1980 figures half a million of the already impoverished Tibetans—over a quarter of the population—were worse off after the mutual-aid groups were communized, and about 200,000 were rendered destitute.[35]

33   *The Making of Modern Tibet*, pp. 170–1; Xizang Nongmuxueyuan Maliejiaoyanshi yu Xizang Zizhiqu Dangxiao Lilunyanjiushi, comp., *Xizang dashi jilu 1949–1985* [Chronicle of Major Events in Tibet, 1949–1985], 1986, pp. 268, 288.

34   [Chronicle of Major Events], p. 390; [Selected Important Documents of the TAR], p. 212.

35   Speech by Guo Xilan at the Fifth Session of the Second Party Committee, June 3, 1980, in *Xizang zizhiqu zhongyao wenjian*, vol. 1, p. 97. The population of Ü Tsang totaled 1,800,000 at the time.

'Redressing the wrongs'

The Great Helmsman responsible for these disasters passed away in 1976. It was another two years before Deng Xiaoping became supreme leader. The process of 'redressing the wrongs' in Tibet began right from the start of the new Reform Era. On 28 December 1978, less than a week after taking power, Deng gave an interview to the Associated Press in which he indicated his willingness to start a dialogue with the Dalai Lama; he received the Dalai's representative in Beijing the following March. The 376 participants in the 1959 Rebellion still serving prison sentences were freed. Over 6,000 others who had been released after completing their sentences but were still branded as 'rebels' and kept under 'supervised reform' had these labels removed. Party management of Tibet made an about-turn once more.

On 14 March 1980, Hu Yaobang presided over the first Tibetan Work Forum of the Central Committee Secretariat; its proposals were released to the whole Party under the title Central Committee Document Number Thirty-One. Two months later, Hu made an inspection tour of Tibet, accompanied by leading officials including then Vice Premier Wan Li, Ngawang Jigme Ngapo and Yang Jingren. Hu stayed in Lhasa for nine days, meeting people from various circles. The day before his departure, he called an extraordinary TAR Party Committee meeting of more than 4,500 cadres, including all those above county and regiment level from the CCP, government and PLA. Hu's speech to the meeting was considered a turning point in Tibetan history, its significance comparable to the extrusion of the Residential Commissioner in 1912, the PLA's entry in 1951 or the post-1959 reforms. It has determined the approach to Tibet ever since. Hu made six major proposals:

1. Tibet should enjoy autonomous rule, and Tibetan cadres should have the courage to protect their own national interests;
2. Tibetan farmers and herdsmen should be exempt from taxation and purchase quotas;
3. Ideologically oriented economic policies should be changed to practical ones, geared to local circumstances;
4. Central government's financial allocations to Tibet should be greatly increased;
5. Tibetan culture should be strengthened;
6. Han cadres should step aside in favour of Tibetan ones.[36]

This was a striking departure from both the Qing court's Twenty-Nine Articles and the CCP's Seventeen-Point Agreement concluded in 1954, both of which had been intended to strengthen Beijing's position of control over Tibet. The Twenty-Nine Articles had been imposed by imperial decree and, while the Seventeen-Point Agreement made various promises, the Tibetans had been forced to sign it after their military defeat, which it sealed. By contrast, Hu's initiative proposed to restore Tibetan rights and pledged substantial aid.

The Six Proposals were unquestionably of benefit to Tibet. The tax and purchase exemptions initiated in 1980 were naturally welcome, as were the pro-privatization policies and the abolition of the People's Communes. Beijing's financial allocations to Tibet soared from 500 million RMB in 1979 to close in on 2.9 billion RMB in 1994, while investment in Tibet's infrastructure increased from around 100 million RMB in 1979 to over 900 million RMB in 1993.[37] The real

---

36 [Selected Important Documents of the TAR], pp. 15–32.
37 *Xizang tongji nianjian 1994* [1994 Yearbook of Tibetan Statistics], Beijing, p. 109; *Xizang zizhiqu jiben qingkuang shouce* [Handbook on Tibetan Essentials], tables 4–15, pp. 4–16.

turning points for the Tibetans, however, were the proposals to strengthen autonomous rule, indigenous culture and Tibetanization—points one, five and six. Even before Hu's visit to Tibet, Document Number Thirty-One had already made the dramatic announcement that:

> Among all the general and specific policies drawn up by the Central Committee and its various departments as well as all the documents, instructions and regulations issued nationwide, those that do not fit Tibet's circumstances may not be carried out or may be implemented after modification by the leading organs of Tibetan party, administrative and mass organizations.[38]

Historically, the central government had always sought the passive submission of the minority peoples of the borderlands. Now for the first time the authorities were, on their own initiative, urging the minorities to question their orders or even to resist them. In the past it would have been simply unimaginable that such a document could be issued to the whole Party. Hu made a further call at the mass Party Committee meeting:

> Are all the secretaries at the level of county and above present here today? You should, according to the characteristics of your own areas, draft concrete laws, decrees and regulations to protect the special interests of your nationality. You really should do this. In the future we would criticize you if you still just copy indiscriminately the stuff from the Central Committee. Do not copy indiscriminately the experience of other places nor that of the Central Committee. Copying indiscriminately is only fit for lazybones.[39]

---

38   [Selected Important Documents of the TAR], pp. 3–4.
39   [Selected Important Documents of the TAR], p. 21.

While Hu's speech did not touch directly on lifting the ban on religion, it put great stress on strengthening Tibetan culture, of which Buddhism was the core. Document Thirty-One demanded 'respect for people's normal religious practices'. Following Hu's speech, the TAR Party Committee and the regional government also issued decrees requiring the use of the Tibetan language in official documents and public speeches, and applying 'competence in the Tibetan language as one of the major criteria for admission to school, employment and transferring one's status to that of cadre, as well as for using, promoting and selecting cadres.'[40] Historically, dominant ethnic groups had always tried to force minorities to give up their own languages—Nationalist officials had even attempted to impose a Chinese-language exam on Tibetan 'incarnates' before they could accede to living Buddha status.[41] It was commendable that the central government now took measures to strengthen an indigenous tongue.

Tibetanization and instability

But the most significant of the Six Proposals was the insistence that Han cadres should step aside in favour of Tibetans. Hu argued that:

40 *Xizang zizhiqu guanche yijiubasi nian zhonggong zhongyang shujichu zhaokai de Xizang gongzuo zuotanhui jingshen wenjian xuanbian* [Selected Documents on the Implementation of the Spirit of the Forum on Tibetan Work, held by the Secretariat of the Central Committee of the CCP in 1984], vol. 2, p. 89.

41 Huang Musong wrote in his Tibetan diary, 'I think in order for the government to reorganize the religion, it has to instruct the senior lama incarnates to study Chinese and pass the examinations when they grow up, and only then permit their succession. This is the key to governing (Tibet).' *Shizang jicheng* [My Mission to Tibet], p. 50.

As the result of our discussion yesterday, in the next two or three years (in my opinion, two years is better), among state non-production cadres—here I am not talking about production cadres, who should be entirely Tibetans, but about non-production cadres, including teachers—Tibetan cadres should make up more than two thirds of the total. [Wan Li adds: I proposed an eight-to-two ratio the other day.] He was even more radical than I am and I also agree. He wants 80 per cent for Tibetan cadres and 20 per cent for Han cadres. [Wan Li: What I meant was an eight-to-two ratio for the county cadres. As for the prefecture cadres, it should be 100 per cent.][42]

This last proposal encountered great resistance from Han officials in the TAR but Hu's instructions were: 'Carry out the policy even if you do not understand; make decisions first and straighten out later'. Fifteen days later, the transfer plan was announced. The total Han population of the TAR stood at 122,400 at the time, of which 92,000—75 per cent—were scheduled to depart within the next two to three years. Among these were 21,000 Han cadres (of a total 55,000 TAR cadres, of whom 31,000 were Han) and 25,000 Han workers (of a total 80,000 TAR workers, of whom 40,000 were Han).[43] The plan was later modified because the departure of so many trained Han workers brought many organizations in Tibet almost to a standstill. Nevertheless, between 1980 and 1985 the Han population was reduced by 42 per cent.

The transfers vacated more than ten thousand cadre quotas and a similar number of 'iron rice-bowls' in the state-owned enterprises; Tibetans were the beneficiaries of this. The

---

42 [Selected Important Documents of the TAR], pp. 29–30.
43 [Selected Important Documents of the TAR], p. 51; *Dangdai Zhongguo Xizang renkou* [The Tibetan Population in Contemporary China], Beijing 1992, p. 200.

implementation of new legislation on 'Autonomous Rule in the Nationality Regions' subsequently ensured that all key positions in the governing bodies were held by officials from the local region; Han officials could only hold deputy positions. Tibetan cadres thus not only comprised the statistical majority but also controlled most of the leading government positions, including the crucial departments of finance, public security and justice. By 1989, Tibetans accounted for 66.6 per cent of total cadres in the TAR, 72 per cent at provincial level and 68.4 per cent at prefectural level. All 'number one' administrative leaders at provincial and prefectural levels were Tibetans, as were the Party Secretaries in 63 out of the 75 counties.[44] 'Redressing the wrongs' also brought tremendous improvements in living standards. In 1979 the average income of Tibetan farmers and herdsmen was 147 RMB; in 1990 it was 484 RMB and in 1994, 903.29 RMB. In 1992, the TAR's total agriculture output was up 69.8 per cent from 1978—and 460 per cent up from its 1952 level. In the cities the improvement was even greater.[45]

Under the new policy, religious practices in both the TAR and the Tibetan areas of the neighbouring provinces were revived to a level comparable to pre-1959—barring only the restoration of the old monastic economy and 'unity of monastery and state'. The clergy were once again given special 'United Front' treatment; the number of monks and nuns increased to 46,000— 2 per cent of the Tibetan population—by 1994. Temples were under construction everywhere. The decision of the Second

---

44   Zhang Shirong, 'Xizang shaoshu minzu ganbu duiwu hongguan guanli chutan' [A Preliminary Exploration on the Macro-management of the Minority Cadres in Tibet], in *Xizang Qingnian Lunwenxuan*, p. 161.

45   [Tibetan Population in Contemporary China], p. 342; [1995 Yearbook of Tibetan Statistics], p. 178; Song Yong et al., *Xizang jingjishehui fazhan jianmingshigao* [Concise History of Tibetan Economic and Social Development], Lhasa 1994, p. 122.

Tibetan Work Forum of 1984 to 'gradually restore about 200 temples by the end of the eighties' was vastly exceeded, with 1,480 temples and monasteries reopened by 1992, and over 300 more by 1994.[46] A considerable part of the capital involved came from local government, while the TAR authorities allocated 260 million RMB for rebuilding between 1980 and 1992. The provincial governments in Sichuan, Yunnan, Gansu and Qinghai also contributed a sizeable amount of money to religious projects in their Tibetan areas. The central government disbursed over 53 million RMB for the renovation of the Potala Palace, as well as 64 million RMB and 614 kilos of gold to construct a tomb pagoda for the tenth Panchen Lama.[47] In the spirit of promoting the religious revival, Wu Jinghua, the first secretary of the TAR Party Committee, participated—in full Tibetan costume—in a Great Prayer Festival in Lhasa which was broadcast to the entire region on TV. The few remaining restrictions were mainly applied to clerical organizations, and even they were largely lip-service; there was hardly any interference in the religious practices of the laity.

Deng Xiaoping's policy in the region was, in all these respects, an essentially open and enlightened one. For most Tibetans, it might have been thought, the situation should have appeared the best in their history. These apparently optimal conditions, however, saw an unprecedented outbreak of discord and social instability. On 21 September 1987, the Dalai Lama appeared before the US Congress. Six days later Lhasa saw its first street demonstration since 1959. Big rallies demanded independence and raised the banned national flag. Arrests immediately followed, and when people heard the screams of monks being

---

46 [1984 Tibetan Work Forum Selected Documents], p. 20.
47 Liu Wei, *Xizang de jiaobusheng* [The Sound of Tibet's Footsteps], Lhasa 1994, pp. 194, 253.

beaten in the central police station, crowds besieged the building and started throwing stones. The authorities were caught by surprise and the situation quickly deteriorated as buildings and vehicles were torched and Han were lynched. Troops opened fire as the confrontations escalated. The next seventeen months saw an increasingly bloody pattern of disturbances, leading ultimately to the imposition of martial law in March 1989, which remained in effect for 419 days. At the same time, the Tibetan question came under more intense international scrutiny, with Beijing's policies eliciting an increasingly wide range of criticism in the West—as if the 80s' turn had been retrogressive. Tibet became a bargaining chip with which to put pressure on China, and the Dalai Lama acquired unprecedented influence.

Getting down from the shrine

In secular terms, the Tibetans' reaction to the liberalization of the 80s is hard to understand. Another form of analysis is required. Within the terms of Tibetan Buddhism, 'redressing the wrongs' destroyed the divine status Mao had been accorded. God did not make mistakes. Even if they could not understand his cruelty and his punishments, he would have his own reasons and did not need to explain—if he did, it would be incomprehensible anyway, like a book from heaven. God did not need to curry favour; he could order people to do whatever he desired. More importantly, he would never admit to any errors. That would reduce him to the status of human. Once that happened, people could settle accounts over all the past cruelties, and demand even more admissions and compensation.

The Tibetans did not necessarily feel grateful, therefore, when they got government money for restoring the temples. On the contrary, they saw it as an admission that the holy buildings had been destroyed by the Han authorities—the standard account now among Tibetan exiles as well as in the West. If the money was to be a compensation for these crimes, no sum could be large enough to earn their praise. In the past, when a new god appeared and demanded they destroy the old religion, they had obeyed. Now, all of a sudden, after they had smashed the monasteries and temples to pieces, they were told that the new god did not exist. It was all an unfortunate mistake and the previous religion needed to be restored. It is not hard to imagine how they felt; and such a feeling could hardly be commuted into gratitude by government grants.

This was also one of the crucial factors in the strong rebound of traditional religion. To all who had once sided with the great Han atheist and taken part in the destruction of the monasteries, the resurrection of the old religion connoted that they had betrayed their god and would face the most horrifying punishments. Terrified by what awaited them they tried, on the one hand, to explain that they had had no choice and, on the other, to 'atone for their crimes' through redoubled, fanatical devotion to the traditional religious regime. It was common to find that those working hardest to rebuild the temples were the very ones who had led the way in tearing them down. Some officials also tried to 'wash off' their guilt by playing up ethno-national sentiments, resisting instructions from their superiors, and discriminating against the Han.

Maoism had fractured the Tibetan national entity through class polarization. Freed from the control of their old masters, the peasants had been the foundation of the communist regime. Under Deng, the class-struggle line was abandoned, and the old aristocrats, clan chiefs and lamas once again were invited to the National People's Congress and the Chinese People's Political Consultative Conference. Lhalu Tsewang Dorje,

commander of the Tibetan forces in the 1959 Rebellion, was
released from prison in 1979 and is currently a vice-chairman
of the regional Political Consultative Conference; his wife is a
member of its standing committee and his son is deputy director
of the regional Nationality and Religions Bureau. Meanwhile,
Tibetan 'activists' who were once in the vanguard of the
'Rebellion suppression', the 'democratic reforms', the struggle
against the landowners and the destruction of the monasteries
have now been cast aside.[48] The majority of such militants had
been production-brigade cadres in People's Communes. With
the Communes gone, they have lost their previous status and
are reduced to ordinary farmers and herdsmen. Many of them
languish in poverty, with no help for their old age. According to
the Organization Department of the Tibetan Party Committee,
the majority of previous 'activists' have sunk into this poverty-
stricken stratum. Based on his survey on pastures in western
Tibet, Melvyn Goldstein also points out that:

> all the former wealthy households are among those with the largest
> herds and most secure income. On the other hand, all of today's poor
> are from households that were very poor in the old society . . . The
> former commune cadres fall between these poles . . . In 1987, ten

48   The *People's Daily*'s reporter in Tibet, Liu Wei, recorded Tibetans'
views after the 1989 Lhasa riot in his *Lasa saoluan jishi* [An Eyewitness
Account of the Lhasa Riot]: 'The government should review its work and its
policies on Tibet. The smiling face has always been given to the people from
the upper strata and no one cares about the grievances of the ordinary people.
This is very disheartening for the masses.' 'Nowadays the troublemakers
are not isolated; the isolated ones are we cadres—isolated in the society as
well as at home. If you ask why? Some people said, the communist party
has changed: it wanted us in the 1950s but wanted the nobles in the 1980s.
There was a saying: all personnel of the upper strata and even dogs were
rehabilitated. But what happened to the masses? The retired workers and
cadres? No money. No houses.'

households (18 per cent) received welfare from the county . . . It is interesting to note that all ten households who received welfare in 1987 were poor in the old society.[49]

On top of everything else, these 'activists' now also have to carry the burden of being seen as traitors to their nation, while their misfortune is perceived by others as well-deserved retribution.

The old rich have become rich again, and the poor have become poor. To the fatalistic Tibetans, this is an omen of God's will. Consciously or unconsciously, many have already started to adjust their behaviour. A cadre with more than twenty years' experience at grass-roots level in the Dingqing County of northern Tibet told me of one small change. During the Cultural Revolution, if an old landowner met emancipated serfs on the road he would stand to the side, at a distance, putting a sleeve over his shoulder, bowing down and sticking out his tongue—a courtesy paid by those of lower status to their superiors—and would only dare to resume his journey after the former serfs had passed by. Now things have changed back: the former serfs stand at the side of the road, bow and stick out their tongues, making way for their old lords. This has been a subtle process, completely voluntary, neither imposed by anyone nor explained. Although the pre-revolutionary era has not made a real comeback, the former serfs have sensed the change in the social atmosphere and feel it would be safer to show their repentance for holding their heads high in the past. This tiny change in conduct reflects the tremendous metamorphosis that has taken place.

---

49   Melvyn Goldstein and Cynthia Beall, 'The Impact of China's Reform Policy on the Nomads of Western Tibet', *Asian Survey*, vol. 29, no. 6, 1989, pp. 637–8, 640–1.

Commercialization and superstition

Annual economic growth in Tibet was over 10 per cent between 1991 and 1999—higher than in China proper. Per capita income for farmers and herders has grown by 9.3 per cent per year, for urban residents by 19.6 per cent. These are not just empty figures. On a visit to Tibet in 2000, rising living standards were visible everywhere, in rural areas as well as the towns, with a lot of new construction taking place. Material conditions are currently comparable with those of inland— not coastal—China. Tibet is more prosperous now than ever before in its history. However, this has not gained the PRC the allegiance of the Tibetans, more and more of whom have become attached to the Dalai Lama, who has never given them a penny. There have been no recent street riots, and things look peaceful on the surface. But there is no difficulty in sensing where their feelings lie. Virtually all Tibetans have the Dalai in their hearts. Every year thousands of ordinary Tibetans risk their lives crossing the Himalayas to join him in India. Not infrequently, CCP functionaries themselves, PLA officers included, become Buddhists right after retirement. Meanwhile, many of the young Tibetans sent to China to be educated become the most radical oppositionists, with the strongest national sentiments. Chen Kuiyuan, the current CCP First Secretary in Tibet, complained in September 1996: 'How many traitors were nursed by us'. It would be wrong to regard the present situation as more stable than in 1987. At that time, it was mainly monks and disoriented youth who led the riots. Nowadays, opposition lurks among cadres, intellectuals, state employees. In the words of one retired official: 'The current stabilization is only on the surface. One day people will riot in much greater numbers than in the late 80s'.

The Han presence has become more variegated. Han cadres were resentful of Hu's policy in the 80s: Tibetans gained a lot of ground in local life, and the Han felt marginalized. Later they turned their grudges against Zhao Ziyang, who blamed the '87–'89 riots on 'Han ultra-leftism' in Tibet. Han officials, on the contrary, felt that the situation had got out of hand because of the incorrect Beijing line of laying all the blame for unrest in Tibet on the Party there, so justifying Tibetan troublemakers and undermining their own ability to keep order in the TAR. They felt condemned to a passive stance, without instructions. In the 90s, however, the policies of Hu and Zhao were reversed: the official line now blames 'the Dalai clique and Western intervention' for the riots, and local Han power-holders feel thoroughly vindicated, viewing the retrospective change as a significant rectification. They are thoroughly comfortable with the 'key point is stabilization' line of the current CCP leadership.

But there has been a new influx of Han over the past decade. Some of these—prostitutes, cobblers, tailors, clock-repairers, vegetable farmers, grocers—have been drawn by the magnet of money-making. They are to be found along the highways, running small roadside restaurants, bidding for construction contracts, flocking to gold rushes, hunting rare species. Even Chinese beggars can make a living in Lhasa. As to their number, the TAR authorities have no idea. They are, of course, concentrated in the towns and along the main roads, giving them a more visible presence than the statistics may justify. A second type of newcomer is the tourist or adventurer, mainly from the Han elite—people such as journalists, writers, painters, photographers, students, and not a few officials, ostensibly on missions, but actually on travel jaunts. These Han differ from earlier cadres in that they don't look to local political power for protection—nor do they get near the core of Tibetan society.

They retain their outsider identities; few intend to stay. The first type are similar to the 'floating population' in the big PRC cities, and will leave when conditions cease to be profitable. The second group come and go anyway. But both bring secularization and commercialization to Tibetan society; the blow they represent to the traditional order is not to be underestimated.

What headway has secularization made in twenty-first century Tibet? A tiny minority—mainly younger urban people with higher education—may view the Dalai Lama in a more detached way, as a human being rather than a god, and embodying the attractions of Western liberalism and capitalist prosperity rather than reincarnated divinity. But within the TAR, those with college education comprised only 0.57 per cent of the population in 1990—including Han living in Tibet, who are better educated. The overwhelming majority of Tibetans are peasants, nomads and poorly educated town-dwellers who have never heard of the Nobel Prize or Hollywood. They worship the Dalai Lama with the same awe as they do the gods whom they would never be lucky enough to meet. It is common enough in Tibet today to see a crowd form and bow down to worship a little boy, merely because he is a reincarnated Buddha.

The Deng era renounced the class line, restored traditional Tibetan religion, and re-engaged the upper classes in a 'united front.' This turn greatly improved the living conditions of the Tibetans, but it forfeited the capacity of the CCP to intervene within Tibetan society, and led to its reintegration as a national community. If China had still remained closed, as in the past, the re-emergence of the Tibetans as one nationality might not have caused major problems for the regime in Beijing. But China was now opened up to the world, and could not insulate Tibet from changes in the international environment—among them the disintegration of the Soviet system, and new interventionist attitudes in the West. In earlier years, the rationale behind the policy shift from the 'United Front' to the class line was precisely that the two banners of religion and nationality had been monopolized by the upper classes, and outsiders were not allowed to play any role in the country. Today, the person who controls the two banners is none other than the Dalai Lama, who enjoys the status both of the highest spiritual leader and the internationally recognized symbol of Tibetan nationhood. With the Tibetan populace coalesced behind these banners, there existed no opposition force that could counter the exiled deity. Only Mao had succeeded in dissolving the religious and ethnic unity of the Tibetans, by introducing the element of class struggle. Renouncing this without creating any new ideology has left a vacuum that can only be filled by a combination of lamaist tradition and ethnic nationalism. Undeniably, the process of 'redressing the wrongs' has brought many positive changes to the Tibetan people, and even if it were desirable, the Mao era could not be reduplicated. Historically and morally, the reforms were absolutely necessary. But they have not solved the Tibetan question to the satisfaction of anyone, and today all the parties to the conflict over it have reason to fear for the future. New ways of approaching the problem must be found.

March–April 2002

2

Blood in the Snows

Tsering Shakya

The starting point of Wang Lixiong's 'Reflections on Tibet' is the proposition that the Tibetan people have been active participants in the destruction of their own culture.[1] The logic of the argument is one often employed by those responsible for injustice—that is, to heap the blame on the victim. It is reminiscent of the view once advanced by apologists for the apartheid regime in South Africa: since blacks made up the majority of the police force, and since hundreds of thousands of black people flocked from neighbouring countries to work in South Africa's dust-choked mines, the system could not be as bad as its critics supposed. But colonialism and injustice are never consensual: they are always achieved through the use of force, and perpetuated through the brutalization and degradation of the native people. It was, after all, Mao who announced that political power grows out of the barrel of a gun.

It is true that Tibetans played an active part in the Cultural Revolution, and this fact cannot be wiped out of history. It should, however, be put into proper perspective, and the actual nature of their participation subjected to examination. The Cultural Revolution is a difficult topic not only for Tibetans but

1   This chapter first appeared in *New Left Review* 2: 15, May–June 2002 and is a response to Chapter 1, Wang Lixiong's 'Reflections on Tibet'.

also for the Chinese. The strategy of China's leaders has been to blame it all on the Gang of Four, with nothing more being said about the others who plundered or killed. The question, 'What did you do during the Cultural Revolution?' is not an easy one to put to Chinese of a certain age; it tends to bring any conversation to a halt, with much being left unspoken or passed over in discomfort. Tibet was swept up in the fervour of the times, just like the rest of China; many did go on to destroy religious buildings, to denounce friends and neighbours as reactionaries, or to revolt against their teachers. It was a mass movement from which no individual was exempt. Nor was there any question of watching passively from the sidelines: it was either denounce or be denounced—the Party allowed no other option. The brave few who refused to participate in the madness paid the price of being branded as enemies of the people and subjected to mass-struggle sessions. Only the crudest notion of freedom could suggest that such participation was a 'choice' for the ordinary men and women of the time.

Millenarian insurgency

Nevertheless, as Wang should know, there were Tibetans who resisted, and faced the full wrath of the Party. In 1969 there was widespread rebellion throughout Tibet, eventually crushed by the PLA. The best-documented episode is the revolt led by Thrinley Chodron, a young nun from the *xian* (county) of Nyemo, who marched her followers—armed with swords and spears—to the local Party headquarters, and slaughtered both the Chinese officials and the Tibetan cadres working for them. At first the Party ignored the massacre, thinking it was a manifestation of the Cultural Revolution—as we know, murders could be exonerated if they fell under the rubric of class struggle.

But the authorities soon realized that these Tibetan peasants were rebelling not in the name of the 'newly liberated serfs' but in defence of their faith. What was more, they targeted only Chinese Party officials and those Tibetans seen as colluding with the colonizing power. The revolt spread from Nyemo through eighteen *xians* of the Tibetan Autonomous Region (TAR), and the Party was forced to send in the PLA to suppress it. Thrinley and fifteen of her followers were eventually captured and brought to Lhasa for public execution. Even today, the Party has expurgated this episode from the historical record as it fails to conform to their image of liberated peasants—or, indeed, to Wang's portrayal of Tibetans joyfully 'casting off the spectre of the afterlife that had hung over them for so long'.

Wang concedes that there was widespread revolt in 1969—although this contradicts his perception of a docile and submissive Tibetan peasantry—but attempts to portray it in a very different light. His account secularizes the rebellion, explaining it in utilitarian terms—the peasants wanted to protect the gains of the initial land reforms from the extension of People's Communes—while stripping it of the cultural and religious elements that reveal its nationalist content. In doing so, he grossly distorts the historical record. For example: Thrinley Chodron told the PLA after her capture that she had been visited by a bird who had come as a messenger from the Dalai Lama, and who had told her to drive out the Chinese. Other rebels claimed to be reincarnations of Ling Gesar, the mythical hero-king of Tibetan epic who fought for the Buddhist religion. There can be no mistaking the symbolism here. Indeed, we can describe the revolt of 1969 as a millenarian uprising, an insurgency characterized by a passionate desire to be rid of the oppressor.

Before Wang claims this as fresh evidence of the retarded mind of the native, he might wish to consider the broader

historical record of peasant and national revolts that have
begun with visions and voices. If the Maid of Orléans is the
best-known European instance, similar cases are to be found
even in Chinese history. The leader of the Taiping Rebellion
Hong Xiuquan, from rural Guangxi, was said to be the Son
of God and the younger brother of Jesus Christ. His illiterate
disciple, Yang Xiuqing, claimed to have spoken with the Holy
Ghost while in a trance. Foreign gods thus inspired the Chinese
uprising against what they saw as alien and despotic Manchu
rule; the Tibetans can at least claim to have heard native voices.
Wang is surely familiar with the heroic status attributed to such
psychotic figures as Hong Xiuquan and Yang Xiuqing within
Chinese national narratives—their promotion to the pantheon
of modern revolutionary heroes. Yet he balks at Tibetans hailing
the revolt of 1969 as a national movement against a colonial
oppressor. Wang tries to suggest that the Cultural Revolution
was a 'liberating' experience for the Tibetans, who could now
cast off their gods and spirits. But the millenarian nature of the
revolt suggests something else: that it was induced, rather, by
the deep fracturing of the self caused by the Cultural Revolution,
which attempted to erase every trace of Tibetan identity.

Wang's argument that the Red Guards could not have reached
remote areas of Tibet because of the lack of transportation and
manpower also needs qualification. The Red Guards were
charged with such revolutionary fervour that they would have
walked barefoot through the mountains to get to Tibet, so
desperate were they to bring revolution to its snowy peaks; but
there was strong pressure from Beijing not to let them go. Far
from being a period of mindless chaos, the Cultural Revolution
was a carefully orchestrated affair in Tibet, and the Party was
always in control. There were sound strategic reasons for
keeping the Red Guards away from the border areas. This was

the height of the Cold War in the Himalayas, India and China were on a war footing after the Sino-Soviet rift, the Russians had moved closer to the Indians and the CIA was still aiding several thousand Tibetan guerrillas based in Nepal. Tibet was a flashpoint and the Party did not want any disturbances in such a militarily sensitive region. Order reigned in the midst of disorder. Another aspect that Wang ignores was the overall division of the Cultural Revolution into two main factions. In Tibet, these consisted of the Rebel Group—supported by Red Guards from China, and seeking the overthrow of the 'power holders'—and the Alliance group, made up mainly of the Party leadership and cadres in Tibet. The Rebels were strong in urban areas, with Lhasa, the capital, more or less under their control, while the Alliance dominated the countryside, forcibly preventing Chinese Red Guards from venturing into its zones. Members of the Alliance faction actually blocked the road leading from Chamdo to Lhasa, and Red Guards trying to enter the region from China were held and beaten up by organized Party mobs. These were the practical political realities of Tibet at the time.

Wang's assertion that most of the destruction in Tibet took place during the Cultural Revolution also fails to tally with the historical record. As he himself admits, the monasteries and temples had been emptied long before, and 'the PLA had bombed them as it re-established control' after the 1959 Rebellion. In fact, the destruction of religious sites in Eastern Tibet—outside the TAR—had begun in 1956, under the guise of suppressing local uprisings in Gansu, Qinghai, Yunnan and Sichuan. In May 1962, the Panchen Rinpoche submitted a long memorandum to the Party Central Committee, detailing the terrible failures of Chinese government policies throughout the entire Tibetan region. Two passages prove categorically that much of Tibet's cultural heritage had already been destroyed. The Panchen Rinpoche writes:

> Our Han cadres produced a plan, our Tibetan cadres mobilized, and some people among the activists who did not understand reason played the part of executors of the plan. They usurped the name of the masses, they put on the mask [*mianju*] of the masses, and stirred up a great flood of waves to eliminate statues of the Buddha, scriptures and *stupas* [reliquaries]. They burned countless statues of the Buddha, scriptures and *stupas*, threw them into the water, threw them onto the ground, broke them and melted them. Recklessly, they carried out a wild and hasty [*fengxiang chuangru*] destruction of monasteries, halls, '*mani*' walls and *stupas*, and stole many ornaments from the statues and precious things from the *stupas*.

Referring only to the area within the boundaries of the TAR when he speaks of 'Tibet'—the situation was probably worse in other Tibetan districts—the Panchen Rinpoche goes on:

> Before democratic reform, there were more than 2,500 large, medium and small monasteries in Tibet. After democratic reform, only 70 or so monasteries were kept in existence by the government. This was a reduction of more than 97 per cent. Because there were no people living in most of the monasteries, there was no-one to look after their Great Prayer Halls [*da jing tang*] and other divine halls, or the lodgings of the monks. There was great damage and destruction, both by man and otherwise, and they were reduced to the point of collapse, or beyond.[2]

---

2 'Seventy-Thousand Character Petition', in *A Poisoned Arrow: The Secret Report of the Tenth Panchen Lama*, London 1997, pp. 51–2 (translation modified).

This memorandum to the Central Committee was written four years before the Cultural Revolution.

There is no need to resort to the kind of cheap psychological analysis Wang adduces to explain why Tibetans turned against the sacred symbols of their religion during the Cultural Revolution. The real reasons are far more straightforward. One of these lay in the Party's need to restrict the inter-factional struggle in an area which, as we have seen, was highly sensitive militarily. As soon as things looked like getting out of hand the Central Committee issued an order that, in these zones, the struggle should not be formulated as a fight between the 'two lines'. Such conflict was thus essentially confined to the towns, especially Lhasa. The result was that, in most rural areas of Tibet, the ferocity of the Cultural Revolution was shifted away from the battle between the two factions and directed instead towards an attack on tradition, under the call to smash 'The Four Olds'. In this effort, no stone was left unturned. The Red Guards may not have entered far into the countryside but CCP rule penetrated every crevice of the vast Himalayan landscape. The Party's hegemony was so deeply entrenched at this time that even the way a peasant slept was said to indicate ideological orientation—someone who lay with their head towards the west was accused of turning away from Chairman Mao, since he was 'the Sun that rises in the East'. One of the crimes of which the Panchen Rinpoche was accused during his trial by Red Guards in Beijing was of having anti-Party and reactionary dreams. (The Red Guards here, it should be noted, were not Tibetans but Chinese students.)

The Cultural Revolution was exported from China to the High Plateau by the Communist Party, much as opium was forced upon China by British gunboats—and eagerly consumed by the Chinese. Do we condemn the starving coolie for resorting to narcotics to escape the pains of his empty stomach, or do we censure the drug-pushing masters of a foreign empire who, despite endless pleas and petitions, directed the expeditions? There is no doubt that individual Tibetans committed despicable acts in the course of the Cultural Revolution; and many of them today hold senior posts in the regional Communist Party. In fact, such deeds are now viewed as a badge of party loyalty. Wang fails to mention the fact that in China, in the 1980s, the CCP purged 'three categories of people' who had committed crimes during the Cultural Revolution, but that in Tibet, despite repeated appeals by leaders such as the Panchen Rinpoche, no such purge took place. Hu Yaobang noted in his speech at the Tibet Work Forum in 1984 that he had received written submissions from both traditional leaders and CCP members, urging the Party to expel such people; instead he promoted them, saying they could be reformed. The real reason was that the Communist Party could not find anyone else they could trust to run Tibet so dutifully. The stark contrast between the policy implemented in the TAR and that applied to the rest of China highlights the classic colonial tactic, often observed in Western imperial practice, whereby the hegemonic power seeks to cultivate loyal and servile natives to guard its interests. China rules Tibet differently from China, because there it faces the problems of being a colonial power.

Colonial attitudes of the Chinese intelligentsia

How, Wang asks, was it possible for supposedly devout Tibetan Buddhists to destroy their temples and smash their holy statues? The answer he urges upon us is that the Cultural Revolution was a liberating experience for the Tibetan peasantry, who now 'forcefully asserted that they would rather be men in this life than souls in the next'—a fine phrase but utterly meaningless, since it ignores the fact that such choices were made by people with bayonets at their back. Wang is, indeed, quite unable to explain the actions of these newly liberated men once the bayonet was removed and—as Wang himself attests—the peasants rushed to rebuild the temples and monasteries and reinstate the Buddha's statue among the ruins. Complaining that 'the Tibetans' reaction to the liberalization of the eighties is hard to understand', he offers some convoluted remarks about how the native now needed to atone for his sins.

Given Wang's current stature among the Chinese intelligentsia, such propositions raise a much more serious and pervasive issue. It seems that asking some Chinese intellectuals—be they Communist Party officials, liberal democrats or dissident writers—to think about Tibet in an objective and reasonable manner is like asking an ant to lift an elephant; it is beyond their capabilities and vision. Their perception is impaired by racial prejudice and their imagination clouded by the convictions and certainties of all colonial masters. Wang's essay exhibits the same arrogance of reasoning and contempt for the native mind—into which he purports to have delved deep, and to have felt the heartbeat of a simpleton. His Tibetans are governed by demonic gods and live in a permanent state of fear, in awe of terrifying spirits—a state Wang ascribes to the Himalayan ecology:

> Encountering, alone, this savage expanse of earth and sky inevitably produced a feeling of being overwhelmed by such preponderance, a terrifying sense of isolation and helplessness, repeated down the generations. Fear provoked awe, and awe gave rise to the totem of deities and monsters . . . Fear formed the core of the Tibetans' spiritual world.[3]

---

3   See Chapter 1, p. 55.

This approach will be familiar to anyone who has studied the implantation of Western colonialism in Asia and Africa, or read the works of early Christian missionaries on the religions and cultures of the peoples they subjugated. The strategic positioning of the natives as living in 'fear' and 'awe' of the gods drains the people of agency. It is a device used by colonizers to strip their subjects of their humanity and of the ability to reason. Wang's text accordingly reveals next to nothing of the native worldview but divulges a great deal about the mindset of the colonizer. This seeks to reduce the native's status to that of an infant—allowing the colonial master, by contrast, to assume the position of a wise adult, and thus justify his rule. The crude environmental determinism of Wang's imagined Tibetan *Weltanschauung* is, in fact, a redaction of the works of such early Western colonial cadres as Austin Waddell, whose book on 'Lamaism', as he disparagingly called it, was published in 1904—the year of the British invasion of Tibet, in which Waddell played a leading role. It is still used as an authoritative source in China. Wang's use of language and tone are strikingly similar to Waddell's. Yet the concept of an awe-inspiring and terrifying physical geography begs an obvious question: is it really the native who is intimidated by the surroundings in which he and his ancestors have lived for thousands of years, or is it rather the foreign visitor to the Tibetan plateau who is struck by the unaccustomed expanses of the grasslands or the scale of the mountains? If anything, history suggests that human beings, far from being intimidated by their environments, have always sought to control their different natural surroundings in order to carve out a living. Wang's theory of Tibet is a romanticized description of his own urban *ennui*—little more than pop psychology, presented as serious thought.

Mao worship

What is more worrying is Wang's failure to reflect upon his own culture and society. His description of the Mao cult is typical of this. Mao, he argues, 'replaced the Dalai Lama as the god in [the Tibetans'] mind' in a process of religious substitutionism—the natives were in awe of the new foreign god, and saw him as more powerful than the local deity. Such simplistic reasoning is, again, reminiscent of Western colonial and evangelizing views—Wang's version of Friday, worshipping the footsteps of his white master: the native is struck dumb with wonderment at what befalls him. As evidence, Wang cites the ludicrous examples of Tibetan peasants marching behind portraits of Mao at harvest-time, and of Mao's picture adorning every household wall—as if this was unique to the Tibetan peasantry. Was it they alone who elevated Mao to the level of a god? Wang—who, as a citizen of China, has had to live in the midst of totalitarianism for much of his life—is peering so deep into the native soul here that he loses sight of where he's standing. In a delirious moment, he is akin to the man so entranced by the buttercup in front of him that he has no perception of the forest he is in.

In fact, there was nothing peculiarly Tibetan about the ritualistic treatment of Mao. Every schoolchild in China sang:

> The sun rises in the East,
> No, it is not the sun,
> But the brilliant rays of the Chairman.

Didn't everyone in China sport a badge of Mao? Didn't the Chinese peasant labour in the paddy field with a banner of Mao fluttering in the wind, and didn't the Chinese, too, recite quotations from Mao when they jumped out of bed every morning? Such behaviour was to be found throughout the People's Republic, carefully choreographed by the CCP. Wang can hardly be unaware that Mao worship was not simply a Tibetan experience. Indeed, the fanatical devotion extended towards the Great Helmsman and the Party by elements of the Chinese population—where we find instances in which the corpses of 'class enemies' were cannibalized, as proof of dedication to Mao—exceeded anything in Tibet. If we applied Wang's own logic, not to the colonized natives but to these members of his own society, we would apparently have to conclude that their preference for eating each other, rather than living in filial obedience to their ancestors, was a sign that they were liberated men.

Wang's argument that the Tibetans were attracted to Mao's totalitarianism because they were, by nature, submissive is identical to that used by Western Sinologists when they explain Mao's sway by essentializing the Chinese peasantry as, again, naturally obedient and submissive to authority. In fact, it was a young Tibetan, the Panchen Rinpoche, who put forward by far the most extensive criticism of Mao's policies of communization and the Great Leap Forward—when millions of Chinese apparently accepted that melting down their household utensils would enable them to overtake Britain in steel production. Similarly, it was the people of eastern Tibet who staged the most extensive revolt in China against the imposition of People's Communes. This hardly suggests a subservient people, taking Mao into their hearts.

Far from seeing Mao as a god, in some rural areas of Tibet the people did not even know who he was. Their first encounter with the colonizer was usually through the local PLA and Party cadres. There is a scene—fictional, but revealing—in a Tibetan novel, *Joys and Sorrows of an Ordinary Family*, by Tashi Palden, which describes a meeting convened by the Party to initiate the Cultural Revolution. The stage is decorated with portraits of Mao and, as the crowd gathers, the heroine asks the person sitting next to her who he is. A local Party activist has to inform her that he is Mao Zedong. Later in the narrative, when Mao dies, the local Party issues a decree setting out the exact form of behaviour and mode of dress required. In the evening, Party activists secretly spy on every house to make sure the correct rituals are being observed.

Such uniformity of behaviour, dress and outward expression of loyalty is clearly indicative not so much of a peculiar Tibetan mindset as of life under a totalitarian regime. When the Tibetan peasants carried pictures of Mao and red flags to their barley fields, they were merely going through the motions required of them. If they really found this behaviour as emotionally gratifying as Wang suggests, we would have to ask why they discarded it as soon as they had the opportunity to do so. The fact that, the instant it was permitted, Tibetans not only shook off the uniforms of the Cultural Revolution but pulled down the red banners and hoisted prayer flags in the valleys, discarded the Chairman's 'Thoughts' and brought out long-hidden prayer-books, restored their native gods to their altars and sent thousands of young people to join the monasteries, hardly supports the notion that Maoist rituals were psychologically irresistible to them. It rather suggests that, given the choice, Tibetans will prefer their own religion.

Manichean iconographies

Frantz Fanon has famously described the colonial mentality as dominated by a Manichean set of oppositions—white and black, good and evil, salvation and damnation, civilization and savagery, superiority and inferiority, intelligence and emotion, self and others, subject and object. Wang offers a rather neat illustration of this type of perception in a footnote in which he contrasts the Chinese representation of the Buddha of Compassion as 'a beautiful woman' to Tibetan pictures of her as 'a dark giant wearing a necklace of skulls'—the classic colonialists' view of their own deity as benign, while their subjects' god is dark and wrathful. As well as a total ignorance of Tibetan Buddhist iconography, the comparison reveals a sad lack of knowledge of Chinese cultural history and tradition. The religion prevailing in Tibet was also the court religion of Chinese emperors for several dynasties, and many in China shared the same faith and pantheon. In fact, hundreds of Chinese came to study in Tibetan monasteries throughout the centuries; some still do.

The religious icons Wang finds so alien were therefore the same as those propitiated by many Chinese followers of Buddhism. The worship of Mahakala, a wrathful form of the Buddha, was introduced to China during the Tang Dynasty, and Chinese monks at the time recorded its widespread popularity. For centuries there existed a Mahakala temple in Beijing, decorated with murals and statues of the same fierce deities that Wang finds so abhorrent. It was destroyed by the Communists in 1970; the Capital Stadium stands on the site today. Such religious imagery is therefore not as alien to the Chinese mind as Wang supposes, and his portrayal of these practices as peculiarly Tibetan only reveals how successful the Communists have been in erasing China's memory, so that the younger generation now suffer from a sort of amnesia in respect to their own traditions.

The great Urdu–Hindi writer Premchand wrote in his novel *Godan* (*Gift of a Cow*) that when one is being trampled by a giant tyrant, there is not much one can do except tickle his foot. The mass adoration for Mao in both China and Tibet was the product of a frenzied fervour, generated by the Party and ritually reinforced by its propaganda machine. Besides the coercion from above, there was overwhelming group and social pressure to conform, coupled with a dismissal of any individual sentiments. A similar, uniform outward loyalty can be found among all those who endure life under a totalitarian regime—it is a form of foot-tickling. The speedy rejection of the Mao cult is the clearest indication that the Tibetan peasants were feigning compliance. I agree that there may have been moments of fervour or frenzied emotion and that, under such circumstances, deep and long-buried resentments can resurface. Indeed, the Party clearly sought to provoke such feelings, and it could be argued that its entire mobilization strategy throughout both China and Tibet was in large part based on them. But as we know, such behaviour is often temporary and does not necessarily indicate a deep shift in people's sentiments or in what they hold sacred. In his discussion of Malay peasants in *Weapons of the Weak*, James Scott makes a more perceptive point about the behaviour of those who face overwhelming odds: they resort to 'everyday forms of resistance', which typically involve a fake compliance and dissimulation. The Tibetan peasants went along with the demands of the Party largely because they knew very well that to do otherwise would meet with cruel punishment. It was not that they felt 'liberated' from their religious bondage, but rather that their fear of the wrath and retribution of the Party was greater than their fear of the afterlife. Visiting temples and monasteries in Tibet today, one often finds old statues and paintings reinstalled on their altars with notes that indicate which ones survived the Gang of Four's destruction because the local people had hidden them away. In other words, the outward display of compliance concealed strongly held values and strategic decisions.

Shadow suzerainty of the Qing

The present Chinese government's claim of sovereignty over Tibet has been acquired by military conquest; its rule rests on might—brute facts, which Wang's highly selective account of the historical relations between China and Tibet effectively blurs. Wang chooses to begin his discussion of Sino-Tibetan relations with the Qing dynasty—which was, indeed, the period when contact between the two was at its most developed, and imperial engagement in Tibetan domestic affairs most marked, although Chinese imperial involvement with Tibet can be traced back to the Mongol era. In practice, however, there was no direct imperial administration, and when the Emperors did intervene it was at times of great internal turmoil there. The establishment of the office of the Amban, or Imperial Commissioner, occurred at a time when Tibet was suffering invasion by the Gurkhas, in 1788 and 1792. For the Tibetans this was a costly war, and they sought the support of the Qing to repel the intruders. The Qing, fearing foreign incursion in such vulnerable frontier regions, naturally sided with the Tibetans, and the Manchu general Fu Kang'an recommended the establishment of a permanent imperial resident in Lhasa. This marked the beginning of the first attempt at direct rule of Tibet, with the Amban being given equal status to the Dalai Lama and the power to supervise the appointment of Tibetan government officials and high-ranking lamas.

The relationship between the Qing court and Tibet did not, however, amount to the establishment of sovereignty by one country over another. Luciano Petech's detailed study *China and*

Tibet in the Early Eighteenth Century (1950), drawing upon both Tibetan and Chinese sources, argues that the Qing position in Tibet can, at best, be described as a protectorate—the Chinese authority of the time a 'shadowy form of suzerainty'. Similarly, Willliam Rockhill, a scholar and American diplomat at the turn of the last century, writes in his study of the relationship between the Dalai Lamas and the Manchus that 'he [the Dalai Lama] had been treated with all the ceremony which could have been accorded to any independent sovereign, and nothing can be found in Chinese works to indicate that he was looked upon in any other light'.[4] Imperial influence in Tibet depended on domestic conditions and external threats: the Tibetans were quite happy to seek the Emperor's support when faced with intrusions from the south, but Qing authority was quickly discarded once the borders had been secured.

At the time of the Gurkha Wars the Tibetans were in no position to reject the imposition of Manchu rule by the army they had invited to assist them. But it is clear that the establishment of the Amban's office was never seen by the Tibetans as signalling their acquiescence to rule from Beijing. As Wang's own account shows, the Amban's role had little effect either on Tibet's domestic or its external relations, and his presence in Lhasa was largely disregarded by the Tibetans as long as their own borders were not menaced. Indeed, three Ambans were assassinated by Tibetans, in 1750 and 1905—contradicting Wang's portrayal of an amicable if ineffectual coexistence. The Qing clearly recognized the impotence of their position, and more than twenty of the hundred or so Ambans appointed by the Emperor never even took up their

---

4   W. W. Rockhill, *The Dalai Lamas of Lhasa and their Relations with the Manchu Emperors of China, 1644–1908*, Leyden 1910, p. 18. Rockhill's work draws only on Chinese sources.

posts—some failing even to begin the perilous journey and others dying on the way.

The lack of Qing authority in Tibet was most glaringly demonstrated in its dealings with British India. By the late nineteenth century, the British were pushing for trade routes into Tibet, and land routes from India to China. At the Chefoo Convention of 1876 the Chinese granted British access to Tibet, leading to the signing of the Anglo-Chinese Convention of 1890 between the Amban and Lord Lansdowne. This gave the British the right to trade and to send missions to Lhasa, as well as fixing the boundary between Tibet and Sikkim. The Tibetans, far from acquiescing in the agreement, proceeded to fortify the border, advanced troops up to the frontier and refused to allow the British to implement the rights conceded by the Chinese. The British soon found that the Chinese were in no position to enforce terms on the Tibetans, who simply would not accept Beijing's right to sign any agreement regarding their territory. It was incidents such as these that led to Lord Curzon's exasperated remark that Chinese suzerainty over Tibet was a 'constitutional fiction'. British frustrations eventually led to the full-scale military invasion of Tibet under Younghusband in 1904. This broke the Tibetans' power to resist the Chinese and, once again, forced them to seek the aid of the Qing court, leading to a disastrous but short-lived retaliatory invasion by the Chinese in 1909. When the Qing regime collapsed in 1911 the Tibetans severed all ties with China, expelled the Amban and his military escort and declared independence, thus ending nearly two centuries of Qing authority in the region. Between 1911 and 1950 Tibet enjoyed total control over its external and internal affairs.

'Under compulsion of circumstances'

On the eve of the Chinese Communist invasion in October 1950, Tibet was to all intents and purposes an independent state. Chinese Nationalist attempts to regain power over the territory had been unsuccessful, partly because of internal problems in China but mainly because the Tibetans were determined to oppose any Chinese presence. After 1904, the British were also prepared to counter any extension of Chinese power in the region, and every mission that the Nationalist government sent to Lhasa was balanced by a similar British delegation. Whatever the nature of the polity that prevailed in Tibet during this period, its authorities were determined to preserve their independence from China and initially did everything they could to secure international support. But by 1950 the situation in the world—and in Asia—had dramatically altered. With Indian independence the British renounced any imperial interest in Tibet, while the new administration in India lacked the military capability of its former colonial master when it came to countering the CPP government in Beijing. The other relevant power was, of course, the United States; but because of Tibet's geographical situation as an isolated, landlocked country, the Americans offered only limited, clandestine support.

The tiny, ill-equipped Tibetan Army was no match for the 40,000 battle-hardened PLA soldiers that invaded in October 1950. After its capitulation the Army's commander, Ngabo Ngawang Jigme, was appointed by the Lhasa government to negotiate with the Chinese. On 23 May 1951 the Chinese authorities and the Tibetan delegation signed the Seventeen-Point Agreement—more formally known as the 'Agreement for the Peaceful Liberation of Tibet'—which formed the basis for the incorporation of Tibet into the People's Republic of

China. As Nehru remarked, it was signed 'without joy and under compulsion of circumstances'. The Agreement virtually guaranteed a special status for Tibet within the PRC, since no other province, nationality or region reached such a formal accord with Mao's newly established government. It placed Tibet in a unique position, theoretically entitling it to enjoy the same status as Hong Kong and Macau today. It pledged that Tibet's traditional polity would be protected and that, above all, the institution of the Dalai Lama and his administration would continue to be the functional government. The only two conditions of real importance to Beijing were that China would conduct Tibet's foreign relations and station PLA troops in the region; these were designed to erase Tibet's international personality and to consolidate China's geo-political advantage.

Wang is right to argue that, in the early period, the CCP's primary objective was to establish the strategic and legal integration of Tibet within the new China, and that Beijing was willing to make concessions to this end. Nine years later, however, the whole of the Tibetan region erupted in revolt. The causes of this uprising were manifold, but its primary source was Beijing's failure to appreciate the ethnic dimension of the Tibetan issue. The Seventeen-Point Agreement and the promise not to impose reforms applied only to the Tibetan Autonomous Region, the area under the immediate control of the Dalai Lama and his government in Lhasa. The Tibetan population in eastern Tibet, situated in the present-day provinces of Gansu, Yunnan, Sichuan and Qinghai, were subjected to the same reforms and political campaigns as the rest of China. The Tibetans in these areas—Amdo and Kham—rebelled in 1956, and it was not until 1960 that the Communists were able to subdue the revolt. As a consequence, hundreds of refugees from the eastern areas poured into central Tibet, turning it into a theatre of anti-Chinese resistance. The fact that the CCP had retained the previously existing social and political system in central Tibet, under the control of the Dalai Lama, did not allay apprehensions about China's ultimate goals. Despite the Party's characterization of the revolt—as upper-class resistance to social reform—the Tibetan Rebellion was a national one, supported by all classes. In fact, the bulk of the protests came from ordinary people and the poor, resentful not only of the Chinese but also of what they saw as the Tibetan ruling class's surrender of the interests of the nation. The Communists, after all, had done everything they could to appease the Tibetan elite and absorb them into their infrastructure by promising them a role in the new regime.

Despite the inequalities of the traditional Tibetan social system, there had been few popular peasant uprisings in the country's history. Struggling to come to terms with this, Wang falls back as usual on his conception of the awestruck native mind:

> What explains such an unusual degree of deference and obedience? The answer surely lies in the deeply rooted religious traditions of Tibet . . . if they [the peasantry] committed the crime of 'defying their superiors' or 'enriching themselves with dubious wealth', the dreadful punishment that awaited them would far outweigh any earthly gains.[5]

Wang's colonial assumptions forestall any serious empirical investigation of Tibetan social reality. The peasantry were certainly badly treated and the system of land distribution unjust; yet because of Tibet's vast size and scant population,

---

5   See chapter 1, p. 54.

there were not thousands of peasants without land or a right to livelihood, nor were they plagued by economic uncertainties about their future. In this sense, they were better off than vast layers of the urban and rural poor in pre-revolutionary China, who proved more open to the CCP's promises of reform. The Tibetan peasantry lived in isolated, sparsely populated areas; traditional society consisted of village and nomadic communities, with few political tensions between the various groups. Down to the middle of the twentieth century Tibet had an essentially pre-modern economy, based on agricultural self-sufficiency. The vast majority of peasant families produced their own food and clothing, and there was little trade or market development. Before the 1950s, it was almost unheard of for *tsampa*—barley flour, the staple diet—to be bought and sold in the market. Even in a city like Lhasa, families relied on relatives from the countryside to supply their basic needs.

This is not to paint a picture of happy smiling peasants—their life was full of hardship. In addition to economic inequalities, the social system was sharply delineated between commoners and aristocracy, with the former totally excluded from state affairs and burdened with heavy taxation by aristocratic and monastic landlords. There was much resentment, resulting in petitions to the Lhasa government from individual families. The reasons why this never led to open socio-economic rebellion are complex—as are the causes of the failure of working-class revolt in the industrialized West. But economic grievances alone are rarely sufficient to spark an uprising; a sense of injustice can be perceived on different levels, and the development of class consciousness is many-sided, involving cultural, social and economic factors.

Politics of reincarnation

The question of how the Tibetans' belief system has impinged upon their social and political attitudes is, indeed, a vital one, but demands far subtler treatment than Wang is able to provide. Certainly, a belief in karma and reincarnation would have a discernible influence both on people's everyday behaviour and in their response to larger issues. Reincarnation is based on the idea that the beneficial effects of working hard and doing good deeds in this life will accumulate in the next one. This does not have to imply passivity—on the contrary, it can inspire one to play an active role in order to alter one's position. The implication of Wang's argument is that the Tibetans' beliefs paralysed any capacity for social change; this is far from true. While not experiencing upheavals on the scale witnessed in some parts of the world during the nineteenth and twentieth centuries, Tibetan society has undergone a continuous process of change and redefinition, clearly visible in the religious reformation that took place. There were also many political conflicts, involving mass mobilizations—often very violent—on the basis of regional or sectarian interests. Assassinations of Dalai Lamas were common—only three lived to maturity; others died in mysterious circumstances, sometimes on the verge of assuming political power. Far from being a paralysing factor, the belief of retribution in their future lives did not even stay the Tibetans' hands in murdering their highest religious authorities. The Rebellion of 1959 is further proof, should it be needed, that the Tibetans have no natural aversion to violence, or resistance. But the uprising was carried out in the name of nationalism and in defence of cultural autonomy, rather than as defiance of economic conditions.

In fact, the rhetoric of modernity had most appeal for the young aristocrats and sons of wealthy merchants who had travelled outside the country and had the opportunity to witness changes abroad. As in most parts of the non-Western world, the call for reform was primarily generated by external influences and supported by the new urban intelligentsia. In 1943, when a group of radical Tibetans met in Lhasa to found the first Tibetan Communist Party, they were all children of wealthy merchant or aristocratic families. The bulwark of a reactionary religious community with mass peasant support meant there was very little chance of internal reform. Earlier attempts—such as the thirteenth Dalai Lama's invitation to English educationalists to run newly established schools, in the 1930s—had been similarly thwarted. The students were all children of Tibetan aristocrats, but the institutions were eventually closed down as a result of opposition from the monasteries, who mobilized the masses through such slogans as: 'In the Holy City of Lhasa, there is an unholy school'. The religious community—the Gelugpa Monastery in particular—viewed any reform as a threat to its hegemony.

Once the Communists took over, there was even less chance of reforms succeeding without coercion. However liberal the early measures of the CCP may have been, they were seen by the vast majority of Tibetan people as colonial impositions. While in some respects the peasantry might have welcomed land reform or the abolition of feudal labour service, the Party's anti-religious policies antagonized them. The positive effects of the early reforms were also undermined by the indiscriminate assault of the Anti-Rebellion Campaign, in which thousands of ordinary people accused of involvement in the 1959 Rebellion were sent to labour camps. The question of reform in such a traditional society is a complex one; but it is impossible to abstract it from the national element in the relationship between China and Tibet. As long as criticisms of 'backward' Tibetan practices were seen as coming from an alien source, the response would naturally be a defensive one. As Lu Xun said, 'If a man slaps his own face he will not feel insulted, whereas if someone else slaps him, he will be angry'.

Wang depicts the traditional society of Tibet as dark and corrupt, with the common people living on the brink of a precipice. This was also the perception of the CCP. Yet their response to the situation when, in 1959, they seized the reins for themselves, was to plunge Tibet into depths of misery it had never known before. The economic and living conditions of the people plummeted sharply between 1960 and 1979; in many areas people were forced to live on a single meal a day. It was not until the 1980s that living conditions began to improve, under the new leadership of Hu Yaobang. But although Hu's reforms were welcomed, for many Tibetans they did not go far enough—as was evident in the widespread unrest of the late 1980s. As Wang rightly suggests, the new reforms were seen as merely redressing the wrongs done in the previous decades. Even liberal leaders like Hu were not prepared to address the fundamental questions of Tibetans' rights. In retrospect, the reforms of the 1980s could be seen as placating Tibetan resentments at a time when the new leadership in Beijing was seeking legitimacy, and the position of the Party in Tibet was growing more precarious.

The limitations of Party hegemony were demonstrated by the popular welcome afforded to the delegation sent by the Dalai Lama in 1979, which was mobbed by hundreds of people in the areas it visited. Their reaction shocked the Chinese leadership; it gave a clear sign that, in the hearts and minds of the people, the Dalai Lama still ruled Tibet. It was while the delegation was in eastern Tibet, on its way to Lhasa, that Chinese officials finally realized there might be an uncontrollable show of loyalty to the Dalai Lama and suggested to Ren Rong, the Party Secretary in Lhasa, that the visit to the TAR should be cancelled. Ren confidently replied that the people of the Region had a heightened sense of class consciousness. Like Wang, he had badly misjudged the situation. The Cultural Revolution, far from liberating the peasantry, had fuelled deep resentment towards Beijing's authority.

Party marionettes

Many of the reforms initiated by Hu have now been discarded and a new process of colonial rule enacted in their place. The 'autonomy' of regional bodies such as the National People's Congress and the Political Consultative Conference is utterly spurious, existing only on paper. It is true that the 1980s saw a steady rise in the number of Tibetan cadres and senior Party officials, and that Tibetan was made the official language of the region. But it was comrades such as Raidi and Pasang—who had held senior posts in the regional Party since 1967 and who were both widely known to be illiterate in Tibetan—that the CPP appointed to leadership positions. The overriding objective of 'Tibetanization' was to place faithful apparatchiks in positions of power. In fact, many of the senior Tibetan Communists cultivated by the Party since the 1950s—or, in the case of Tian Bao, since the Long March—were incapable of reading their own language. Tibetan leaders both inside and outside the Party complained bitterly about these appointments, but even Hu Yaobang could not dismiss them. As he told the Tibet Work Forum in 1984, they were the ones considered most loyal to the Party and Fatherland. Hu's attempts at reform were further confounded by resistance from the Chinese cadres who refused to surrender their power in the region, or to accept that the last thirty years of their work in Tibet had been, as Hu termed it, 'a mistake'. When Hu and Wu Jinghua later fell from power, these officials celebrated openly and seized the chance to undo all the liberal policies they had established.

Tibetans are indeed well represented on bodies like the National People's Congress and the People's Consultative Conference. In fact I would go further and say that they are over-represented, given the size of the Tibetan population. But their presence in such august institutions does not mean that they have either the power or the voice to articulate the actual views of the people. It is a symbolic gesture, designed to show the inclusiveness of the Fatherland. Tibetan members of these bodies are selected and approved as model citizens by the CCP, and very often their positions are given as a reward for loyalty to the Party. Among most ordinary Tibetans, they enjoy neither respect nor trust. There is a joke about these people, which goes something like this. What are the responsibilities of the People's Congress representatives and the People's Consultative Conference members? They are three: one, to shake hands when they enter the meeting hall; two, to clap hands after the speech; and three, to raise hands when the vote is counted. It would be utterly naive to suppose that the Tibetan presence on these bodies demonstrates a genuine inclusiveness. Whether at regional or national level, these Tibetans carry out only what I would call a 'messenger' role: they serve as a caste whose duty is to provide a symbolic presence, and to act as mouthpieces for the CCP. Their role is not to voice the will of the Tibetan people, but to disseminate the Party's will to them.

Today, the Party has managed to subdue the Tibetans' anger not through gaining their consent but by instituting a greater degree of integration within the PRC. The policies of the last few years show that the Chinese government has adopted the classic colonial strategy of containment and absorption. The most vocal opponents of Chinese rule over the last decade have come from the religious community. Monks and nuns have been virtually confined to the monasteries while the Party has carried out purges of religious influence in public life. However, this has not been an easy matter, with thousands of followers in religious groups presenting a formidable challenge to the CCP. The Chinese authorities know that religion represents a powerful nationalist ideology in Tibet, with the ability to mobilize the public and to contest the authority of the Party. This was starkly highlighted during the selection of the new Panchen Lama in 1995. While Beijing was able to impose its own candidates, Tibetans refused to acknowledge the Party appointee. The incident may have caused the final loss of CCP authority over the religious groups, united in their opposition on this matter. Even Tashilhunpo Monastery, the traditional seat of the Panchen Lamas and always seen as loyal to the Party in the past, refused to cooperate or provide an abode for the official candidate. All senior Tibetan lamas have spurned the Party's decision and have refused to endorse the appointment, except when made to do so by force. This showed the ability of cultural groups to organize and mobilize their members for a common purpose. Religious followers have remained loyal to their faith.

The problem is heightened by the fact that, although almost all Tibetan religious leaders are in exile, the Party knows that they occupy the people's hearts and minds. Furthermore, religious faith is closely associated with ethnic identity and nationalism. Monks and nuns have been at the forefront of anti-Chinese demonstrations and are viewed as defenders of Tibetan culture and traditions. They command the loyalty and respect of the local population, while the local CCP leaders are seen as alien and corrupt. Beijing is engaged in a contest with the public, with the issues of leadership and legitimacy at stake. It fears above all the loss of control in terms of social, moral and political authority. But it knows that the people have lost any faith in Communism or in the Party, which can no longer generate support by appealing to its past revolutionary achievements or to the evils of its predecessors.

Dissolving the spell

The combination of religious faith, ethnic identity and social and economic disadvantage, real or perceived, provides fertile soil for Tibetan nationalism. Despite economic improvements over the last decade, the majority of Tibetans view their position as marginalized and disadvantaged in today's China. In this sense, Wang is right. While on the surface the Party has managed to contain the latent nationalistic aspirations of the Tibetan people, these factors, together with the presence of a powerful leadership in exile, do indeed provide a major threat to the CCP. The solution to the Tibetan problem, however, is neither complex nor difficult; nor does it require any major concession by the Chinese government. The notion of Tibet as an integral part of China is a recent invention by the Communist Party in its process of nation building. Tibet has never been central to the Chinese imagination. There was never any Chinese Woody Guthrie to warble, 'This land is our land, from the crest of the Himalayas to the shores of the South China Sea': the Party conjured up this sentiment after 1950. The spell can vanish as quickly as it was made to appear. Tibet is not Palestine or Kashmir, with extreme passions on both sides backed by centuries of religious bigotry.

In fact, China's main interest in Tibet is strategic. But since the Dalai Lama has declared that he does not want independence for Tibet and is willing to meet China's concerns by agreeing to relinquish control of foreign affairs and defence to Beijing, China should recognise that giving Tibet genuine autonomy would not endanger either the PRC's security or its position in the world. If Tibet were to be granted this autonomy tomorrow, or even independence, China would not collapse. The Chinese leadership should be wise enough to accept that the Dalai Lama's offer would meet their own concerns and at the same time allow Tibetans the genuine freedom to practise their culture and tradition.

May–June 2002

Analyses

3

Two Imperialisms in Tibet

Wang Lixiong

Having been denounced and rejected by civilized societies, imperialism is no longer simply defined by territorial expansion or the plunder of foreign wealth.[1] Although it still involves military force and politics, adhering to practices of occupation and colonization, imperialism must now disguise itself as benefiting the ruled minority, which includes providing economic assistance. By assuming their own civilizational superiority and material benevolence, present-day empires manifest themselves more often in the realm of cultural life. Political imperialism has been transformed and extended to become a cultural imperialism as well.

Culture has become the focus of current debates on Tibet. The Chinese government responds to worldwide criticism of its actions by enumerating its efforts to protect Tibetan culture, including its renovation of temples, its conservation of Tibetan cultural heritage, its promotion of Tibetan language education, its usage of both Tibetan and Chinese languages in the Tibetan autonomous regions, and its rescue of endangered arts. On the other hand, most of the critiques lodged against China by the international community and exiled Tibetans are based on these

---

1   This chapter was translated by Susan Chen.

same issues. Both sides are equally able to produce examples in support of their cases, though their conclusions are often in direct opposition to one another.

But because national cultures are primarily forms of national self-articulation, I think that such cultural debates distract from what ought to be the focus. National articulation is not simply about repeating one's history or acting out one's traditions. More important is the expression of what the nation's people feel, think and demand from their present realities. Only when rooted in the spirit of the nation and linked to its realities does such an articulation of national history and tradition become a part of live culture. Otherwise, this culture, divorced from a national sense of self and disconnected from present reality, is but an empty shell or a puppet—a form without life. On the subject of language, for instance, no matter how carefully a nation's is preserved, if it is only allowed to reiterate the words of the ruling empire and not to articulate the true feelings of the nation, then how culturally meaningful can the language remain? The primary measure of cultural protection within a nation is not whether its traditions have been conserved, much less the abundance of economic investment from the empire.

It is in light of this that the damage to and suppression of Tibetan culture under Chinese rule is most apparent. Despite any benefits it has brought to this region, it has categorically suppressed Tibetan self-articulation. The empire seeks to control all forms of expression so that all transgressions are punished. The actions taken against Tibetan writer Woeser, a former editor for *Tibetan Literature* (*Xizang Wenxue*) (the official journal of the Literature Association of the Tibet Autonomous Region), are merely one example: despite the popularity of her 2003 prose anthology *Notes on Tibet*, it quickly attracted the attention of the censors. At first, the United Front Work Department of the Chinese Communist Party (CCP) claimed that the book had made 'serious political mistakes'. This accusation was soon followed by orders from those in charge of ideological work in Tibet that the book be examined. Meanwhile, its sale in the Tibetan Autonomous Region (TAR) was banned. Not long after, the Bureau of Journalism and Publication in Guangdong Province was ordered to ban the book completely, with the TAR Literature Association— the working unit to which Woeser had formerly belonged— concluding its comments on *Notes on Tibet* with the following statement:

> It exaggerates and beautifies the positive function of religion in social life. Individual essays convey the author's faith in and reverence for the Dalai Lama. Certain contents reveal a rigid thinking on nationalism and opinions that are harmful to the unification and solidarity of our nation. Some of its contents render the great achievements of Tibetan reform over the past decades invisible; meanwhile, it indulges in nostalgia for the old Tibet without tangible examples. The book appears to have made false value judgments and divorced itself from the correct political principles; the author has abandoned the social responsibility that a contemporary writer ought to have, and lost her political commitment to the progressive civilization movement.

Shi Jifeng, Deputy Director of the General Bureau of Journalism and Publication, outlined the official charges against *Notes on Tibet*:

> The book praises the XIV Dalai Lama and the XVII Karmapa, and it encourages reverence to, and belief in, religion. These are serious mistakes in the author's political stance and her point of view. Some

of the chapters have, to a certain degree, stepped onto the wrong political terrain. For instance, in [the chapter] 'Nyima Tsering', the author depicts the confusion that the famous religious figure Nyima Tsering felt when he encountered the supporters of the Dalai at an international conference. It reflects that the author is not clear about the essence of the Dalai's separatism and promotion of Tibet independence. Also, chapters such as 'Tenzin and His Son' reveal her misunderstanding of the history of Sino-Tibetan conflict in the 1950s.[2]

The charges cited here reflect a completely imperialistic attitude, which denies any self-consciousness on the part of the Tibetan nation. To identify 'reverence to, and belief in, religion' as serious mistakes in a writer's political stance and viewpoint is ridiculous, no matter what society we are speaking of. Woeser herself is a follower of Tibetan Buddhism, and so it is natural for her to praise her religious leaders, including the Dalai Lama and Karmapa. Only a colonizer intending to suppress minority nationalities would think that such an attitude towards religion is a crime. To accuse a publication of having 'made false value judgments and divorced itself from the correct political principles', and its author of having 'abandoned social responsibility' and 'lost her political commitment to the progressive civilization movement'—is this not the language of violent domination and imperial manipulation?

To a certain degree, the fact that *Notes on Tibet* was published at all under Chinese censorship was itself a miracle. Perhaps it was because Guangdong Province currently has the most commercial environment in China, with a relatively relaxed political atmosphere, that the book was able to reach the public. The aforementioned chapter 'Nyima Tsering' articulated

2   Shi Jifeng, *Publication Newsletter*, no. 22; posted on *www.intelnet.com* on 23 February 2004.

in depth the repression and lack of choices faced by China's suppressed nationalities. The sympathetic responses the story received are exemplified in an email to Woeser from a Uyghur reader—written in poor Chinese:

> I could not control myself and naturally allowed myself a good cry.
> I read it several more times. Who knows why, when reading the
> paragraph on Nyima Tsering's answer to the girl, I could no longer
> control myself. I cried loudly. I was alone crying for a long time,
> feeling something pushing badly into my heart. It is unbearable to
> my weak heart. I want to shout loudly, but I don't have the courage.

Woeser happened to be in Beijing attending an advanced seminar when the ban was imposed on *Notes on Tibet*. Before the incident, the TAR Literature Association had considered promoting her to vice editor-in-chief of *Tibetan Literature*, but once the book became a problem her studies were immediately suspended. She was summoned back to Lhasa. An 'Aid and Education Committee' (*Bangjiao Xiaozu*) was organized for her ideological education. She was asked to perform 'self-criticism' and 'overcome her obstacles'.

These phrases belong to the special terminology of the CCP. They constitute a set of methods for mental control that are vividly described as tools for 'fixing' people. Their purpose is to make individuals bow before dominant authority and surrender their independence and dignity. He is repeatedly interrogated and forced to confess, even though the authorities have already compiled their own record on the individual. Only once the Party is satisfied is the subject allowed the opportunity to 'remake himself'. Presumably, he won't dare to transgress again and will sincerely bow before the Party, though at its mercy. The Party has utilized this mechanism for decades—it permeates every level of the system and is automatically put to use once the need arises. If they get into trouble, the majority of the Chinese population might just surrender to its mechanisms in order to sidestep the problem. This has been the practice in China for years—people have long gotten used to it and do not experience any shame in giving in.

Although Woeser was no longer eligible for promotion and was even threatened with the possibility of reeducation in the countryside, she may have at least retained her monthly salary if she had given in, and in Tibet, where the space for individual survival and development outside the system is so narrow, such a salary is certainly essential. 'Having a salary is like keeping a cow; it guarantees one's daily milk supply', as Tibetan's say. But Woeser was unable to 'overcome this obstacle'—at the most basic level, she could not repudiate her faith.

Since she had been accused of 'praising' the fourteenth Dalai Lama, the only way to redeem herself was to attack him, or at least to repeat the statement of Li Ruihuan, an ex-member of the Party's Politburo in charge of the affairs of minority nationalities, who had said: 'the Dalai is the head of the separatist clique for Tibetan independence, the loyal instrument of the international campaign against China, the fundamental root and origin that inspires social unrest in Tibet, and the biggest obstacle to Tibetan Buddhism establishing a normal order'. But how could she repeat such criticisms of her own religious leader? Was it not absurd to say the Dalai Lama had created social unrest in Tibet and, furthermore, blocked the establishment of Tibetan Buddhism's normal order? Regardless of whether it was because of her religious beliefs or her conscience, Woeser could not repeat such words. To attack one's guru in Buddhism creates serious negative karma. And after all, who was it that chased away the Dalai Lama, killed hundreds of thousands of Tibetans and destroyed nearly all of the monasteries in Tibet? It is they who were the leading perpetrators in creating social disorder in Tibet and disrupting the establishment of Tibetan Buddhism's normal order!

During his campaign to reorganize monasteries, Chen Kuiyuan, former Party Secretary of the TAR, ordered all Tibetan monks and nuns to copy out Li Ruihuan's charges against the Dalai Lama by hand. Whoever resisted the order would be ejected from their monastery. However, the difference between 'is' and 'is not' in written Tibetan is just a dot. Many monks added a barely visible dot above their 'is' to complete the task without attacking their guru. Yet Woeser could not do this. She writes in Chinese, and in this script 'is not' is a whole extra character. She could not overcome the obstacle so easily.

Various officials took turns to carry out 'ideological work' with (or on) her and her family, though in actuality, this was simply to abuse and damage her spirit. At the same time, she was ordered to 'receive education' at a construction site for the Qinghai-Tibet Railway due to her critical stance against its construction. The constant harassment by the authorities was stressful and became an unbearable burden for Woeser, and knowing that she did not have the strength to fight against the system—either directly or indirectly—she chose to leave Tibet.

Before she left, she wrote a letter to the TAR Literature Association's highest decision-making body, the Leading Party Group. The letter is entitled 'I am Forever a Tibetan Writer and Follower of Buddhism'. It reads:

14 September 2003
Wenlian Leading Party Group:

The charges against *Notes on Tibet* have mainly centred on my perspectives on religion and the present realities in Tibet. Asking me to 'overcome my obstacles' is to demand that I verbally renounce my faith in Buddhism, admit that my first-hand observations of the current realities in Tibet were mistaken, renounce religion in all my future writing and follow official directives in describing the situation in Tibet. Regarding all of these demands, I can only say that I am both unable and unwilling to overcome such an 'obstacle'. From my perspective, to cooperate is to violate the calling and conscience of a writer. Under current circumstances, remaining in Lhasa to undergo reeducation—reeducation that I will not freely accept—would have no positive results. It will create unnecessary troubles for everyone and make it difficult for the Association to close my case. Therefore, I think the best choice is for me to leave Lhasa temporarily and wait elsewhere for the final decisions of the concerned offices. I am willing to face of the consequences of this decision.

Woeser

Woeser was punished for the publication of *Notes on Tibet* in several ways. She was forced to resign ('voluntarily') from her post at the TAR Literature Association and was deprived of her income, housing and social security, including medical and retirement insurance. She is barred from applying for a passport and cannot therefore leave the country, so that, short of imprisonment, she has been deprived of all that could be taken from her. But for those living in free societies and inland China, the significance of such forms of punishment to Tibetans might not be clearly understood. The options available to those living in inland Chinese society have proliferated to the extent that individuals can survive and prosper without depending on the official system—enough opportunities now exist beyond it. By contrast, the process of modernization in Tibetan society has been completely dependent, financially, upon Beijing, so that no one can detach themselves from it.

With the sole exception of the monasteries, nearly all other cultural workers and intellectuals have been absorbed into the system. In other words, only as part of the system can one be a culture industry professional—otherwise, even basic survival is not guaranteed.

I found it striking that while dissenting intellectuals were active in the public sphere in the former Soviet Union, Eastern Europe and inland China today, this is not the case in Tibet, despite international support for the oppressed Tibetan people and their spiritual leaders. Why have we only heard about quiet resistance from the monasteries or at extremely localized scales? I think one important reason for this is the lack of space for Tibetan intellectuals to survive outside the system. The system thereby retains power over individual life and death. The system that feeds the cultural industry is also the system that disciplines it totally. Fear of the system precludes resistance against it. The current suppression of Tibetan culture is enabled by such systemic control. Woeser's punishment acts as a warning to the rest.

The egoism of cultural imperialism

Imperialism still involves force and politics, as we can see in Woeser's case, but it can no longer be simply seen as the work of a handful of colonizers. It is concerned with culture and involves the participation of ordinary people in the empire. If the collapse of political empires now seems inevitable, potentially coming to an end through institutional revolutions, a similarly drastic change is unlikely to befall cultural imperialism, since it has taken root in the minds of every member of the ruling nation. Since it has become a part of collective subconsciousness, to overturn it will be a difficult task.

Cultural imperialism first of all manifests as an egoistic pride: a feeling of cultural superiority that has—both collectively and individually, consciously or unconsciously—permeated every aspect of life. In Qushui County, located on the way from Gongkar Airport to Lhasa, sits Taizhou Plaza: a project meant to promote Tibet that shows typical characteristics of cultural imperialism. The plaza is huge and its construction swallowed up acres of good farmland, but apart from showcasing the wealth and crude taste of the builders, it is hard to explain the necessity of its existence. It features a pavilion, stone bridge and an artificial creek, all of which are elements of Han Chinese-style landscape design and do not mesh well with the local surroundings. At the centre rests a metal sculpture, above which sits a large stainless steel ball to symbolize the mainstream ideology of science and progress. Billboards along its periphery are decorated with portraits of Party leaders and the Party's ideological slogans. The financial investment in the plaza must have been immense; yet it appears to have nothing to do with the local surroundings. I sometimes even wonder if it was constructed for anyone at all. The reflection from the white concrete bricks on the ground irritates the eyes and makes you feel as if you're are standing on a baking sheet. The grass is fenced off with a sign prohibiting access; the artificial creek runs through a deep concrete ditch and is out of human reach. There are only two stone benches sitting opposite each other in this huge open space, which were erected only because they are formal requirements in such plazas, but being exposed to the intense sun and devoid of shade, they are not made for sitting and resting. I walked through the plaza on a Sunday, which one would expect to be a busy day for visitors. But there was no trace of anyone at all: the wide streets surrounding the plaza were deserted.

The plaza embodies the bird's-eye view from which the empire looks downward, its cultural pride and its extravagant display of wealth. The local people and culture have no place within the empire's horizon, being irrelevant and not worthy of concern or consideration. One might go even further and suggest that the plaza was designed to make the locals feel inferior: looking upwards, they might follow the cultural model imposed by the empire. Either way, it is a symbol of naked cultural violence and occupation.

The feeling of cultural superiority is common among Chinese officials governing Tibet. We most often hear them complaining that the locals are lazy, crude, conservative, lacking in culture, and ignorant about science, business and the marketplace. At the same time, they brag about their successes in forcing the locals to change their ideas, in reorganizing local business practices, and in encouraging hard work and punishing laziness. A cadre in charge of agricultural production in the TAR and meant to 'promote Tibet' once showed me a photo he had taken, which proved how lazy Tibetan peasants were. Apart from laziness, he explained, what else could explain their refusal to remove these hand-sized stones from the field? He was apparently unaware that the summer rains in the farming regions of Tibet are usually heavy and intense, capable of quickly washing away the topsoil, and that the sun is extremely harsh on the plateau, which results in rapid vaporization. Leaving those stones in the field is the Tibetan way to protect the earth: to make sure it isn't washed away when it rains, and to keep it moist under the intense sun. The problem is that it never occurred to this Han official that Tibetans might know better than himself.

Yang Song, former Secretary of the Party's Bureau of Politics and Law Enforcement and Chief Director of Bureau of Public Security in the TAR, has stated: 'The Dalai has not seen Tibet for decades. What is his right to speak about Tibet? I have crossed through every county in Tibet; I have more right than he does to speak'. But even ignoring the lack of awareness in such a claim (Yang seems to have forgotten that the Dalai Lama has been unable to see Tibet for decades precisely because of Chinese imperialism) all Yang might have acquired by travelling widely in Tibet is information—which does not necessarily deliver understanding. That can only be achieved by considering culture. Yet it is often the case that the officials sent by the empire maintain the chasm separating themselves from the culture of the local nationality. They are full of prejudice. Yang's claim illustrates perfectly his ignorance of the cultural factors involved in the Tibetan situation. Such a mediocre understanding fails to recognize even the simplest fact: that while countless colonizers have died in their colonies without ever understanding their people, twenty-seven long years of imprisonment did not undo Mandela's right to lead South Africa.

But this kind of imperialistic pride doesn't just exist among officials; many Han residents in the Tibetan region consider themselves superior to the locals, including rickshaw drivers, fruit vendors, construction labourers, who look down on Tibetans and think them to be stupid and backwards. A female writer who had travelled extensively in Tibet once told me that she had nearly given up writing entirely to advise on economic development everywhere she had gone. She worked hard instructing the local officials on how to develop a market economy, devising investment plans and even working out all the practical details. She was upset by the indifference of local officials to her efforts, which she concluded was due to their conservatism and laziness. It is amazing to me that a poetry and prose writer could think herself the supreme authority on such matters simply by having visited Tibet. What is this conceit but the sentiment of cultural superiority and egoism? I believe that she saw her own intentions as good, but to me they are disgraceful.

Many of my Han friends went to Tibet of their own accord after graduating from university in the 1980s. They differed from their predecessors, who had surrendered their careers and lives to the Party, as well as from the opportunists that moved there later purely for the sake of self-profit. The mark left by their fleeting presence upon modern Tibetan history cannot be erased, but analyzed around the viewpoint of cultural imperialism, they remained members of the empire and conspirators in its cultural intrusions. While they were not cogs of the imperialistic nation-state but instead highly individualistic, they still saw themselves in the position of Robinson Crusoe, who, on his own, enlightens and controls Man Friday. Tibet was only the prop and backdrop to their demonstration of cultural superiority. They kept their distance from Tibetans and clustered in a small social circle with the other Han Chinese. Many of them had travelled throughout Tibet, including the rural and nomad areas, and visited the sacred mountains and lakes. But they remained pursuers of the exotic—treasure hunters who appropriated Tibetan culture in their writing and films.

This tight-knit circle is represented in an oil painting by Yu Xiaodong entitled 'A Toast to Tibet' ('*Ganbei, Xizang*'), which depicts twenty-three figures crowded around a table, in the religious style of 'The Last Supper'. Apart from three of the writers depicted, who are half-Tibetan and half-Chinese but know no Tibetan, all the other figures are from inland China. In its use of a religious style, the painting emphasizes the noble sacrifice they made in going Tibet, but the people it represents are not without ignorance. An anecdote about Yu demonstrates their attitude toward the religion and culture of Tibet:

> Yu Xiaodong lived in a dorm converted from a classroom. The room was huge and Yu used giant prayer flags to divide it . . . He said that those giant black-and-white flags could only be found next to a holy river or on top of a sacred mountain where Tibetans had left them. It took him a lot of planning and hard work to acquire them secretly after having just been put up during the Tibetan New Year celebrations.[3]

To use these prayer flags—which carry the devotion, reverence and wishes of Tibetans to the divine—to decorate and divide one's room could only occur in the absence of any cultural understanding and respect. Moreover, Yu was not the only one who had done this: it had become a habit within their circle. Having looked through their collections, I can attest to the fact that nearly all of them owned piles of stolen Tibetan objects.

I would not imply that I myself am immune to the influence of cultural imperialism. The desire not to take part in it isn't simply resolved through individual choice. I cite one of Tsering Shakya's responses to my writing in his essay 'Blood in the Snows':

> It seems that asking some Chinese intellectuals—be they Communist Party officials, liberal democrats or dissident writers—to think about Tibet in an objective and reasonable manner is like asking an ant to lift an elephant; it is beyond their capabilities and vision. Their perception is impaired by racial prejudice and their imagination clouded by the convictions and certainties of all colonial masters.

---

3   Zhang Ziyang, 2004. *Tibetan Cultural Geography* 1: 86.

I can understand the radical emotion in Shakya's writing, since even Chinese supporters of democracy, who have relatively more awareness regarding questions of national identity, are afflicted by the mindset of cultural imperialism. They typically take the idea of Great Unification for granted, so that while believing in and promoting democracy, they still subconsciously place themselves in a superior position, from which they have the right to judge the claims of minority nationalities. They support demands for democracy but not independence for suppressed nations. There is no openness to even considering or much less understanding their positions.

But most Han Chinese supporters of democracy, in their belief in Great Unification, deny the existence of suppressed nations within China anyway. According to their rationale, there is only autocratic suppression, and since the Han people also suffer under its yoke, minority nationalities should join forces with the Han to fight for China's democratization. For this reason, minority peoples should not only pursue the goals of their nationalities. Yet the fact is that the autocracy, despite its suppression of all, is still discriminatory in dealing with different nationalities. When Han intellectuals pen articles critical of the Party, their positions within the system are never affected, yet Woeser's single sentence praising the Dalai Lama and her description of Nyima Tsering's confusion were enough to deprive her of everything. How can we say that all these acts of suppression are the same?

Most minority people who have travelled to inland China have experienced the difference directly. 'We would have been thrown into jail long ago if, as a minority, we dared to articulate what you Han are saying', it is frequently said. At the same time, there is an unspoken understanding even among democratically-minded Chinese that a democratic China, once achieved, should continue to wage war against minority nationalities demanding independence, simply for the sake of maintaining a unified nation-state. In that case, each nationality would not be suffering under a shared autocracy—rather, it would simply be the Han nation that would dominate the minorities. But even under the autocracy, ordinary Han people also frequently follow the lead of the empire on the issue of minority nationalities, and particularly in areas where they coexist alongside other nationalities. The civilian workers recruited from inland China by the Xinjiang Production and Construction Corps were not only under orders from the empire to exploitation of the locals but appeared in many cases to have carried out this task with great enthusiasm.

A popular and seemingly equitable perspective on the issue emphasizes the shared humanity of different nationalities and plays down their unique features. It proposes an objective standard under which the law and democratic procedures are identical for everyone. To avoid conflict, no nationality should be given special treatment. But no standard, law or procedure can be completely objective: they are all intimately bound up with culture. Cultural imperialism is not going to disappear simply due to democratization. Instead, it will survive for a long time in the consciousnesses of much of the majority nation—democracy blind to national differences will only lead to domination by the majority nation, which will create concrete inequalities for the minority nationalities. Particularly where a large population gap exists between the majority and minority populations, representative democracy will be relatively unresponsive to minority rights and interests. If there is no insistence on nationalism once that day comes, minority cultures will be suffocated under the rule of the majority. Otherwise, minority claims to resistance will be voided under the banner of democracy and the discourse of modernization.

Edward Said made the acute observation that cultural imperialism still prevails in democratic societies of the modern world. It need not exercise political suppression or violence but instead can rely upon democratic methods to form a 'mainstream', which itself can marginalize minority others and their cultures. There on the periphery, they may become withered or even completely obliterated. This is why nationalism is a necessary part of minority movements for cultural resistance. In fact, the common anti-globalization stance already opposes such a mainstream, so as long as this nationalism does not take on a political form or become violent, it can be constructive. This kind of cultural nationalism should be allowed a reasonable place in an open and fair society.

Disarming cultural imperialism through national articulation

National culture can best be protected by building an independent nation-state. But the conditions for achieving independence are not always in place and are usually achieved at a high cost. It only really becomes feasible when the power distribution between the majority and minority populations are highly disproportionate. On the other hand, if independence is only perceived as a means to protect a nation's culture, it can become less important if other ways of protecting the national culture are accepted and carried out.

Through what practices might a minority nationality's culture then be protected within the context of a larger nation-state? Apart from ensuring that the basic political system is responsive on the issue, the imperialistic attitude of the majority nationality would have to be dissolved. After all, the construction of political mechanisms to relax national tensions are dependent upon support by the majority within the nation-state. But we cannot simply expect cultural imperialism to disappear automatically as the majority national group becomes more enlightened. National minorities must therefore become competent in articulating themselves, which requires cultural strength, patience and a willingness to persist.

Articulation involves many aspects—achieving a good grasp on one's national language, including the ability to speak and write clearly—but the one I wish to discuss here is the ability to utilize the majority language. Many people will object to Tibetans having to learn the Chinese language, whereas Han Chinese needn't learn Tibetan, and it is indeed unfair that this has become the case due to the cultural pride of the Han and the fact that, in China, learning Tibetan simply isn't necessary. But media and the spaces for expression in imperial systems are dominated by the language of the empire, so that minority groups simply become unable to articulate themselves in public space if they refuse to master the majority language out of spite.

It is justifiable to demand that majority groups learn minority languages and to take the initiative to understand minority cultures. But the possibility of achieving this is very slim, and in the long run, the minority group would still be Woesers—marginalized within the game. But if the majority way of thinking is to be modified, then wielding the language of the other strengthens one's position in interactions. It is similar to embracing and building on air and sea technologies adopted from the enemy. Linguistic competence might then become less entangled with questions of national pride and identity.

Articulation is not an exercise in solitary contemplation: it means being heard by others. Quietly clinging to one's national culture is certainly a form of passive resistance, but it cannot finally halt the expansion of the dominant culture or prevent itself from being subsumed. Violence is equally useless in the face of cultural imperialism. The Manchu conquered China but were at last swallowed up by Chinese cultural imperialism.

Only in the realm of culture can cultural imperialism really be fought. Imperialistic sentiments will only be abandoned, respect for minorities granted and equality achieved if the strength of the minority culture can be demonstrated to the imperial other. This kind of active engagement is the best way to protect national culture and help its further development. In light of this, the ability to articulate one's national culture in a competent way is even more vital. Such competence is to a large degree dependent on being able to wield the language of the empire in sophisticated literary ways.

On this note, many talented Tibetan writers have emerged through a convergence of historical events. Hundreds of Tibetan authors and poets make up what is known as Tibet's 'Chinese Writers' Group', of which the most outstanding members include Woeser, Methuk, Serpo, Alai and Tashi Dawa. Their command of Chinese is better than that of many Han writers. Woeser, for one, though born in Lhasa and raised in the Tibetan region of Sichuan Province, studied Chinese language and literature then worked as a reporter for *Ganzi Daily* and as an editor for *Tibetan Literature*—both Chinese-language journals.

This phenomenon has been explained in different ways among Tibetans themselves. Some feel that it is a result of colonialism, which is certainly supported in examining the upbringing of these writers. To begin with, the majority of them grew up in the Tibetan region of Sichuan Province, which is a result of China's decision to divide the Tibetan areas outside of Tibet into the four provinces of Qinghai, Gansu, Sichuan and Yunnan. The degree of Sinicization in the Tibetan areas of Sichuan is high and education in Tibetan language has been poor. The authors listed above do not write in Tibetan; some of them cannot even speak the language. Besides Methuk, none of them is fully Tibetan: Woeser and Serpo are both a quarter Han Chinese; Tashi Dawa is half; and Alai is half Tibetan and half Muslim. All have Chinese names that are regularly used, and all have Han spouses, including Methuk. In addition, all apart from Alai (who comes from a peasant family) are children of Party cadres. Woeser, Serpo and Tashi Dawa's fathers (and, in some cases, mothers) were Khampa Tibetans recruited into the vanguard units when the CCP army first arrived in the area.

Should these writers be viewed as an embarrassment to the nation, or as its treasures and weapons? The answer is clear if we admit that national articulation can contribute to resisting and disarming cultural imperialism. In fact, Tibetans have been greatly successful in expressing their national identity—particularly when compared with Uyghurs. Where most Han Chinese saw Tibet as a dark and backward society just thirty and even twenty years ago—a place where criminals were punished by being skinned and having their eyeballs gouged out—today many Chinese see Tibet as a spiritual destination and admire Tibetan culture and religion. Tibetan self-articulation has, to a large degree, produced such a change. Many Tibetan exiles have been persistent in publicizing the situation internationally over the past few decades, providing information to the West, which it has in turn conveyed to a reopened China. Nor should the contributions of Tibetan cultural and religious professionals in Tibet be underestimated.

Uyghur society currently possesses neither of these two assets, although the coexistence of different ethnic groups in Xinjiang has, in practical terms, necessitated the use of Chinese as a common language. Many Uyghurs speak Chinese very well, but I know of no Uyghur authors who write in Chinese, nor of any religious teachers who preach in that language. This is a big difference between the Tibetan and Uyghur cases, which might be explained by the latter's staunch adherence to their culture. Uyghur intellectuals have unanimously rejected the use of the Chinese language in the media and other public spheres. Uyghur language reforms of the 1960s and 1970s, which replaced the traditional Arabic script with a Roman script (known as the 'new script'), have since been abandoned, while at the same time, many Chinese terms that had been absorbed into spoken Uyghur are now gradually being replaced by English words. This process doesn't seem to have occurred through any concentrated effort but has instead been spontaneously driven by the social atmosphere of nationalism. Even prison inmates laugh at anyone using Chinese. A Uyghur friend who had grown up in Beijing was sent back to Xinjiang by his parents, who expected him to learn Uyghur there. But because his Uyghur was so poor, other Uyghurs thought he had lost his 'Uyghurness' and no one was then willing to help him learn the language. Everywhere he went, he was looked down on and excluded. In the end, he never really learned his own language, and it is easy to see that in such a social environment no one would want to be a Uyghur author writing in Chinese.

Although more Han Chinese live in Xinjiang than in Tibet, Uyghur society has appeared to be more successful than Tibetan society in preserving their national language and avoiding linguistic assimilation. Their internal solidarity also seems stronger. But in terms of national articulation, the Tibetans have been much more successful. For one, most Uyghurs do not think it worth making themselves heard by the Han population. Even in foreign countries, where one does not have to worry about the possibility of political persecution, exiled Uyghurs still refuse to engage in dialogues with Han Chinese or to participate in their activities. Moreover, few Uyghurs possess Chinese language skills that can be deployed at the aesthetic level, with acts of expression rarely going beyond political claims or slogans. These are neither moving nor convincing, and can easily stir up conflicts.

While books about Tibet and Tibetan culture are usually in abundance in quality bookstores in inland China, often remaining as bestsellers for long periods of time, there is little interest in books on the Uyghur people and their culture. The Uyghur people have a long and rich culture like the Tibetans and are even larger in population, so why is there such a discrepancy in the amount of attention they each attract? In fact, a few publishers were interested in Uyghur and Islamic culture in the 1980s, but the few books that were published had been written by Han Chinese authors and expressed uneasy sentiments toward Muslims, leading to strong protests and street demonstrations by Muslim people in China, including many Uyghurs. Some even went as far as issuing fatwas, similar to those the Ayatollah Khomeini issued regarding Salman Rushdie. The lives of the authors and editors were threatened. Since then, writers and the media world in inland China have tended to keep at a distance from anything to do with the Muslim population. At the same time, few Muslim writers write and publish in Chinese. This all perpetuates an unhelpful cycle: the scarcity of pieces on Muslim society and culture published in Chinese makes it more difficult for the Han population to understand the Uyghur people, which in turn makes it yet more difficult to develop a market for publishing on these subjects. The Chinese media is subsequently even less motivated to understand the people and their culture. Today, the Uyghur people are complete strangers to most Han Chinese, who know nothing about Uyghur history and culture and follow the official propaganda on the Xinjiang issue almost completely. They feel only fear and enmity toward the Uyghur people, which is hardly beneficial to the Uyghur people themselves.

By contrast, the inclusiveness of Tibetan religion, its commonalities with Han religion, the Dalai Lama's active efforts to reconcile with the Han Chinese, the plethora of Tibetan cultural professionals who write in Chinese (explaining Tibetan culture and establishing close communication between the two cultures)—all of this has helped to make Tibetan culture popular and even fashionable in China today. There is now a Chinese subculture built around 'Tibetan fever'.

In the meantime, this cultural articulation at the aesthetic level has publicized Tibet's political agenda to the Han Chinese; it is gradually producing an understanding and sympathy for the Tibetan position. The strength of the Tibetan movement in using their peacefulness and flexibility to overcome the dominant power should provide a lesson to other minority nationalities. Here, I recall Genghis Khan's great military might that no nation was able to confront. But he did not defeat the Tibetans. Rather, it was the Mongolians who finally converted to Tibetan Buddhism. This proves the power of culture.

Compensating for a lack of proficiency in the national language

Being unable to master the Tibetan language is admittedly a common problem among Tibetan intellectuals whose major competence is in Chinese. As a result of colonial education, many of them cannot write or even fluently speak Tibetan. Woeser's generation was schooled during the period of the Cultural Revolution, when barely any Tibetan was taught in the schools of Tibetan areas of Sichuan. But the payoff is that their Chinese was good enough for them to choose writing as their profession.

It is generally accepted that one can only master a single language to the degree of becoming a writer, and Chinese is indeed these Tibetan writers' first language. When Tashi Dawa, in his capacity as chairman of the Tibetan Writers' Association, met with Tibetan exiles overseas, the two sides could only communicate through Chinese, the language of the Chinese empire. No wonder the exiles question how, if a nation's language is the carrier of its culture, someone unable to master the language can grasp the culture and spirit of the nation, much less speak for the nation. But it is also true that a nation is not a race; that culture rather than blood is the essence of a nation. If one can no longer communicate with one's own national culture, linguistic mastery of Chinese will not strengthen the Tibetan nation but only shepherd more people into the majority culture of the nation. They would culturally become Han Chinese. The poor command of Tibetan is indeed a major handicap of Woeser's generation. But it is the result of a history for which the authors themselves cannot be held responsible. But on the other hand, their nationalism and faith in religion give me high hopes in their potential to shoulder the burden of articulating Tibetan national aspirations. These two factors compensate for their lack of Tibetan language mastery, keeping them connected to their nation's culture and nurturing their desire to speak for it.

Nationalism is the primary manifestation of national consciousness today, but its articulation does not have to be based solely upon inherited culture (including language). So long as one identifies with one's nation, one can speak—and this needn't occur in the national language. In fact, one is more likely to be heard by the Chinese government and the rest of Han society if one uses Chinese to express what that nation means. A Tibetan consciousness prevails among Tibetan authors writing in Chinese, even if that sentiment is usually not articulated openly in the political domain. But it can be felt everywhere in their various forms of cultural expression.

The articulation of nationalism through aesthetic and cultural forms has not, admittedly, been done out of choice, but instead because of restrictions on other channels. Yet it might actually be more effective than its political form. Although political nationalism can be used to express the people's needs or as a force of resistance, its main objective is to demand power. Its concerns are, by and large, purges, confrontation and exclusion. What is missing here is compassion, compromise and peace. As a result, political nationalism tends to enhance enmity and conflict between nations rather than improving their relationship. By contrast, cultural nationalism is primarily an embodiment and manifestation of one's passion for and commitment to one's national culture. It needn't confront other nations and thus allows for the simultaneous blooming of diverse cultures. In light of this, the current way that Tibetan writers (writing in Chinese) express their national concerns through cultural forms may generate better results in the long term.

On the other hand, culture is undeniably formed through the accumulation of history and, to a large degree, relies on language for its transmission. Where Tibetan national culture largely revolves around religion—which has in turn been central to the formation of Tibetan national consciousness—for Tibetan writers who cannot write in Tibetan, national religion becomes the only connection with their culture. While folk traditions, inherited from the past, are becoming mere formalities, religion is a live practice that continues to develop. So despite their lack of Tibetan language skills, as long as their ties to Tibetan religion are maintained, these writers remain deeply connected to the national consciousness and culture.

In this regard, the belief of Tibetan intellectuals writing in Chinese in Tibetan Buddhism becomes particularly important. I am not talking here about the importance of religion per se, but about religion as the sole link between these intellectuals and their national culture. What makes Woeser the voice of the national spirit and a defender of its culture is precisely her devotion to Tibetan Buddhism.

I should specify here that these statements only refer to the small subset of the Tibetan population who speak Chinese as their first language and whose command of the language has allowed them to speak successfully for the Tibetan nation. The price they've paid in losing their national language can also be seen as a gain—in Chinese fluency. But such logic does not stand up when the issue concerns average Tibetans who are not burdened with the responsibility of expressing nationhood. Their loss of the Tibetan language is not positive in any way. The Tibetan nation should learn here from the Uyghurs, who defend their language and every aspect of their culture on a daily basis.

Beyond whispers within the nation

Some might argue that even absent these Tibetan writers who write in Chinese, Tibetan articulations of their national consciousness exist nonetheless. Even under the most severe forms of suppression, Tibetans have never stopped expressing their discontent in private venues, in the form of complaints, jokes and gossip. But this rarely goes beyond whispers among family, friends and relatives. At best, they may be spoken as private words among nationals wherever Tibetans gather.

Since Tibetan voices will never be heard by the Han majority through these means, the authorities can interpret this superficial silence as evidence of an unprecedented degree of stability. The use of this kind of expression is thus very limited. Instead, it is more important to speak publicly and face the audience of Han people, Chinese authorities and international opinion. Otherwise, the average Han Chinese person has no option but to go along with government propaganda on Tibet. The Chinese authorities have only the biased reports of intelligence agents and policy studies to rely on in controlling Tibet. Reality is either distorted or ignored when the nation itself is voiceless.

In 2003, the famous Chinese swimmer Zhang Jian swam across Tso Ngonpo, a lake Tibetans view to be sacred. For Tibetans, to swim in the lake is an insult. Many similar incidents had occurred in their other sacred waters and holy mountains, but despite the distaste most Tibetans felt toward such behaviour, they only complained in private. After swimming across Tso Ngonpo, unaware of Tibet's sacred geography, Zhang declared that he would repeat his feat at Nam Tso, another of Tibet's sacred lakes. This time, the *Tibetan Cultural Web* (*Zangren Wenhuawang*), a Chinese-language website run by and for Tibetans, posted a public letter to the relevant government departments. Meanwhile, Woeser drafted a petition demanding that Zhang cancel his Nam Tso project. The public letter and the petition were immediately and widely circulated on Chinese websites. Woeser's petition recieved hundreds of signatures, nearly half from Han Chinese people. The overseas Chinese media also reported the story, which by then had become a major news item. In the face of public criticism, Zhang cancelled his Nam Tso swim. In addition, after being mentioned in Woeser's petition, the pop singer Han Hong also cancelled her concert at Lhasa's Potala Palace. These incidents show that articulating demands in the public domain can achieve results that differ drastically from what is achieved through whispering among nationals.

The Dalai Lama and Tibetans-in-exile have been speaking out for a long time, and this is responsible for the bulk of international coverage on the Tibetan issue. But because of censorship and language barriers, their influence on Han Chinese thinking is very limited. Many Chinese also believe that overseas Tibetans cannot represent their compatriots in Tibet, and that their statements are propagandistic rather than descriptions of reality. It is therefore necessary for Tibetans inside Tibet to articulate their nationalism in Chinese, if Chinese audiences are the target.

What happened to Woeser is no doubt the price that Tibetans inside Tibet must pay for speaking out. But it would be strange indeed if there was no price to pay! These are the necessary and inescapable sacrifices involved in a nation's fight against imperialism. Until now, the articulation of national consciousness in Tibet has only manifested in the form of sporadic dissent. While many anti-imperialist movements around the world have been led by the activists of minority nations, there is still a long way to go for Tibetans to form such a movement. But rather than being totally silent, the sentiments of the Tibetan people should still be publicly and continuously voiced. Sustained protest and going public are two crucial principles here. The latter refers not only to public occasions but also the use of Chinese as the medium of communication.

In 1999, when the National Minorities Traditional Games was held in Lhasa, a Tibetan individual slipped through security, sneaked into the dance performance during the opening ceremony and shouted out 'Free Tibet!' in Tibetan. But because there was no loudspeaker nearby, not many people understood what he was doing. Even those audience members who heard him did not understand Tibetan and thought he was a part of the program. This person clearly did not lack courage, but his actions had little effect. No one knows what happened to him afterwards. This incident was only related by word-of-mouth among Tibetans. A similar incident took place in 2004 at a New Year's concert in Urumqi, the capital of Xinjiang, when a Uyghur man walked on stage and recited a political poem in the Uyghur language. Although it too was a public occasion, his actions were just as ineffective as those of the Tibetan man. Most of the audience members did not understand the Uyghur language and did not understand what was happening. Such incidents eventually get reported outside of China, but because by then they are no longer 'news items', the media simply loses interest in discussing them.

Protests like this happen all the time. But they are isolated events that produce few lasting effects, with protesters usually growing quiet after getting arrested and being locked up in prison. The events usually involve little more than a few slogans that express one's courage but are not persuasive, moving or capable of generating cultural interaction. These events may leave an impression on some people but they hardly constitute lines of reasoning that can change the way people think.

The ones who bear responsibility for expressing national consciousness in widespread and lasting ways are those of Tibet's public intellectuals who have strong Chinese-language skills. They are able to communicate directly with the Chinese population and authorities; they are able to spread the word through the media, since internet connections are still available even if they've been censored; and they can participate in mainstream Chinese society, and through it access an international, China-focused audience. They are relatively more protected by international observers of China and therefore have more leeway than the average citizen to probe at the limits of autocracy.

Being a public intellectual means that one's acts and deeds are publicly visible. Their probing of this limit can in turn encourage others. Although the courage of a people is only accumulated over time, large changes can come about in society as a result of this, just as a succession of water droplets can eventually carve through a rock. Chinese society is much less fearful than it was twenty years ago, though this is not because the control of authorities over society has weakened, or because the nature of the autocracy has changed. Rather, the autocracy itself is faced with the major challenge that its laws no longer rule the people. As long as the majority of the people remain united, tyranny will be very limited. If public intellectuals, who are relatively better protected, take the lead, it may be possible to inspire the courage of the people and move forward together—so long as the collectively agreed-upon bottom line is not transgressed. This may expand the space of freedom under autocratic rule, overcome the loss of the national language and initiate a movement of dissent.

But because all of its intellectuals have so far been recruited into the system, Tibet has produced few public figures of this kind to date. Meanwhile, dissidents are not tolerated by the system, which dominates Tibet's cultural space almost completely, and a cultural market that is at least partially independent of the official system has yet to emerge in the Tibetan province. Given these constraints, the existence of Tibetan intellectuals who are fluent in Chinese are significant in yet another way: where public intellectuals have to be able to make a living through the market in order to shake off the system and freely express alternative viewpoints, intellectuals with Chinese-language skills are able to circumvent the system through their mobility. Intellectuals who use Tibetan as their main language of expression are confined to the Tibetan areas where the cultural market does not exist, and so distancing themselves from the system is to lose their means of basic livelihood. But a large cultural market has developed in inland China. Tibetan intellectuals fluent in Chinese can access this market to gain their livelihood, and thereby shake off the system's control.

The Woeser incident should not simply be seen as a human rights case. To do so merely adds it to a list of many such cases. Rather, it should be seen as an inspiration for thinking about the situation in Tibet in various ways. How might Tibet challenge these two kinds of imperialism? How might we cultivate and produce public intellectuals with the ability to articulate a nation's wishes in the way that I've described? What is the function of those Tibetan intellectuals who are adept at writing and speaking in the Chinese language?

As a part of its imperial policy, China has nurtured its Tibetan allies through a Sinicized education system, and while the policy has in some ways been successful, it has also produced no small number of Woeser-type figures. Rather than eroding their national consciousness, this education has in fact enhanced it. Meanwhile, its students have cultivated a good command of the language of empire. This generation is gradually becoming the backbone of Tibetan society. In the future, some of them may become the leaders and pioneers in various professions in Tibet. At this time, will a group of dissenting intellectuals arise, who are adept in reasoning and possess strong Chinese-language skills—perhaps a Tibetan Andrei Sakharov or Vaclav Havel? How should Han Chinese people think about the future implications for both Tibet and China in resolving the Tibetan problem? How should we respond to such future possibilities? How might each of us reflect upon and banish the cultural imperialism that hides deep within our minds?

August–October 2004

4

The End of Tibetan Buddhism

Wang Lixiong

Monasteries and temples seem to be everywhere in Tibet today. They are packed with worshippers, who are busy making their offerings of butter lamps and incense.[1] Monks and nuns are present in abundance, and lay people are free to worship and do their circumambulations. Passing quickly through Tibet, many Chinese and foreign tourists commonly conclude that Tibetans now have complete religious freedom. Then having caught wind of these touristic impressions, the Chinese government changed its defensive closed-door policy and began more actively to encourage outsiders to visit Tibet, inviting more foreign reporters and politicians. We are just beginning to see the effects, which were expected by the government, of such a shift in policy.

But in January 2003, Lobsang Dhondup, a common Tibetan, was executed following a death sentence in Nyagchu County (Yajiang in Chinese), located in the Karze Tibetan Autonomous Prefecture (KTAP) of Sichuan Province. The Tibetan monk Tenzin Delek Rinpoche (A'ngag Tashi in Tibetan) was also sentenced to death (though given a suspension of two years). Tenzin Delek Rinpoche is a reincarnated Gelugpa lama (the

---

1 This chapter was translated by Susan Chen.

Gelugpa school being one of the most well-known in Tibetan Buddhist traditions today), who is highly respected by the locals in the region. The authorities accused him of plotting and instructing Lobsang Dhondup to carry out a series of terrorist explosions. He was thus arrested and sentenced.

Back in January 2001, a bomb was set off on a bridge crossing the Zheduo River in Dhartsedo, the capital of KTAP. No one was injured in the explosion, but it shocked the entire city. It was in Dhartsedo again on 1 August 2001 that the gate to the KTAP Party Office was bombed. Two armed policemen on duty that night were injured. On 2 October, another explosion took place in Dhartsedo, this time at the gate to the KTAP's Traffic Police Division office. The elderly guard of the building was killed at the site.

The authorities claimed that Tenzin Delek Rinpoche and Lobsang Dhondup were responsible for all of these bombings. I have written elsewhere questioning the evidence that had been used to prosecute them. Rather than rehashing them here, I want to raise a broader question here: if Tibetans actually enjoyed the religious freedom claimed by the Chinese authorities, why would these bombings have happened? I am unconvinced by the official charge that Tenzin Delek Rinpoche was behind these incidents. Yet, like many residents of KTAP, I accept the hypothesis that Tibetans were involved in these bombings and that these bombings were indeed motivated by religious concerns. Neither did the Dhartsedo locals associate the explosions with Tenzin Delek Rinpoche after they took place. Instead, they were thinking of the Serta Buddhist Academy in Larung Valley, several hundred kilometres away from where Tenzin Delek Rinpoche lived.

Larung Valley is about twenty kilometres from the town of Serta, where the Nyingma lama Kenpo Jigme Phuntsok once established his Buddhist Academy. The Academy had only thirty-some students in the 1980s. By the late 1990s, it had attracted nearly ten thousand pupils, including monks, nuns and laypeople. Thousands of Han devotees joined as well. People arrived from everywhere, and the number of the participants only kept increasing.

The Chinese authorities fear and mistrust any institution that is not completely under their control. When I was travelling in the Kham region with a plan to visit the Serta Academy in August 1999, I heard that the authorities were about to launch a purge of it. Rumours were spreading that the police had already gained control over the Academy. Because I had just been released from a jail in Xinjiang Province and my travel companion did not want to invite further trouble, we gave up the idea of going there. Apparently, the goal of the authorities was to reduce enrolment in the Academy, in turn limiting its influence. Following their demands, only 10 per cent of the four thousand Tibetan female and 25 per cent of the four thousand male Tibetan students were allowed to stay; meanwhile, all of the one thousand-odd Chinese pupils were ordered to leave.

In the beginning, the authorities expected Kenpo Jigme Phuntsok and the other tulkus (reincarnated lamas) and teachers in the Academy to help send the students away. Together, they refused the government's demand, because to tell others to disrobe themselves is a serious violation of their own monastic vows. The authorities thus hired Chinese labourers to demolish the huts that students had built. Most students in the Academy lost their shelters and were forced to leave. On 1 July 2001, the authorities' actions came to a climax: 1,700 houses were knocked down on that single day. I heard from witnesses that, while noise and dust covered the scene, the loud crying of thousands of nuns seemed to have shook the earth. For a while, clustering in groups, wandering nuns could be seen in the surrounding hills. They camped out to avoid government pursuit. Please take note of the dates: twenty days after the climactic demolition of the Academy's residential huts, the gate of the KTAP Party Office was bombed. Furthermore, the three bombings in Dhartsedo that I mentioned above all occurred in 2001, when the purge of Serta Academy had reached an extreme.

Of course, I am not suggesting that the high lamas of the Academy participated in or ordered these explosions. But the purge had forcefully removed thousands of its pupils and participants. The moment they were chased away, they were no longer under the discipline of the Academy, while at the same time, many of them may not yet have achieved the level of Buddhist discipline characterized by total patience and freedom from anger. If a bystander like me could be upset by the thought of those harmless nuns being forced into homelessness and fear because of their religious beliefs, why should we expect the victims to remain calm and unreactive? It is not unthinkable that some of them turned to the idea of protest through bombing.

Every religion has visible attributes, such as monastic architecture, the mantras and texts recited by monks and nuns, and the worship, offerings and pilgrimages performed by the devotees. A religion also has less visible elements, which include its philosophical foundation, monastic lineage, institutions and educational system. The former is the form of the religion; the latter its substance. Since the form mediates the substance, a religion merely sustained by its forms without any substance can no longer be considered a religion. Instead, it has become superstition. Currently, religion seems to have been granted a large degree of formal freedom in Tibet. Tourists passing through in a hurry rarely notice the limitations imposed upon the actual practice of religion. But one only needs to go one step further to realize that religious confinement not only exists but prevails.

Next to the Tibetan Autonomous Region (TAR), the part of the Kham region belonging to KTAP has the largest Tibetan population in China. However, the two tulkus most widely accepted by their Khampa followers—Kenpo Jigme Phuntsok from the northern part of the region and Tenzin Delek Rinpoche from the south—were both in trouble with the authorities. The bulk of the student body at Kenpo Jigme Phuntsok's Academy had been dismantled, as I described above, and Tenzin Delek Rinpoche himself was behind bars and facing a death sentence. Why had the authorities done this to them? Religious freedom is the central aspect when we try to comprehend these events. The authorities could not accept the kind of religious freedom that they demanded. What happened to Tenzin Delek Rinpoche was clearly linked to his difficulties with the local government over the course of many years. The KTAP authorities had long seen him as a heretic. As far back as July 1997, the KTAP Religious Affairs Bureau acted on the will of the Party and released a document criticizing the Rinpoche, accusing him of having converted a tent temple into a permanent infrastructure; expanding the size of the temple; setting up a gathering place for chanting; confirming the reincarnation of two tulkus; and intervening in the relocation of another monastery.

It is easy to see that all these accusations concern religion. The government would not have made these claims had there been decent religious freedom. But they didn't stop there— they revoked his tulku status, ordering him to be a normal monk; denied his confirmation of the two tulku reincarnations; suspended his participation in events held in other monasteries; and withdrew his seat in the Nyagchu County People's Political

Consultative Committee. Of these four measures, only the last one falls into the realm of politics and can be decided by the authorities. The other three no doubt represent an interjection of politics into religion. Yet there is a further problem regarding the legitimacy of their intervention. Since the recognition of reincarnated lamas concerns the issue of succession within the religion, it can only follow the internal rules of the religion, and according to Tenzin Delek Rinpoche, he had been recognized by the Dalai Lama himself. Tulku identity is religious in principle and cannot simply be changed by political power— how can an atheist political party step in to decide who is and is not a tulku? This was unacceptable to both the Rinpoche and the local believers, and he actually gained in reputation because of the charge. The government was embarrassed when over ten thousand people signed a petition supporting their Rinpoche and finally had trouble implementing the charges. They felt their authority had been neglected and challenged, with certain officials even feeling personally humiliated, yet Tenzin Delek was the only one they blamed. In this society, where power is believed to be everything, those with power could not just stop because of people's protest. They had to keep raising the stakes. If they could not win in the first round, they would return for another. It would continue like this until they emerged victorious.

The function of religion in Tibetan society

I had been closely observing Tenzin Delek Rinpoche even before his imprisonment. I was interested in examining his experiences as I was thinking about how social security could be maintained in the Tibetan areas. Kham—and especially the part falling under the KTAP—is an area where violent crimes frequently occur, which I had experienced personally on a few occasions. I once stayed at an inn a few kilometres away from the seat of Nyagchu County, and as I drank butter tea the morning after, the Tibetan innkeeper pointed to something outside the window that he wanted me to see. It was a dead body covered in a shroud. The innkeeper said it was a bandit shot by the police the night before—one of two Tibetan bandits who were believed to have robbed a truck coming from Chengdu. After the driver ran into town and reported it to the police, they arrived at the inn in pursuit, and just as the bandits were about to pull their knives, the police opened fire. One was killed and the other escaped, vanishing into the mountains. The inn owner seemed remorseful. He said that the bandits wanted to check into his inn, but because they could not show their identification cards, he had turned them away. They were caught by the police as soon as they left. 'If I had let them stay, no one would have been killed.' He continued: 'It's okay to kill robbers like this. There was another killed a few years ago. It gave us peace for a while. The robberies have become more frequent lately. To have one killed means another while of peace.'

Not long after we spoke, several county police cars showed up to check the scene. I chatted with one policeman. He said that these sorts of crimes had been happening more frequently. Ten years ago, just after joining the County Police Bureau, they were made up of only thirty policemen. There were now more than seventy, but there are still more crimes than they can handle. The main problem is that the Tibetan region is vast and sparsely populated. Road conditions are often poor and driving is very difficult. People sometimes have to travel for days on horseback just to report a crime, and then it can take several more days for the police to arrive at the crime scene—also by horse. By that time, the culprits are long gone, and there is no way to search people out in the endless expanse of grassland and mountains. The policeman thought that the methods employed by Mao were still the best in handling security in Tibet. In his view, the people were in charge then. Everyone was vigilant and on alert. Local organizations served the function of maintaining social order, so that even without the police force, no one wanted to run the risk of getting caught; even if a crime was committed, the criminal could not run too far before being arrested. The local organizations no longer serve this function. When something happens, everyone pretends not to see. No one wants to get involved. The police force has become the only way to maintain social order. Anywhere out of reach of the police force is a place where criminals can do whatever they want.

But Mao's time has come and gone, and things will not be reversed. That reliance on class struggle to maintain social order could only have been temporary—there were no guarantees. If Mao's method of rule is no longer effective, what might be the long-term solution for maintaining social security in the Tibetan regions? This question could not solely have existed in Mao's era and ours. How was it handled through the thousand years of Tibetan history?

Nyagchu County borders a heavily Han-populated area. It is a frontier region where Tibetans encounter modern life, commercial economy, market value and Han migrants very intensely, and where the social order has been greatly deteriorated. But conditions in the rural and nomadic regions west from Nyagchu are much less severe, and here I once stayed with a Khampa man named Karma, who was tall, strong and built like a warrior, as many Khampa men are. When I met his two close friends, Ribu and Chodrak[2], for the first time, I was surprised that none of them smoked or drank—a common habit among many Khampa men. Noticing my reaction, Karma explained that they had been heavy drinkers in the past. Like many Tibetans in the neighbouring regions, they had been addicted to smoking, gambling, fighting, hunting and stealing. Karma had a knife scar on his forehead and admitted that he had once swung a knife at someone's head. At one point, he lost more than 13,000 yuan gambling. His life was a mess: getting drunk, going wild, fighting and handing money to whomever he met. Sometimes he and his friend would spend hours going back and forth, drunk, escorting each other home, and then would still remember to beat their wives. But none of them had touched alcohol for years and had stopped smoking, gambling, stealing, robbing and fighting (which had sometimes ended in death). They were not alone. More than 90 per cent of the locals in the nearby villages had done the same.

What had produced such a change? Apparently, it was Tenzin Delek Rinpoche. The Rinpoche was sent to the monastery when he was seven years old, and was recognized as a tulku in India at thirty. He returned to Kham in 1987 and was active in religious affairs from Nyagchu County to Litang. Karma said there had been other tulkus who came to the region before Tenzin Delek Rinpoche, but they did not care about the people. They left as soon as they received their offerings. But Tenzin Delek Rinpoche was different. He did not keep the money offered for himself, instead using it for public purposes. He supported sixty or seventy widowed elders and fed those who were needy. He paid for road construction in remote villages and even joined in on the construction work. His school consisted of about 130

2   To avoid getting Karma and his friends in trouble, I have decided to conceal their real names here.

students—orphans, disabled children and children from poor families—and though it cost about 13,000 yuan per month to run, Tenzin Delek Rinpoche took it upon himself to foot the cost.

Having gained their trust, Tenzin Delek Rinpoche became highly influential among the people. When he advised people to quit drinking and gambling, his suggestions were accepted, and after enough people followed his advice it actually became trendy to do so, and more people then deferred. Every year, he travelled from village to village giving teachings, usually lasting two weeks at each stop. Knowing everyone in the village and everything that happened there—who had recently gotten into fights and who were thieves—he would call on people in the course of his teachings, singling them out and scolding them before the crowd. They would not be allowed to join when he led the chanting. To Tibetans, such punishment is humiliating, but it effectively demonstrates the lesson of karma. Because of this, it is psychologically effective. Having been made to confess in public, these guilty individuals usually took their promises to change very seriously.

I asked Karma what he did for fun now that he had quit smoking, drinking and gambling, and he replied that there were many ways to have fun—dancing, eating good food and chatting with friends. He was very sincere in his realization about his past activities: 'They are just small pleasure lasting for only a short while. I would feel regretful afterward.' He may have been built tall and strong—capable of moving mountains— but his eyes were full of childlike honesty. That night, Karma, Ribu and Chodrak were still chatting next to the campfire as I was drifting off to sleep. I could hear them laughing outside. It was laughter from the heart: joyful, pure and touching. I could not understand how, despite seeing each other every day, they still had so much to talk about and laugh about together. They laughed more in that one hour than I probably do in an entire year. Their happiness had nothing to do with material wealth or sensual enjoyment. Chen Kuiyuan, Party Secretary of the Tibet Autonomous Region from 1992 to 2000, and one of the most powerful figure in the social sciences in China today, has said that 'religion cannot bring to people real freedom or joy in any country at any time'.[3] But this does not appear to be true of Karma's case.

Deng Xiaoping's statement that development is the absolute principle has become a motto throughout China today. Even in the Tibetan grasslands, such rhetoric appears on billboards everywhere. The Chinese Communist Party (CCP) has pinned all its hopes on the concept of 'development' for building stability in the Tibetan and other minority nationality regions. So long as the economy keeps developing and the living standard keeps improving, people will feel settled and happy. In the meantime, conflicts over nationality will gradually die off.

But will development and the generation of wealth necessarily lead to social stability? Let's return to Karma's story once more. In recent years, annual events have been staged in Kham to showcase culture and boost the economy, one of which is the selection of the 'Khampa Eagle'. A beauty pageant of sorts, its goal is to select the most well-built, good-looking and handsomely-dressed Khampa man. Karma satisfies all of these conditions and has been elected each year to represent Nyagchu County for the prefecture-wide competition. He has won the title several times—a big honour for him—and each

---

3   From a speech by Chen Kuiyuan at a meeting of Lhasa residents on 23 July 1996. This meeting was intended to mobilize participation in the construction of a spiritual civilization.

time took very seriously the task of preparing his outfits, which usually includes silk chubas brocaded with tiger or leopard skin, expensive and complex ornaments, a knife inlaid with gold and silver and the compulsory ornamental gun—the latter is what highlights the masculinity of the Khampa man. But as soon as he returned home from the pageant in 2002, Karma was arrested and detained by the Public Security Bureau, ostensibly for carrying a gun.

What events had led to his arrest? First, Karma's village had been chosen as a site for investment in developing Nyagchu County's tourist industry. The village was designated in a project called 'Tibetan Homestay' to host tourist groups in the homes of local Tibetans. The stays were usually arranged by the county Tourist Bureau and tourists would directly pay the host families. More sociable families with bigger and cleaner houses and better cooks were favoured by the Bureau, and for these reasons, Karma's family was the most favoured of all. They received more tourists than anyone else in the village and surely profited from this arrangement as well. But this attracted the jealousy of others, and when the head of the county's Tourist Bureau visited the village, its residents went to complain and demand a fair share. They were told to go look at their reflections in their own piss, and so out of frustration, someone decided to make Karma's gun an issue.

In theory, tourist development has brought new wealth to the entire village, with everyone being wealthier now than before. But although the village used to be poorer, people generally got along, and especially when Tenzin Delek Rinpoche was around. Everyone wanted to behave well and conflicts were rare, then when arguments occurred, the Rinpoche—their 'Big Lama'—would quickly be sought out to settle the issue. Now, everything had changed. Even though the authorities had ordered the locals to turn in their guns several years ago for the purposes of social stability, few had handed in their good guns, giving up only their shabbier ones, so that when Karma borrowed a good gun from his friend for the competition, neither of them thought for a moment that it would be a problem with the Public Security Bureau (PSB). The competition was a government-organized event, and Karma had been officially elected to represent Nyagchu County. The gun was no different from a prop in a play, and nobody could have thought it was a mistake. Even if the gun had been noticed, it would be thought of as permitted by the government. But now someone had reported Karma to the PSB—out of spite.

So Karma was arrested. The gun was confiscated, and he was fined and jailed. But worse than all these insults, the police also shaved his head, which he had worn long for his whole life. His long hair had been a part of who he was, and to shave it off was no different than chopping off his nose. Desperate, he offered to pay an extra fine of 10,000 yuan to save his hair but was ignored. By the time he was released, Karma looked like a naked eagle. He no longer looked noble and proud, and became the butt of people's jokes.

The locals in Nyagchu County have asked why the improved standard of living has worsened the human relationships in the community. They also wonder how the cycle of revenge will eventually be stopped. In light of this, development is certainly not the absolute principle. Economic development alone is insufficient for creating political stability or loosening ethnic tensions. Perhaps it resolves older conflicts, but it creates newer and more complicated ones in turn. I think of the bandit who was shot by the police; Karma and his shaved head; the imprisoned Tenzin Delek Rinpoche; Lobsang Dhondup, who has been jailed and sentenced to death; and their family and friends, and

I ask what sort of final outcome we might expect. Will these situations be resolved through economic development?

Development and ecology

Songrong, a kind of wild fungus, has been one of the primary factors in making Kham more prosperous than other Tibetan areas. It was collected in the 1970s mainly for domestic consumption—one person could collect a basket in a half day and it cost less than 0.25 yuan per kilogram in the local markets—but is now exported to Japan. The price has increased to 1,000 yuan per kilogram. It now seems like everybody in Kham is involved in collecting or selling the fungus, constituting at least 60% of the local annual income. In the places where songrong growth is common, it can add 1,000 yuan to the per capita annual income.

I have heard that some Tibetans now pray to the Buddha for the health of the Japanese: this would guarantee prosperity through the songrong industry. But the transformation of this industry has created problems in Kham itself. Where a county cadre reported to me that approximately 1,000 tons of songrong were gathered in his county annually in the late 1990s, the number dropped to 700 tons by 2000, and 400 tons in 2001. This has resulted from improper gathering. Songrong ages quickly once the spores reach maturity, so that it must be gathered quickly before the spores begin to ripen, but because songrong also cannot reproduce itself until the spores mature, the volume collected has decreased with each cycle. Attracted by increased prices, more people join the hunt. They dig up everything, including the young fungi that have yet to sprout from the earth. Overturning the top level of dirt exposes and damages the layers below, and nothing remains to enable new fungus to grow. Although everyone knows that this will soon cripple the industry, no one is willing to stop.

Similar to this is the practice of digging up caterpillar fungus in the TAR and Amdo, which used to be considered in Tibetan religion to be the intestines of the mountain gods, and not therefore something to be dug up. But it is believed to have great health benefits, primarily being consumed by wealthy inland Chinese, and like songrong, the price of caterpillar fungus has also jumped—from less than 20 yuan per kilogram to about 1,000 yuan per kilogram today. The collection of caterpillar fungus requires digging up 20 cm of dirt, which is also the average depth of vegetation in most of the mountain regions in Tibet—which has accumulated over several thousand years. It is not uncommon to see acres of land that used to be covered in short grass now completely destroyed. This is the aftermath of digging up caterpillar fungus and can lead to landslides in the rainy season.

Meanwhile, the quantity of collectible caterpillar fungus is also dropping. In the 1980s, a single adult could gather 2–3 kilograms within a month, and has since dropped to less than half a kilogram. Similar circumstances surround other wild medicinal herbs. With the investment in Tibetan medicine in the Tibetan areas doubling from 1999 to 2002,[4] large-scale extinction of many herbs of the plateau has occurred. As more people join in collection, less is left behind to be collected, then as supply decreases, the price goes up. These increased prices then attract yet more people to join the hunt. The entire industry now follows this counter-productive cycle.

The balance of the ecological system in the Tibetan region is much more fragile than in many other locales. Where

---

4   In 1999, there were thirty-four Tibetan medicine companies in China. The number was approaching one hundred by 2002. See *www.tcmgap.com*.

biological diversity is fundamental for a balanced ecosystem and relatively fewer species are able to survive under the tough natural conditions of the Tibetan plateau, the degree of biological diversity is very low and the entire ecological balance can be damaged when merely a few links in the food chain are disrupted. It differs from the ecology of tropical rainforests, where multiple food chains form a complex web capable of supporting one another. At the same time, several of China's major rivers originate on the Tibetan plateau, so that the effects of this ecological imbalance are multiplied downstream, where the rivers reach the plains. The destruction of the ecosystem is not only disastrous for the Tibetan region; it affects inland China as well.

The Chinese government has certainly taken notice of this problem. Following the Yangtze River flood in 1998, it finally acknowledged the relevance of upstream ecology to downstream environment, which experts had been discussing for years. The government ordered a moratorium on the lumber industry and set up conservation projects in the upstream regions of the country, nearly all of which are predominantly Tibetan. But we cannot merely depend on government action to protect the ecosystem. In such a remote area as Tibet, where police already have difficulty capturing criminals, it will be easy for violators of environmental regulations to avoid punishment. Then at the same time, the fragility of the food chain in the Tibetan region means that even small disruptions can throw off the balance of the entire system. Will the government be able to regulate each link in the system and always keep them under watch?

It is with this in mind that I return to the social function of religion. Its meaning and values are not only capable of providing inner balance to individuals, but also of achieving harmony between human beings and nature. This has been a very important pragmatic function of religion in Tibet. Its humble attitude toward nature and its emphasis on compassion for all sentient beings have helped to protect the fragile ecosystem on the Tibet plateau. Where, in Tibetan Buddhism, all sentient beings are equal, human beings do not possess the unique right to assert their power or satisfy our desires at the expense of other species. Buddhism does not share the Christian viewpoint that God grants human beings the superiority to overcome nature and dominate the other species. Instead, it emphasizes respect for and maintenance of a balanced world. Harmony among sentient beings is its goal. In traditional Tibetan religion, killing even an ant is something not to be taken lightly, because according to the belief in karma, the ant could have been one's father or mother in a previous life. By the same token, Tibetans were generally hesitant to damage the grassland in any aggressive way, because they would still have to depend on it to survive in the next lifetime—whether reborn as human or animal.

The Chinese authorities are keen to promote the idea that nothing beyond the mundane exists. Then because there is nothing transcendent to think about, the only concern is to satisfy desires in the present. Why should one worry about a flood that might happen after one's death? Sometimes, environmental concerns are framed in terms of the environment our offspring will be living in. But this stance is often dropped as soon as our own self-interests are at stake. Instead, in Tibetan Buddhism, environmental protection within karmic logic is not for our offspring but for ourselves, since any consequences left unresolved in this life will still have to be resolved in the next.

In the Tibetan regions, the lands next to monasteries are often the most well protected. The traditional ways in which the monasteries deal with the modern environmentalist concerns are often surprising. And these monasteries are numerous on the Tibetan plateau. They represent the authority in the minds of common Tibetans and are an intimate part of local life. They should be mobilized as a social force to achieve the kind of environmental responsibility promoted by the government. But the Chinese government cannot see the picture from the broader perspective. It is only concerned with the potential of the monasteries to challenge and transgress its own power. When KTAP authorities launched their second purge of Tenzin Delek Rinpoche, one of the charges included his encouragement of locals to stop the Forest Bureau from cutting down trees. Even if this charge was true, these actions were completely in line with the environmental policy of the state. It was cast as a criminal charge only because, as a monk, Tenzin Delek Rinpoche had presumably intended to mobilize the people. He had transgressed the authority and power of the government.

In fact, on the issue of hunting the Rinpoche came up with an even more efficacious solution. Where discrimination against hunters in Tibetan society was quite severe, it was also seen to be necessary for the sake of natural protection. But rather than simply condemning the hunters, the Rinpoche purchased sheep and yaks for them to help in their transformation from a hunting to a nomadic life. If more lamas educated people and initiated grassroots efforts on environmental protection the way that Tenzin Delek Rinpoche has done, not only would the government save on its financial investments toward resolving this issue, we would also likely see very different results.

Once, when I was travelling in Markham County in Tibet, I saw an image along the road that affected me greatly. It was a residential house built in the Tibetan style, which sat on the hill next to the road, upon which someone had written the Chinese character for wealth—*fu*—in large letters and white paint on one of its walls. It was shocking even from a distance. It suggested the owner's eagerness to become rich. Meanwhile, it occurred to me that the character had been written where religious symbols or pictures used to be drawn. Tibetan society used to be based on the principle of living for happiness rather than the pursuit of self-interest, which is perhaps closer to the true essence of life. But once moral frameworks were broken down, it was easy for things to begin going downhill. Religion was the foundation of the Tibetan moral system. Once religion ceases to provide an all-around restraint, the future of the Tibetan people becomes at stake.

If Tibetans have forgotten their religion and are simply focused now on gaining wealth, where will the cycle of desire and satisfaction end? To earn more money, they can only keep increasing their livestock, and this will lead to higher consumption of grass and then the desertification of the grassland. Less water will accumulate upstream of those rivers flowing down to the plains, and then the drying-up of rivers is a factor in inducing large-scale sand and dust storms in inland China. How much can the government have to invest to deal with these problems?

In recent years, the Chinese government has begun investing heavily in environmental protection, but its efforts have so far had only limited effects. Those in charge of the Kekexili Nature Reserve, which has become infamous for the controversial issue of the endangered antelope, have discussed using helicopters to stop illegal hunting. This same solution has been suggested on the question of social stability as well, where the head of a PSB office in Tibet once claimed that the most effective way to achieve security was to equip the police force with helicopters. The prefectures in the Tibetan region are vast, and only helicopters can overcome geographic barriers and reach crime scenes in a timely manner—which is true enough. But because the altitude of the Tibetan Plateau is extremely high—at an average 4,000 metres above sea level—it is beyond the reach of normal helicopters so that specially-designed models are required, which China has been unable to produce. As a result, all the helicopters serving on the plateau are 'Black Eagles' imported from the US, at a cost of more than 10 million US dollars each. This is more than ten times more than the annual income of any single prefecture in the Tibetan region, and I have not even included the cost of shipment and maintenance. The Chinese authorities have for years criticized religion as wasteful, and the monasteries as social parasites, but they ignore the role that religion can play in reducing criminal behaviour, which could alleviate the cost of public security. On the question of the environment, we should ask why the Tibetan ecosystem was previously balanced and well-protected when, historically, there was no official attention paid to wildlife preservation: perhaps it had something to do with the religion and superstition.

In Tibet, religion has helped to reduce criminal behaviour, and the money that can be saved from investment in public security could be significant. It does not require government investment or organization, and so long as the government does not suppress religion, instead allowing it actual freedom, religion can provide organic solutions to the issues I have just discussed. In investment terms, it can reap great profits with very few expenses. Nevertheless, the Chinese authorities today have gone in the opposite direction. While spending huge amounts of resources to crush Tibetan religion, they are also forced—in the name of aiding Tibet—to bring in even more resources from inland China to satisfy the increased material desires of the Tibetan population. These two things are also connected in a cycle: as religion becomes less important, the material desires and appetites of people increase. The TAR has been receiving financial support from Beijing for half a century now. The notion of cutting it back now—not to mention actually ceasing this financial support in the future—can present an immediate challenge to China's stability. How can we break this cycle of support, and can this support provide a foundation for real stability?

The greed of humans acts as a major destructive force toward a balanced ecosystem and stabilized social order. While it leads to moral deterioration at the individual level, it can result in natural and social catastrophe at the level of civilization. Theft, robbery, hunting, destroying nature . . . what does the greedy heart care? No matter how strict the laws, how strong the police force, how expensive helicopters might be, they cannot control what goes on in people's hearts. Morality is necessary for individuals to police themselves from within, and this often derives from religion.

Capitalist societies have profit-making as their highest goal. 'Capital comes dripping from head to foot, from every pore, with blood and dirt', as Karl Marx wrote. China is just now moving into the primitive stages of capital accumulation. But whereas religions were historically respected and protected by European and US states, the Chinese state has not only tolerated and encouraged the greed now permeating society, it has also mobilized all its resources to destroy religion—the only mechanism that can prevent society from absolute deterioration.

An actual police force can be established in a society in a relatively short period of time. It will take much longer to reestablish mechanisms that allow individuals to 'police' their own actions from within—its religion and moral system. For an entire nation that has lost this framework, recovery could take generations. The concept of 'police' barely even existed in traditional Tibetan society (with the exception of Lhasa), where religion was popularly practiced, and criminal behaviour was also rare. The explanation for this was the ability for individuals to 'police' themselves from within.

At the same time, laws and police power are actually less effective than religion in creating social stability, because they only act as a negative deterrent and operate through the principle of punishment. They do not produce or promote goodness in society. China currently has millions of policemen and national guards, not to mention all kinds of joint forces for national security and neighbourhood protection. But crime rates continue to rise, and the annual budget for fighting crime keeps increasing as well. If police power and laws are the only way to achieve security, then what check is there on police and government actions in turn? With limited resources, how can they look after an area as vast as Tibet? The restraints provided by religion and morality are necessary alongside physical policing. It is a mistake to treat religion as the enemy. China is making such a mistake.

Fatal damage to Tibetan Buddhism

Monasticism has been an important part of all religions. But in my opinion, Buddhism relies on it more than other religions. Christianity, Islam and Judaism are all based upon single texts, which followers can directly read to understand their divinity and doctrines. Although monasteries may be important to these religions, they are not as central for followers to understand the religion. There has been only one Bible for the past two thousand years, which generations of Christians have read from a very young age on. Compiled in a storytelling style, its language is relatively easy, making its doctrines easily accessible to readers.

But Buddhism is not based on a single master text. Instead, it is a giant system consisting of many texts, one that is vast and complex. The language is often difficult, its logic often subtle and full of dialectical arguments and enlightening riddles that are not always immediately comprehensible. So many different schools have evolved, each with its own unique textual tradition, so that it would be impossible for even the most diligent student to master the entire religion within a lifetime. It may be even more difficult for the average follower to grasp the religion on his own. Because of this, a strange dichotomy exists in Buddhist culture between its extremely rational philosophy (Buddha Dharma, or the way of the Buddha), which resides largely in the ivory tower, and the popular dimension of the religion, primarily based on superstition and blind devotion. Only the monasteries can narrow this gap in an organic way and unify the two poles into a complete religious system.

Through a centuries-old educational system and the diligence of individuals, Buddhist monasteries have developed into places where the essence of the religion can be understood and clarified for followers. Their two missions are to protect and continue to generate the Buddha Dharma, and to deliver it to the public, making it relevant to the lives of the common people. This bridges the two ends of the Buddhist dichotomy. For this reason, Tibetan Buddhism would not be able to survive without its monasteries, and its threefold emphasis on the Buddha, dharma, and monasticism thereby possesses an inner logic. No matter how great Buddha or dharma might be, without the monasteries as their messenger, they are still just big buildings in the sky: unreachable and thus irrelevant to the mundane world.

In practice, the size and complexity of the Buddhist repertoire has made it relatively easy for monasteries to monopolize the practice of interpreting the religion. Meanwhile, there are no mechanisms in place to allow commoners to limit their power in this practice. This has been true of Tibetan society historically, where the belief in Buddhism was universal and a theocracy was in place. No alternative resources existed to evaluate the monasteries, so that the unconditional obedience of the common people to the monasteries largely derived from superstition.

Tibetan Buddhism has developed a very high standard for its monasticism under this context. According to the logic of the religion, obedience will follow if the monastery can maintain its purity through self-discipline. Monasteries that follow the dharma guarantee that the dharma and its devotees remain connected, maintaining the unity of the religion. The monastic leadership is the key element here: the tulkus, kenpos, abbots and other high lamas within the individual monasteries, who are responsible for the management of the institution and its members. This form of leadership is characteristic of Tibetan Buddhism. As long as these leaders follow the dharma and dutifully supervise and educate the members of the monastery, they have performed their monastic duties responsibly.

Honoured as 'rinpoche' or great gurus, the importance of these leaders to Tibetan Buddhism is unquestionable. Kenpo Jigme Phuntsok and Tenzin Delek Rinpoche were both revered leaders of this sort. The goal of Kenpo Jigme Phuntsok's Serta Academy was to train the next generation of monastic leaders, and while Tenzin Delek Rinpoche may not share Kenpo Jigme Phuntsok's expertise in Buddhist philosophy, in serving his lay followers he carried out another one of the monastic functions dutifully. In his regular travels from village to village, he impacted people's lives through religion in practical ways. Only through such efforts can Buddhism really have a social impact.

In light of this, the deterioration of the monastic leadership can constitute a true nightmare for Tibetan Buddhism: it can throw the entire religious institution out of balance and result in large-scale damage. Hence the emphasis on monastic vows and teaching lineages in the Buddhist tradition, for these are its very lifelines. The lineages are described as chains of pure gold, of which not even one link should be polluted. Each transmission from teacher to disciple should be as pure as each that came before it, and every one after. The disciples are blessed and endowed with the potential to succeed on the spiritual path. But if a tulku or lama violates his vows, the lineage would be interrupted. The wisdom accumulated through this line would be interrupted. From the perspective of social function, these rules are intended to prevent moral degeneration in the monastery. But from the religious perspective, such degeneration could halt the transmission of the dharma from one generation to the next, realizing what Buddhists would call the age when dharma comes to an end. This end is apparently rooted in the total deterioration of the monastic leadership. What then follows is the corruption of the entire monastic system.

That unlimited power leads to corruption is common sense. What then can limit or restrict the actions of the monastic leadership? It has to come from the inner force of the religion. If Buddhism is expected to provide the moral compass for people to police themselves from within, then the monks and nuns must put this into practice first. Many monastic vows viewed by outsiders of the religion as tortuous forms of asceticism actually have nothing to do with supervision or punishment over mundane needs. Instead, they represent the strong faith of monks and nuns in karma. Violation of these vows not only damages one's chance to attain the positive results of karma but also invites its unwanted negative effects.

The strength and purity of the monastic community's faith is largely determined by the purity of the monastic teaching lineage. It is a complex system involving listening, contemplating, and practice. It demands a clean environment and an unbroken continuity. In the tradition of Tibetan Buddhism, many monks and nuns begin their monastic education at a very young age to limit the internalization of mundane desires. To distance themselves from the pollution and temptations of this world, many monasteries are built in remote and hidden mountain locations. The retreats of the Kagyu and Nyingma schools of Tibetan Buddhism, which are well known in popular culture and last three years, three months and three days, mark the victory of spirituality over material desire. Only those who pass this trial can be referred to honourifically as 'lama' by the lay population. Only those monks and nuns that have uprooted all mundane desires qualify to act as the bridge between the dharma and lay followers; only having reached religious maturity in an unpolluted environment are monks and nuns ready to confront worldly distractions, to stand on their own feet and to concentrate on spreading the dharma and helping people. Undisturbed surroundings in which purified teachers can pass on their lessons to the unpolluted pupils are the crucial element here. Total disruption can be precipitated by a single event. That is enough to pollute an entire generation of the monastic community and its teaching lineage.

Such a complete disruption occurred once in Tibetan Buddhism following 1959. Not only banning the religion and its hereditary tradition, the Chinese Communist authorities also launched large-scale projects to reform tulkus and other members of the monastery. They forced monks and nuns to violate their religious vows and to accept the mundane standard of life. A tulku educational group established in Lhasa in 1964 is a typical example, where more than ten tulkus under the age of twenty were gathered for thought reform and labour—specifically as butchers and hunters of wild animals. Some of the things learned from the study group became lifelong addictions the tulkus later had trouble shedding. By the 1980s, with the death of Mao, the religion had somehow recovered, and the environment for its continuity had been drastically altered. Not only had an entire generation within the monastic community become polluted in their views on the religion, but a new generation had grown up completely in an atheist environment. This crisis was unprecedented in Tibetan Buddhism and has lasted into the present. The Chinese authorities now allow some freedom to practise the religion—they claim that their citizens enjoy religious freedom—but there still remain all kinds of restrictions on the tradition of teaching lineages.

Kenpo Jigme Phuntsok was one of the few high lamas who had survived the catastrophe. If the authorities had given him sufficient freedom, the interrupted tradition might have had a chance of being reconnected, but as soon as the authorities realized that he and the other lamas might succeed in building the Serta Academy, they could only think of the threat to their own political power and employed tough measures to suppress their efforts.

The numbers support this analysis. Before KTAP was taken over by the Communist authorities in 1950, there were a total of 604 Buddhist education institutes in the region. There are now only 93. Of these, only nine are officially registered, so that in theory, the remaining 84 are illegal.[5] Even if we include the illegal institutions, there are only one-sixth as many institutions as there were previously. So while people are now

5   These numbers were reported by the KTAP Buddhist Association and are available at the Anchu Monastery.

free to burn incense and prostrate themselves, the disconnected tradition of dharma study has not yet been rebuilt. From this perspective, the disruption of Tibetan Buddhism has lasted longer than the two decades from 1959 to 1980: it has continued into the current moment. It might have been possible to repair a twenty-year-long disruption, but forty-odd years is a very long time—long enough to exhaust an entire generation of achieved lamas. Meanwhile, all of their successors came of age in an era dominated by a resolute belief in absolute materialism. They were later impacted by the increasing force of self-interest in dictating relations within society. The possibility of reestablishing a decent teaching lineage has greatly declined.

I've mentioned that, apart from self-discipline, monks and nuns are also limited by the monastic order, who can punish and even expel those who violate their vows. But because the order is managed by the leaders, its control over its leaders is relatively weak. This is especially true of leaders that also happen to be tulkus, for one can only be born a tulku—no external force can deprive him of his status or impose restrictions on him. Of course, the Dalai Lama and other lamas from different sects still have higher authority to regulate monastic leaders below their rank. In traditional Tibet, the system of theocracy also provided ways to restrict and punish monastic leaders of all levels. But all of these conditions are now gone. The highest leaders of the major sects are all in exile and unable to intervene in monastic affairs inside Tibet. In seeking to control the religion, Chinese authorities have also strategically cut off the internal connections within the Tibetan Buddhist tradition. They treat each monastery as a single unit and prohibit any horizontal associations that would allow different monasteries to take part in one another's internal affairs. (We can see this clearly in the charges of the KTAP Religious Affairs Bureau against Tenzin

Delek Rinpoche.) As a result, there is neither a vertical system from within the religion to regulate monastic leaders, nor are there horizontal mechanisms that allow for mutual supervision among the leaders. Local political power has become the only controlling force, one that obviously demands the surrender of monks and nuns to its authority. It has nothing to do with respecting the dharma or observing monastic vows.

The Chinese Communist Party (CCP) is itself an organization characterized by religious zeal. Possessing the fundamentalist traits of extremism, fanaticism and exclusivity, it has to deny other belief systems completely. Only during Deng Xiaoping's time when the party gave up its ideology and moved towards a practical policy, religion had a chance to come back to life. However, the leaders of the CCP still could not see the value of religion.

When the US President Bill Clinton visited China in 1998, a dialogue between him and the Party Secretary Jiang Zemin was broadcast on TV. In their conversation, Jiang mentioned something about Tibet: 'Speaking as the nation-state chairman of PRC, the fact that I am a communist and an atheist has no influence on my respect for Tibet's religious freedom. Yet, I do have a question. Last year when I visited the USA and also some European countries, I found many well-educated people actually believed in the doctrines of lamaism. I think this is a problem which needs to be studied. Why? Why?'

What these words suggest is that Jiang believes it abnormal and problematic for well-educated people to believe in Buddhism. It reveals his deep-seated disapproval of Tibetan Buddhism. Only because they have been unable to abolish the religion completely do the Chinese Communist authorities continue to tolerate it. But despite this tolerance, they also feel it necessary to fragment it and take a zero-tolerance stance toward any challenges from it. Within this logic, it is therefore extremely important to control the monks and nuns, and particularly their leadership. In Jiang's words, this is 'to actively guide religion to complement socialism'.[6] He explained his expectations from the monastic community with even more detail:

> [We are] asking them to love the motherland, to support the socialist system and the leadership of the Communist Party . . . Asking them to keep their religious activities in line with and in service to the highest interests of the country and the total interest of their nationalities. [We] support their efforts to interpret religious doctrines according to the demands of social progress . . . We don't allow religion to be used to confront the leadership of the Party and the socialist system.[7]

It is evident here that all of his concerns derive from the perspective of CCP power. They are not measured by the religion's needs. (In the vocabulary of the CCP, the Party itself represents the 'motherland', 'socialist system', 'country' and 'progress'). Religion can only be a component under the leadership of the Party and function as its instrument. The essence of the relationship between the monastic leadership and that of the Party can be concluded with two sentences: 'Whoever obeys me will prosper; whoever goes against me will be ruined'.

There are two primary ways that Chinese authorities deal with monastic leaders. First, they do not allow monastic leaders

---

6   From Jiang's speech at the 1993 Working Meeting of the United Front Work Department.

7   From Jiang's speech at the National Committee of the Chinese People's Political Consultative Conference (CPPCC) Working Meeting on Religious Affairs, on 12 December 2001.

to become leaders of the people. It is fine for the lamas to satisfy the superstitious needs of the masses—they are free to engage in activities like fortune telling, consecration rites or giving blessings—but providing teachings and using the dharma to influence the local communities only raises the suspicion of the authorities. That would make them spiritual leaders, as Tenzin Delek Rinpoche had become. So activities of this sort are tightly restricted. Some high lamas are even denied the freedom of movement. The authorities keep a close watch over all charitable efforts initiated by the monastic community. For instance, Tenzin Delek Rinpoche was accused of having followed his own path in starting a school for orphans without permission. The school was thereby confiscated and soon collapsed. The fear is that public appreciation for the lamas' charitable activities will transform them from religious to community leaders, who can in turn weaken the government's authority. Once again, the Rinpoche's case shows that the power accumulated through this two-fold leadership was viewed as a potentially uncontainable threat by the authorities, one capable of challenging their power. Many locals had participated in the protest he led against the government-run lumber business, and even earlier, hundreds had signed petitions in his support when he went into hiding in fear of potential government persecution. These were no doubt causes for worry on the part of the authorities.

Second, the CCP orchestrates the decline of existing leaders. As a warning to the rest of the monastic leadership, those who insist on the principles of the religion or refuse to be used as instruments of the authorities—such as Tenzin Delek Rinpoche and Kenpo Jigme Phuntsok—are all threatened with expulsion or even sentenced to imprisonment or death. Chadrel Rinpoche from Tashilunpo Monastery in Shigatse, for instance, was sentenced to eight years of imprisonment for following the Tibetan Buddhist custom of reporting to the Dalai Lama regarding his search for the reincarnated young Panchen Lama. For those with higher rank in the lineage but who are willing to keep quiet and avoid trouble, the authorities use the strategy of the carrot and stick. As for those driven by self-interest, who are opportunistic, willing to sacrifice their religious principles and become instruments of the government, these people are granted all kinds of privileges, including positions in People's Assemblies and even governments. By approving and providing resources for activities organized by such monastic leaders, the authorities represent them as role models for the others. A low-ranking tulku from Nachu in TAR publicly condemned the Dalai Lama on several occasions and was made a member of the Standing Committee of the Chinese People's Political Consultative Conference (CPPCC).

Third, authorities seek to control the makeup of the monastic community. They wish to sanction and even directly select tulkus and abbots, which would make Tibetan Buddhism dependent upon the authorities, while also gradually replacing deceased monastic leaders with leaders trained to become their ruling instruments. As a part of the same effort, important monastic leaders are forced to study in government-managed Buddhist academies in Beijing and elsewhere, as a way of reshaping their modes of thinking in ways that are favourable to the authorities. Meanwhile, the Serta Academy and other institutes of Tibetan Buddhist education not under government control are systematically shut down.

It is evident that the power of the institution of Tibetan Buddhism to restrict its own monastic leaders has been taken over completely by the authorities—whose power in this sphere has been greatly enhanced. These attempts to manipulate the monastic community have impinged upon the pursuit of the essence of Buddhism. Theoretically, the monks remain bound by their religious vows. But the power of the monastic community and the authority of Buddhist teachings derive from the faith of its believers, and the devotion and faith of monastic leaders chosen and educated under the mundane standards of the CCP are now questionable. Moreover, while the flexibility allowed by the complexity of Buddhism is attractive in many ways, it can be easily appropriated by a degenerate monastic community to justify their selfish behaviour.

So although the CCP claims it has guaranteed religious freedom, its religious policy is as damaging to Buddhism today as it was in Mao's era. While Mao had indeed sought to abolish Buddhism completely, and while it was nearly achieved in certain eras of Tibetan history, it has survived by a faith in people's hearts that violence cannot touch. But this widespread degeneration of the monastic class, achieved through the current CCP religious policy, amounts to the most intense threat faced by Buddhism yet. Without monks and nuns as the bridge, the practices of lay people will cease to be connected to the Buddha's teaching and may lead to a rise in superstition and the loss of faith in the dharma. It is said that Shakyamuni Buddha predicted what would happen when dharma comes to an end: 'Those wearing my garments will be the ones destroying my religion'. Of course, monks and nuns today are not the root cause of their own degeneration. But such fundamental damage to Buddhism can only result from the deterioration of the monastic community.

I once witnessed a homecoming orchestrated by Party workers in Kham. They travelled thirty kilometres out of town to welcome a tulku and the wealthy Han Chinese merchants who had escorted him home from inland China. Tents were set up along the road. Police cars were sent to clear traffic for the group, whose vehicles stretched one kilometre long. All the vehicles were decorated with yellow *khata*, a traditional ceremonial scarf. This all resembles the Tibetan ritual of receiving important guests. But the county authorities performed these gestures to the tulku not only as a demonstration of their 'united front'—it was also part of the project of economic development that currently prevails throughout China. The Party and governmental offices of all levels in China today are focused on the economy—that is, they are busy converting everything into an economic resource. The Tibetan regions are not exempted from the scheme. All famous monasteries have to be transformed into tourist sites, while high-ranking tulkus are utilized as attractions for commercial investment. To rich Han businessmen, the county governors and secretaries of the Party are little more than minor, low-ranking officials, but the tulkus are something to get excited about. That is how they became a valuable commodity.

At the same time, the tulkus naturally want the support of (or at least to be tolerated by) local political power, either out of self-interest or for the sake of monastic development, and some work very hard to please the government. For instance, the tulku I just described, who was welcomed in the grand homecoming ritual, was once asked by the local government to convince Tibetan peasants to use pesticide, guaranteeing to them that he had performed rituals to enable the rebirth of the insects. The peasants could thereby use pesticides without fear of violating the prohibition from killing other creatures. The tulku was subsequently promoted to the position of Vice Governor of the county, while another tulku from the same monastery was made Vice Governor of the prefecture. On the one hand, those enthusiastic about gaining political power adopt aggressively patriotic and anti-separatist stances to enhance their political capital, but on the other hand, they also appropriate Tibetan myths and mysticism to create all kinds of unbelievable stories. Capitalizing on the ignorance and romantic admiration of the Han Chinese toward Tibetan Buddhism enhances their own interests, but it also enables their benefactors to cheat people and corrupt the religion.

Nowadays, many tulkus devote much of their time and energy to managing this triangular relationship between power, money and religion, which diverts time from their studies and religious practices. Rather than providing dharma teachings to the lay people or serving the well-being of the community, they are more interested in mingling with wealthy devotees from Hong Kong and Macau, rich businessmen from inland China or government officials. They spend their time flying between cities, staying in upscale hotels and frequenting bars and restaurants. It is not uncommon to see four or five tulkus surrounded by rich Han Chinese men and women just outside Maji Ami, a Tibetan restaurant in the foreign embassy district in Beijing. What can be implied from this is that these tulkus live off the offerings of the rich, who expect blessings from them. As a result of this, some tulkus can now afford luxuries like pricey cars. I have also met tulkus who are eager to break into the movie and TV business and want to become pop or movie stars, or others that have become merchants. Being stationed near-permanently in inland China, where they have become accustomed to various material enjoyments, they are able to disregard their monasteries and home areas almost entirely.

These tulkus justify their conduct by claiming that their religious enterprises need financial support, for instance, or that donations are necessary for building temples and erecting statues. 'Without large donations, how will I build the monastery? How will I collect enough money simply through donations of one or two yuan each from individual Tibetans? How will I do this without seeking donations from the inland?' a tulku once asked me. Some provide even loftier-sounding justifications: 'The Buddhist mission should not be confined to the Tibetan region. It should be made accessible to Han Chinese and other people in the world. So to spread the dharma for the benefit of more people, it is necessary for monks to stay in inland China to study Chinese and English. Ideal hermits should be confident enough to remain in the earthly world without being scared by it'. Tenzin Delek Rinpoche has made it clear that he disagrees with such forms of self-justification. Building temples and stupas, printing sutras, and releasing captured animals are tasks for the lay followers. The merit of the monastic community should not be built upon them. Instead, they should engage fully in their studies of the dharma, and in their contemplation and practice. As for the ideal hermits, who are intimidated by the earthly world, the question is how many of these exist in the monastery? If you cannot prove your readiness, who should believe in the purity of your intentions, and why would you risk exposing yourself on a regular basis to mundane influences? Unfortunately, Tenzin Delek Rinpoche's high standards have made him a controversial figure among the monastic community in Kham.

I never met Kenpo Jigme Phuntsok. But I know why people in Ngaychu County love and respect Tenzin Delek Rinpoche: he is willing to forego his own personal comfort, and he gives back to the community through his public service. I visited him once at his home. He lived very simply, even compared with most of the other tulkus that I knew. He slept on a mat on the floor, upon which rested only a cushion and some Buddhist books. A soda can sitting on a Tibetan-style table held his pencils. The wooden walls were unpainted and without the usual carvings. A poster of Potala Palace hung from the wall. I stayed for dinner, and because I was the guest, he offered me some beef and peanuts while he ate only a bowl of dumplings. His chopsticks were no longer in pairs—they varied in colour. The only item in his room that would not be considered a necessity was an offering vase holding flowers.

So there are two different kinds of tulkus in China today, and for those unlike Kenpo Jigme Phuntsok and Tenzin Delek Rinpoche, it is fair to say that the freedom they experience is only a freedom to proceed on a downhill secular path. It is not true freedom of religion.

I have now shown how the degeneration of the monastic leadership leads to the deterioration of the entire monastic class, which in turn threatens the practice of Tibetan Buddhism as a whole. While this development has resulted from the religious policy of the Chinese government, it is not clear that this series of events was spelled out in their strategic designs. The authorities don't often appear to be able to see strategically beyond their own immediate interests, so that this has mostly resulted from a series of short-sighted political power plays by various players in the government.

Of course, there are some alternative voices coming from within the CCP. For instance, Pan Yue, the ex-deputy director of Economic Restructuring Office of the State Council, is well known for being open-minded. In an article from 2001 regarding the need to reform Marxist views on religion along with the changing times, he calls for the CCP to deploy a new political ideology, one that is functional and reevaluates the role of religion'.[8] Showing that religion has a social function, he

---

8   *Shenzun Tequbao* [Shenzhen News], 16 December 2001.

suggests that the CCP should no longer simply take a reactive stance against religious institutions in seeking to control them. Instead, they should control it in an active way, utilizing it and guiding it in a way that complements the work of the Party. Compared with the Party's current policy of destroying (or at least encouraging the destruction of) religion, Pan's thoughts do have some positive significance. But his way of thinking remains within the official policy of preserving the 'essence' of a religion—that is, what is useful for the Party—while doing away with the parts considered non-essential, or its 'residue' (to use language inherited from Mao). I do not wish to be too critical of Pan. But the ideology behind his words will not help to bring into practice the functionality that he hopes for.

Tibetan Buddhism is an independent system. While it resides in the mundane world, its main concern is with the transcendent. But as a complete system, its sphere of interest also includes all dimensions of human experience—the mundane vs. the super-mundane, or the material vs. the spiritual. And because of its multidimensional quality, different figures within the system are designated different roles, including monastic organizations and members, sects and their leaderships, who might be concerned with education and qualification systems, canons and lineages of textual study, teachings and vows for lay followers, religious holidays, and complex rituals and practices. Within this structure, there is no need for each participant to know every detail about the system or to manifest the meaning of the religion in its entirety. Instead, it is sufficient for everyone to play out their function, to ensure the complete nature of the system. So long as the system is intact, the meaning of Tibetan Buddhism will manifest through the combination of its multiple parts. Where the different parts of the religion support and also define each other, it is difficult to separate the necessary from the disposable. Viewed separately, individual elements may appear useless, yet they are still part of the whole, and removing even one of them can have a domino effect, damaging the system's unity.

So while I've argued that religion has a social function in Tibet, it is wrong to judge it purely on this basis—which is to say pragmatically or opportunistically. That would be to concede to it only where it is useful and to prohibit those aspects that appear to threaten government authority. What some might consider the 'essence' and 'residue' of a religious system are actually two sides of the same coin; outsiders might consider the practices of retreat, celibacy and other forms of asceticism as strange or even ridiculous, but these activities are the different components that have, through a long process of historical accumulation, mutually shaped each other to form a complete system. To think about them separately is to miss the point —a vast system cannot be reduced to one of its elements but includes all its diverse phenomena. The analyses and criticism of bystanders reflect only their own value judgments. Because of this, religious reform cannot be carried out through secular initiatives or transplantation. It has to be driven from within the religion in the form of a balanced and natural evolution, one that possesses total coherence. Only in this way can a positive and balanced outcome be achieved.

So Tibetan Buddhism should not be schooled, modified or appropriated by external forces. Its mundane functions and effects are actually the natural outcome of the path it defines to the transcendent world. This path is unidirectional. You could deny that it leads from the mundane into the transcendent, but from the perspective of the believer, the transcendent world could not possibly be led and transformed by secular powers. This view would violate the principle of Tibetan Buddhism. The most effective way to harness the power of Tibetan Buddhism for social and ecological ends would be to simply leave it alone and grant it the freedom to function as it should. Its positive effects will naturally arrive in the mundane world.

Back before the Chinese authorities intruded, when Tibetan Buddhism was still a complete system, lay devotees simply knew how to follow the dharma—even if their level of education was lower than it is today. A poor and illiterate old woman might only have owned one butter lamp, yet she would have travelled thousands of kilometres to offer it to the Buddha. Her prayers would likely have started with her wish that all sentient beings be protected, including all human beings, the nation of Tibet, her village, family, relatives, friends and finally herself, as well as that the Dalai Lama live a long life.

By contrast, what do we see today? Temples brim with burning incense and butter lamps, which well-dressed people can afford to light in the thousands at once. Yet they only want the Buddha's blessings to help with job promotions and increasing their wealth. They don't mind essentially bribing the Buddha, promising in such a mundane fashion to make more offerings if their wishes are fulfilled. Monks in Jo Khang have become sick from constantly inhaling the smoky air inside their temple, while so many people now offer gold dust to the statue of Jo Wo, applying it on his face like makeup, that the deity always looks fat and swollen.[9] In the past, monks only needed to remove excess gold powder from his face once a year. Nowadays, they have to perform this procedure four or five times a year to keep it looking healthy and slim. Misunderstanding how karma works,

---

9   To cover the full body of Jo Wo with gold powder costs about 6,000 yuan (roughly 900 USD). To cover only the face costs about 300 yuan (roughly 50 USD).

some people believe that the consequences of their misdeeds can be prevented by offering butter lamps and incense, releasing animals or making donations to monasteries. They believe there is no need for them to repent or to reform their behaviour. Thinking in terms of financial transactions, they see these small expenditures—paying off any negative karma accumulated with money acquired through corrupt means—as a true bargain.

A lama at the Serta Academy once told me of a young Tibetan who had released all of his family's two hundred yaks. He assumed that if he preemptively performed these good deeds, they would accumulate to balance out any bad conduct or crimes committed in the future—and what he had in mind for this future was to go to India to join the military struggle for Tibetan independence. At the same time, he was also convinced that anyone who participated in the struggle for the independence would be reborn in Buddha's pure land. So on one level, he appeared to be unaware that, under the karmic principle, the consequences of different deeds are not exchangeable. What seeds he planted in releasing the yaks is not equivalent to the seeds he might later plant through corrupt behaviour: they are each distinct causes that will produce different outcomes, which cannot cancel each other out. His ignorance toward this basic, common-sense understanding of Buddhism suggests a lack of knowledge about his religion, which is a direct result of Chinese religious policy. But at the same time, his logic also betrays a tendency toward extremism that is uncharacteristic of Buddhists—something that sounds more like the words of Jihadist militants. Surely this is not the outcome that the authorities had anticipated.

But the Chinese authorities should recognize that this young Tibetan's extremism is not rooted in the Buddhism he has learned. On the contrary, it proves precisely that he does not understand his religion. Tibetan Buddhism's infrastructure and philosophic core has deteriorated as a result of the CCP's current religious policies, which in turn makes it an easier object to be manipulated. It has become much easier to incite the superstitious excitement of the masses for those who choose to do so. Once religious faith is seen as irrelevant to the wider social horizon, for the achievement of a diverse space for thought and for striking a complementary social balance, it can only become more narrow-minded and extreme. Religious rites can be confused with witchcraft. The politically ambitious can easily posture as religious leaders, spouting prophecies and performing wacky magical feats to produce social unrest. In theory, Buddhism is perhaps the most non-violent religion in the world. But if this young Tibetan has now connected his religion to the potentially violent actions he intends to take, we should not be surprised to find other youths thinking along the same lines in the future. Let us not forget the bombs set off in recent years in Dhartsedo, Litang, Chengdu, Lhasa and Chamdo.

In the long term, the destruction of religion in Tibet will not bring stability. These policies, aimed at the deterioration of the monastic class, only sacrifice those high lamas who still insist on religious principles and encourage the opportunists among the monastic community. But opportunists tend to turn with the tide. They might suddenly switch sides and proceed down a different extreme, overturning what they have done before. By seducing Tibetans from their religious commitment through material desire, the authorities might be able to detract from the question of nation for the time being. But this issue will not simply disappear. Once the compassion and morality entrenched in Tibetan Buddhism have been made inconsequential, this material desire will become much more difficult to control. An entire society can be made to see everything in terms of its economic value, but the negative effects will eventually have to be faced. The balance that money can achieve is far less than the imbalance it can cause. Rather than expecting long-term stability to be achieved through economic growth, we should see how economic growth can be transformed by religious belief. Otherwise, a crisis is imminent.

I have described how the complete religious system of Tibetan Buddhism has been an effective and necessary mechanism for maintaining social and ecological stability in Tibet—and it may also be useful for achieving those same aims within the wider scope of the Chinese nation-state. Although Buddhism has never been made the state religion, it has existed in China for a very long time (even outside of Tibet and in non-Tibetan forms), and has long been a part of Chinese society. Where Confucianism (one of the three major traditions, alongside Buddhism and Taoism, that have historically constituted Chinese culture) has now been relegated to the dredges of history, Buddhism can act as a spiritual resource for reorganizing society—especially since it remains a robust force among the Chinese masses. But in any case, it certainly must be seen as such a precious resource in Tibet. Particularly since the Chinese government keeps claiming that Tibet is a part of China, it should treat Tibetan Buddhism as an important national treasure to be appreciated and protected. The stories of spiritual corruption, moral deprivation and petty crime that I hear so often today, all over China, make me extremely sad. If such a nation still wishes to destroy religion, then where is its intelligence, where is its conscience and where can its future possibly lie?

February–March 2003

March Incident

5

Tibetan Questions: Interview

Tsering Shakya

Your landmark history of modern Tibet, The Dragon in the Land
of Snows, *suggests a broad four-part periodization for developments
since 1951.*[1] *During the first period, 1951–59, the Chinese Communist
Party sought to work in alliance with Tibet's traditional ruling
class under the Seventeen-Point Agreement: a 'one country, two
systems' arrangement, with autonomous rule by the Dalai Lama's
government. After the flight of the Dalai Lama and the crushing of
the 1959 rebellion, the second stage, 1960–78, saw the extension of
Communist reforms on the plateau and the redistribution of monastic
and aristocratic lands, accelerating with the collectivizations and
mass mobilizations of the Cultural Revolution. Following 1980,
there was an era of much greater liberalization and 'Tibetanization'
under Hu Yaobang, accompanied by open-door trade and migration
policies—followed by a clampdown after 1989. Looking back, how
would you characterize the situation in Tibet in the 1980s, under Hu
Yaobang?*

The 1980s reforms were welcomed by Tibetans, who saw them
as a major transition, and still regard Hu as one of China's best
leaders. At the time, many said that things had never been so

---

1   This interview first appeared in *New Left Review* 2: 51, May–June 2008.

good. It marked the start of a period which people thought would bring a certain cultural and economic autonomy for themselves as individuals, and for the Tibetan region as a whole. It was seen as an opportunity to revitalize traditional cultures—the first noticeable sign of this being when people reverted to wearing traditional Tibetan clothes, instead of the blue overalls. Economically, the region also now emerged from a period of real deterioration, running from 1960 to 1980, which was even worse than the years leading up to 1959. The slump was partly due to a total mismanagement of the region's production, which had been drastically altered by the imposition of communes and co-operatives; these were disastrous for the indigenous economy. They were disbanded under Hu's reforms, and traditional systems were revived. Living standards returned to what they had been before 1960, a change that was naturally welcomed by the Tibetan plateau's overwhelmingly rural population: at this time, 95 per cent were engaged either in herding or in agricultural production.

So what accounts for the protests in the late 80s?

The immediate trigger was the growing tension between the monasteries and the Communist Party. The government had expected the reforms to bring increased consumer spending, but in many cases people simply put the extra money they had towards rebuilding the monasteries. There was a big expansion in the number of monks, and in some rural areas there were more people going to monasteries than to local schools. The government was concerned at this growth, and also about the monasteries' funding: they received large quantities of donations which they did not have to account for. By the mid-80s, leftists in the CP were pointing to these developments as an example of

Hu's liberal policies going wrong, and the government moved to restrict the number of monks and gain control of monastic finances. This created opposition, and it was the monasteries and conservative elements that were the main groups leading the protests in the late 1980s.

At the time, people were turning strongly to religion—something they were denied during the Cultural Revolution, but that they now had access to. There was a powerful impulse to fight for greater tolerance of religious practices. But the protests were also responding to changes taking place in Tibetan society under the reforms. There was a major debate at the time about the directions Tibet could take in the future—traditionalists believing that we must revert to time-honoured ways in order to preserve Tibet; younger, college-educated people feeling that it will only survive if we abandon such traditions, and seek a modernized Tibetan culture, creating new identities, new literature and art. In this view, it was Tibetan Buddhism and its traditions that had hampered the creation of a Tibetan identity that might have better resisted conquest and subjugation; and it was a new, stronger identity that was needed to overcome Tibet's current condition. This indigenous critique of the Tibetan past—a self-examination mainly proposed by the younger, educated elite and writers—was seen by the conservatives as somehow a disguised attack by the Chinese on Buddhism. The two groups were not just divided by age, though: there were many young people who shared the conservative view. In general, those educated in the monastic community or through the traditional system were much more conservative than those who went to universities and colleges. These students did not join in the protests at all. Even now, many college-educated people tend to think the 80s protests were unnecessary—that the reforms were taking

Tibet in the right direction, and the demonstrations did great damage in altering that course.

To what extent were the protests of the late 1980s stimulated from outside—by the Dalai Lama's addresses to the US Congress and European Parliament?

The 1980s were a sort of opening for Tibetans—those inside Tibet were allowed to travel to India and go on pilgrimages to see the Dalai Lama. They established new links with the Tibetan diaspora and political leadership, and became much more aware of the organized politics of the Tibetan question. At the same time, the Dalai Lama's speeches to the European Parliament and the US Congress gave them a sense that there was more support for the Tibetan issue in the international community than really existed. Western countries would make statements about some social issues, but their desire to engage China as it emerged from isolation in the 1980s meant that Tibet was never going to be a major obstacle for Beijing.

How would you characterize Chinese policy following the imposition of martial law in 1989–90?

There had been concerns within the Chinese leadership about the direction of the reforms: some felt Hu Yaobang's policies were too extreme and were undermining China's position in Tibet. When the monks' demonstrations began in the late 80s, the hardliners saw it as proof that more liberal policies had led to heightened Tibetan nationalism, encouraging demands for independence. The period from the imposition of martial law to the present has seen a dramatic change in how Beijing deals with Tibet. There were to be no more compromises; Tibet was to be brought under tighter administrative control, and its infrastructure integrated more closely with the rest of China. The plateau had been isolated from China by poor roads and communications, and the PRC leadership believed that the separate provisions made for Tibet in the 1980s accentuated its difference from the rest of the country. So the first policies adopted under Hu Jintao, Party Secretary of the Tibet Autonomous Region from 1988 to 92, were aimed at economic integration— establishing infrastructural links by building roads, opening the Qinghai–Tibet railway, improving telecommunications and so on. Billions of dollars have been spent on the development of the region since 1990.

This means that the Chinese government is to some extent justified when it says that the Tibet Autonomous Region can only survive through government subsidies. The Regional government cannot even raise enough money to pay salaries to its own employees; its ability to levy taxes is very weak at present. All the major infrastructural initiatives—railways, roads, power systems—have been dependent on injections of funds from the central government. This chronic dependence on the centre is one of Tibet's biggest problems—the region has no economic clout to negotiate with Beijing and has to follow its directives, because it is essentially the Central government's money that is paying for the Region's development.

Have there been any moves towards self-sustaining development— in industry, for example, or increased agricultural production?

This is one of the contradictions the Chinese government faces in Tibet. When you look at the statistics for government spending there, the vast bulk of the budget goes on infrastructure, and less than 5 per cent on agricultural development—yet even today,

85 per cent of the population is dependent on farming. This has to do with Beijing's decision to prioritize industrialization over agriculture; but it is also because the authorities see that Tibet has economic potential, which cannot be realized until the infrastructure is built. For example, Tibet has huge quantities of mineral deposits, but they are useless unless you have the means to exploit them. You can mine for copper, gold, silver and so on, but without further developing the railways it will be too expensive to transport them, making them unaffordable on the international market. So the Chinese government's long-term plan is to develop the mining industry, and in the last two years they have invited international mining companies to operate in Tibet. The idea is that, with the infrastructure and power systems in place, resource extraction will make the region profitable. The real day-to-day needs of farmers and herders are not reflected in this planning process.

How much of the infrastructural development involves Tibetan labour?

The majority of the workforce in railway construction, for example, consists of Chinese migrants from poorer regions, such as Gansu and Shaanxi, where many farmers now do not have jobs. The Chinese government encourages them to go to Tibet as a way of letting off steam in these hard-pressed provinces, since if they remain it will create problems for the authorities there. For many people, going to work in Tibet is an opportunity to make a living for themselves: the regions they come from are in fact much poorer than Tibet. Generally, Tibetan farmers are far better off than most rural communities in China—the population is smaller, just under 6 million, and land-holdings are much bigger. No one in Tibet will go hungry: people can produce enough for their own survival, although they may not have enough of a surplus to sell it on the market. But Tibetan farmers face another problem: what they produce, mainly barley and mutton, does not have much market value. For example, Tibet produces a great deal of barley, but it is actually cheaper for Chinese beer companies to buy it on the international market, from Canada or the US, than from Tibetan farmers.

How many incomers are there in the Tibet Autonomous Region at present?

This is a very complex issue, because the Chinese government has not produced any statistics on the number of migrants working in Tibet. The simple reason is that Chinese census data are compiled according to official place of residence, rather than where you are at the time the census is taken. Most of the migrants do not have permits to live there, and will instead be counted as living elsewhere in China; they are a floating population. The government also points out that many migrant workers in Tibet are seasonal—they go there to work in summer, and so could not be counted as permanent residents. But in any case, the census is only taken every ten years; the last figures are from 2000, and a lot has changed in Lhasa in the eight years since then. Change is so rapid and dramatic in China as a whole, the mobility of the population so great, that the figures we have are very unreliable. But it is certainly true that even to the casual visitor, Lhasa now feels much more like a Han city than a Tibetan one, in terms of its population. Chinese migrants tend to be more numerous in urban areas, and used to be concentrated mainly in Lhasa; but now they have begun to penetrate into rural areas, opening restaurants or doing small trade as peddlers across the Tibetan plateau.

How does the development of the Autonomous Region compare with the other Tibetan areas—in Qinghai and Sichuan, for example?

The Tibetan population in Qinghai and Sichuan is economically better off, because they are much more closely integrated with the rest of China, and they have more ways to supplement their income. The Autonomous Region also has the problem that there is very little border trade, from Tibet southwards to India and Southeast Asia. Historically, this was where Tibet's trade was focused, since its goods found much more of a market in South Asia than China. The nearest port is Calcutta, which is two days away, but if you go across the rest of China it is eight to thirteen days. So, for example, wool produced on the Tibetan plateau cannot be exported profitably today since it cannot travel southwards—the borders are closed. The India–China trade relationship is at present essentially based on maritime rather than land routes. The reason for this is that, despite some improvement in relations, the border dispute between the two countries has not been settled. It is partly a security question, but also, neither India nor China are quite sure what will happen if that region is opened to border trade—whether the Indian market will penetrate more forcefully into Tibet or vice versa.

How would you describe the political and cultural atmosphere in Tibet over the last decade?

The government's policy seemed to be that, as long as you did not talk about independence or human rights, everything was permissible. Many more magazines and newspapers started up, and the government allowed a lot of local, indigenous NGOs to emerge, which have been very effective in campaigning against poverty. Tibetan diaspora communities in North America and Europe were allowed to set up NGOs in their home towns, funding the construction of houses. The number of Tibetans going abroad to study—to the West, to Europe, to America—increased during the 1990s. There were more openings to the outside world. In that sense, it was quite a hopeful time.

Culturally, there have been two separate kinds of development. On the one hand, there has been a revival of traditional Tibetan culture and arts and crafts. On the other, a new practice is emerging of modern, figurative painting by Tibetan artists. There is a group of them in Lhasa who have established an artists' guild; they sell paintings and contribute to international exhibitions. There is nothing immediately Tibetan about their work; conservative elements in fact see it as somehow a rejection of Tibet, an imitation of the West—they do not see it as Tibetan art. But this is something new and vital in Tibet, produced by a younger generation whose outlook is very different from that of conservative elements in our society. Similarly in literature, the younger generation writing in Tibetan do not use traditional verse forms, but produce poetry in a free style, novels on new and different subject matter. Again, conservatives would not see this as authentically Tibetan unless it imitates an existing tradition. But for me, the emergence of modern Tibetan literature—novels, short stories and poetry, from 1980 onwards—is a very exciting development, expressing much more of what is happening in Tibet, the desires of ordinary people and the region's possible future direction, than various forms of political protest or movement. There are also a number of Tibetan novelists who write in Chinese, and since 1985 these have gained a real literary presence in China. The most famous is Alai, whose *Red Poppies* appeared in English in 2002; there is also Tashi Dawa, referred to as the García Márquez of China for his introduction of something like a magical realist style. Those who write in the Tibetan language, of course, do not have such a high profile. It is a similar situation to that facing Indian writers—if you write in English you have access to a world market, but if your work is in Hindi far fewer people tend to know about you.

For the traditionalists, what is important is the cultivation of the past; they see the continuation of traditional forms of art as vital for maintaining Tibetan identity. All over Tibet, such forms have re-emerged in painting and crafts, and are still very popular. They are popular in China as well, despite the recent patriotic fervour and hostility towards Tibetans. Since around 1980, interest in Tibetan culture and traditions has been growing there. Tibet is seen as being quite other, and having unique characteristics that China has lost. Its attachment to traditional forms of dress, painting and ways of life is seen as admirable. Many Chinese writers and artists have travelled to Tibet and drawn inspiration from it, as an example of how to live in harmony with nature. In fact, a much more romantic view of Tibet has emerged among the Chinese population than in the West.

There has also been a flourishing of modern Tibetan historiography, including oral history projects on rural life, as well as recording proverbs and popular folk songs. There has been a lot of biographical writing, and some very interesting memoirs written by Tibetan women, who of course are always left out of the traditionalist conservative accounts; in Tibetan schools in Dharamsala, the history textbooks stop at the tenth century. In fact, I was attacked for dedicating *The Dragon in the Land of Snows* to my wife, instead of to the Dalai Lama.

I am currently working on a historical project on banditry. There is almost a Wild West element to Tibetan history: travellers across the vast plateau would be attacked and robbed by bandits. There are many oral sources and other accounts, and I am looking into who these people were—seeing them not as negative characters, but more along Eric Hobsbawm's lines, viewing banditry as a form of social protest. People often became bandits after running away from traditional Tibetan society, from feudal law. According to the master narrative they were bad people, but almost all of them were actually resisting local rulers or governments. When you identify who they were and what happened to them, you often find these were marginal groups in Tibetan society.

Is Tibetan still the official language in the Autonomous Region?

According to the constitution, the regional language of education and administration in the TAR should be Tibetan, but this has not been implemented in practice. The reason is that the leadership of the CP in Tibet, the party secretaries and undersecretaries, are all Chinese and do not speak Tibetan. In terms of education, in rural areas this is carried out in the native language, but in urban areas, and especially in Lhasa, there is an increasing use of Chinese in schools; at university level, courses in Tibetan literature and history are taught in Tibetan, but otherwise everything is taught in Chinese. This is not necessarily a matter of government policy: many parents prefer to give their children a Chinese-medium education, simply because in the long run they will have better job opportunities, and because the majority of Tibetans in further education—at present there are nearly 3,000 new graduates per year—tend to go to universities elsewhere in China. There

are also now the so-called 'inland schools': boarding schools
for Tibetan children, who are recruited in Tibet and then sent
to schools scattered across China—some of them as far away
as Liaoning and Fujian. The ostensible reason they are not in
Tibet is that the government cannot recruit enough teachers
there, nor persuade qualified teachers from elsewhere to go to
the Autonomous Region; it is also a way for the more developed
coastal provinces to meet their obligations to aid the poorer ones,
by paying for these schools to be built in their own area. This is
part of an attempt to foster a sense of 'national unity' and loyalty
to China. Of course, some Tibetans and outsiders see it as a
sinister ploy, comparable to the way the British, Canadians and
Australians tried to Christianize the natives by sending them to
boarding school. Teaching in the 'inland schools' is almost all in
Chinese, and the education is very good. But Tibetan students
tend to come out of them much more nationalistic—on blogs
and websites they are often the ones leading complaints against
the Chinese government, for depriving them of their cultural
identity and their language.

How has the language itself changed since the 1950s?

A new standardized literary Tibetan has emerged, much closer
to colloquial language, along with a simplified writing system—
the idea being that it should be easier to communicate with all
those who are literate. But in everyday speech, there has also
been an increasing use of loan-words from Chinese. A PhD
student at Oxford was researching 'code-switching' in Tibet,
where people would vary in their use of Tibetan and Chinese
depending on the context, and he found that on average, 30 to
40 per cent of Lhasa Tibetans' vocabulary is borrowed from
Chinese. In general, now that fewer Tibetans are studying the

language at a high level, the standard has declined. But it would be a serious mistake to think that it is disappearing. In fact, since 1985 Tibetan-language publishing has been flourishing. There are two newspapers in Tibetan, the *Lhasa Evening News* and *Tibet Daily*, and numerous journals and magazines have appeared, both in the Autonomous Region and in other Tibetan areas. In part this is because each province is required to have a literary journal, and under the PRC's constitutional provisions on the right of association, in Tibetan areas there must also be Tibetan-language publications. Not only the TAR but also Qinghai and Yunnan have Tibetan literary journals, for example. Up until about 1995 these had large readerships—*Tibet Literature* used to print 10,000 copies, and because it was well subsidized it was distributed freely to schools and universities, and to anyone who wanted a copy. But state subsidies have gradually been reduced or withdrawn, and these journals are now required to make money. *Tibet Literature* today prints something like 3,000 copies, and people have to pay for it.

The same applies to books: the withdrawal of subsidies has meant the price of books has gone up tremendously, making it difficult for Tibetan-language publications to break even. In the 1990s there was a real renaissance of Tibetan publishing, driven in part by the reprinting of more or less every title ever published in Tibetan, since the seventh century. That initial wave seems to have ended, and the lack of funding means writers have to seek patronage or pay for publication themselves. For example, a novelist writing in Tibetan might have to pay the publisher 10,000 yuan ($1,400) to get his book printed; he would then be given half of the 3,000 print run and told to sell it himself. I have seen other cases where a village boy becomes a poet, and the village will club together to pay for the costs of printing his poems; other times it will be a local businessman who sponsors the edition.

What about television and radio?

There is vibrant television programming in Tibetan, but people tend to prefer watching Chinese shows, simply because Tibetan-language production is very small-scale, and seems to be much more heavily controlled and censored than the wealth of new Chinese channels that are available. This is also true of print media: none of the Tibetan-language journals or magazines are independent—they are all produced under the auspices of different government offices. Now that more and more people in Tibet are competent in Chinese, they have much more choice of what to read, and will turn to the huge variety of Chinese magazines. To a certain extent, this choice of language that people now have is responsible for a decline in readership of Tibetan publications.

What has been the evolution of the monasteries since the late 1980s?

New restrictions were imposed on the number of monks allowed in monasteries, and anyone wanting to become one had to seek permission from the county-level authorities; under the law, you have to be eighteen or over to become a monk or join a monastery. But no one pays the slightest attention to these restrictions. Anyone who goes to Tibet now will see hundreds of youngsters in the monasteries. The government found itself caught in a dilemma: if it forcibly implemented its own policies and removed these children, it would have a wave of protests on its hands. So as long as the monasteries did not actively engage in politics, the government was willing to turn a blind eye to the situation. But relations between the monasteries and the Chinese authorities deteriorated after 1995, when the Chinese leadership insisted on selecting their own tenth Panchen

Lama, disregarding all the wishes and conventions of Tibetan Buddhists. This has had a lasting effect.

As for the number of monks and nuns, it is quite complicated because the government only issues statistics covering those who have permission to be in the monasteries. Officially, the figure is 120,000 in all Tibetan areas, including 46,000 in the TAR. But the real number including those without permission is far larger; I would estimate the total at 180,000. The fact that the numbers are so large in some ways also reflects the economic changes that have taken place. Monasteries do not receive money from the government; they are totally dependent on alms given by the local community and pilgrims. With the economic reforms of the 1980s, people became wealthier and gave them more money. Economic success helped to generate the revival of the monasteries.

Is there any social distinction between the children who go to monasteries for their schooling, as opposed to public schools?

It is mainly children from rural areas who go to monasteries, whereas very few urban families will send their children to them. There are two reasons for this. Firstly, rural families tend to be much bigger, so parents will often send a child, or even two, to a monastery, and still have several at home; whereas urban families only tend to have one or two children at most. The second element is that people in rural areas are, broadly speaking, more conservative in their outlook and view of traditional Tibetan culture.

The fact that monastery schooling was free also became an important factor in the 1980s, when state provision of education was largely abandoned as part of the turn to the market. Across China, people were now supposed to fend for themselves in every area. School budgets were devolved to provincial governments and to the county level; these did not have enough money to run primary and secondary schools, so although education was supposed to be free, all kinds of fees were levied—for textbooks, uniforms and so on—as a way of raising funds. In Tibet, many farmers could no longer afford to send their children to school. And because agricultural production had been privatized, in farming areas many parents kept their children at home—they needed them to work in the fields and increase their output, which was more urgent than getting them educated. School attendance had been compulsory during the Cultural Revolution and the earlier 'leftist' period, and literacy increased as a result. After 1980, there was a visible drop in the literacy rate.

In these circumstances, the monasteries acted as an alternative source of education. This was not just because they did not charge fees, as the public system had begun to do; parents also felt that the monastic tradition had collapsed during the upheavals of the Cultural Revolution, and that they could contribute to its revival by sending their sons or daughters to a monastery or nunnery. It was seen not only as a way of getting an education, but of helping to regenerate Tibetan culture.

What about the health-care system—do the monasteries provide an alternative here too?

As in the rest of China, since the turn to the market, medical care in Tibet is no longer free. In many cases it has become extremely expensive: relatives of mine in Lhasa recently said it would cost them as much as $15–20,000 to get treatment— ten years' salary for a normal family. The Lhasa area has quite good, well-equipped government hospitals, but the cost has prevented most people from using them. The monasteries tend to have a doctor trained in traditional medicine, who may have a look at patients in exchange for payment in kind—a basketful of eggs or a leg of mutton. These practices have been very popular, again because there is no fee.

Judging by Western reports, there seem until recently to have been fewer social protests in the Tibet Autonomous Region than in many other parts of rural China over the past decade.

This is true to some extent. But one has to remember that Tibet is not like the rest of China, much as Northern Ireland is not like the rest of Britain. Because of the demonstrations that took place in the late 1980s, the level of police surveillance and control is far higher than in other areas of China.

How would you compare the protests that began on March 10th this year—the 49th anniversary of the 1959 rebellion—to those of the 1980s?

The first distinctive feature of the 2008 protests is their geographical spread—they seemed to take place simultaneously in almost all the areas where Tibetans live. I think the reason for this is the use of mobile phones and text messaging to spread news and mobilize for demonstrations; in China, it is a far more popular means of communication than the internet or email. It is noticeable that very few protests took place in western Tibet, where there is no mobile phone network in operation, whereas many took place to the east and in regions on the borders of Sichuan and Qinghai, where the system is well developed. These demonstrations erupted within a matter of days, after the initial March 10 monastery protests were put down by the police.

Second, there is a major social difference: the 1980s demonstrations were essentially led by the monks, but this time the protests involved groups from across Tibetan society. There were schoolchildren, students, intellectuals, city workers, farmers, nomads—as well as Tibetan university students in Beijing and other cities. This level of involvement from different sectors of Tibetan society was unprecedented.

How many people were mobilized in these protests?

It is very hard to say how many people took part. The Chinese government say they detained over 6,000 people, which shows that the demonstrations were very intense, and involved large numbers of people. But they have also been sustained at a very high level for several months—they are still going on now, in mid-May—despite the repression. From the start, tear gas and baton charges were used against the protesters. The monasteries were surrounded by riot police. Armed forces were sent into Lhasa on March 15; prisoners were paraded through the streets in military vehicles the following day. But protests continued despite the mass arrests—there were student sit-ins in many schools and universities, and demonstrations outside government offices in Gansu, Qinghai and Sichuan. A 'Most Wanted' list was issued daily from March 19, Chinese websites published pictures of 'wanted' Tibetans, and China Mobile sent a text message to all its users in Tibet asking the public to send any information on those participating in the protests. In a March 23 Xinhua report from the Gannan TAP in Gansu province, there were said to be 'serious protests' at the administrative buildings of some 105 county- or city-level work units, 113 town-level work units and 22 village committees. The protests included Maqu, Xiahe, Zhuoni, Hezuo and other counties and cities. The best reports on all this were on Woeser's blog; they are translated into English on the *China Digital Times* website.

Was the issue of Tibetan nationalism the overriding one, or were some of the protests focused on economic or social issues?

People talked about many things, but if you look at the slogans and banners the protesters were carrying, there was no explicit demand for independence; I think the main issue was getting China to allow the Dalai Lama to come back to Tibet, as well as human rights. It's true that the protests in Lhasa were against the Chinese government and the Party, but also against ordinary Chinese people who have settled in Tibet—Chinese shops were burnt, ethnic Chinese were beaten. But it was really only in Lhasa that this took place. In other regions the demonstrators rushed to government offices or Communist Party headquarters, taking down the Chinese flag and hoisting the Tibetan one, ransacking official buildings; there were very few attacks on ethnic Chinese. The reason they were the target of public anger in Lhasa and not elsewhere is that the disparity between the migrants' success and the status of the indigenous is so glaringly obvious there— the Chinese own hotels, shops, restaurants, and are therefore much more visible. In rural areas, by contrast, the economic disparity between Tibetans and Chinese is minimal, so there was little resentment based on economic grievances. There are, of course, tensions between Tibetans and outsiders: in eastern Tibet, for example, farmers supplement their income in summer by collecting mushrooms, medicinal plants and *yartsa-gunbu*—the caterpillar fungus, much prized in traditional Chinese medicine. Now many Han migrants are also going into the hills to harvest these things, and though the government has tried to restrict this by charging them a fee, the profits are still large enough for them to continue. Locals object to what they see as the indiscriminate way the outsiders collect the mushrooms and fungus, claiming they are doing long-term damage to the pastures. This competition over resources has become more intense in recent years.

But personally I do not think the demonstrations were principally to do with economic disparities or disadvantages suffered by Tibetans. Rather, I think these were defensive protests, concerning questions of national identity. Beijing interpreted the 1980s protests as not just stemming from religious differences, but as the expression of a separate Tibetan identity. Under Hu Jintao, as TAR Party Secretary, policies were targeted against any manifestation of national identity politics; even demands for Tibetan language rights were tarred with the mark of nationalism and separatism. Every Tibetan's loyalty to China was questioned. Everyone became a suspect. The campaign against separatism also became an excuse for clamping down on dissenting voices— within the Communist Party, anyone who opposed a government directive was often accused of being a separatist. But the policy backfired. The Chinese government became unable to distinguish between those who did actively oppose its policies and the rest, and so succeeded in creating a gulf between the government and the whole Tibetan population. The effect was to unify Tibetans, much more than would have been the case if the monastic community alone had been targeted. Indeed, the recent protests have expressed a much more unified nationalistic sentiment than those of the late 80s. The scale of Han immigration has also been a significant factor. Throughout their history, Tibetans on the plateau have always lived in homogeneous communities, but this is no longer the case—they feel much more acutely than ever before that this land is no longer exclusively Tibetan terrain.

March 24 also saw the start of the Beijing Olympics torch relay in Athens, where there was a token protest, followed by high-volume pro-Tibetan and pro-Chinese demonstrations along the torch's route in London on April 6, Paris on April 7, and San Francisco on April 9; and demonstrations against Carrefour supermarkets and CNN TV in the PRC. Since Berlin in 1936, the Games have been a byword for profiteering and political spectacle—what part has Olympomania played in the Chinese and Tibetan mobilizations this year?

The Beijing Olympics were definitely an important element in the 2008 protests. The fact that there would be this spotlight on China internationally is crucial to understanding why similar protests did not happen previously. Both Tibetans within the PRC and exiled political groups understood the importance of the Olympics to the Chinese government, and sensed an opportunity to make a statement, to make their voices heard. In certain symbolic ways, China also politicized the Games, seeing them in part as a way to advertise to the world its ownership of the Tibetan plateau—hence the plan to take the torch up Mount Everest and the adoption of the Tibetan antelope as one of the mascots for the Games. In that sense, both the Tibetan protesters and the Chinese government saw this as an important moment to highlight Tibet, for different reasons.

Nevertheless, when China first lobbied to host the Games, I think they naively assumed that they were not going to be the focus of protest. But since their inception, the Games have always been a source of international tensions. In every one there has been some degree of confrontation—the Israelis and Palestinians in Munich in 1972, the boycotts of the Montreal,

Moscow and LA Olympics in 1976, 80 and 84. All of them have involved a huge political gamble for the host country.

How would you characterize the political spectrum of the pro-Tibet movement outside China, and its relation to Western governments' policies?

The participants in protests in the West are quite a diverse set of people—not necessarily Buddhists or Tibetophiles. Pro-Tibetans tend to come from traditional middle-class, left-of-centre or liberal groups; in the 1970s and 80s they might have been involved in solidarity with the ANC, CND, Greenpeace and so on. The human rights organizations have also shifted their focus: in the 1970s and 80s, Amnesty and Human Rights Watch were more concerned with what was happening in Eastern Europe and the Soviet Union, and China did not figure much in their reports. Now they have directed their attention more to China, and Tibet as an underplayed concern. But I would separate Western government policy from popular sentiment. Most Western governments are essentially very pro-China. This is mainly connected to economic questions: Beijing and the West are in broad agreement on matters such as developing market economies, privatization and the globalization of trade. Since these governments' primary objective is to integrate China into the global economic order, the issues of human rights and Tibet are very much secondary for them.

By the same token, internet claims in the US and China that the Tibetan protests were engineered by Western NGOs, funded by the US National Endowment for Democracy, are wide of the mark. There are Western-funded NGOs in China— for example, the Trace Foundation, which supports health and education projects in Tibet—but the CCP obviously carries out rigorous security assessments of them. Trace is well known for distancing itself from any anti-government groups or activities, which is one of the reasons why it has been able to operate in the PRC for decades. In fact it is often accused by pro-Tibetan lobbyists of being too supportive of China.

Tibetan exile groups in India do get NED funding, but that does not translate into an ability to mobilize in the PRC. There is a huge social and cultural gap between Tibetans in India and those in the TAR, illustrated even by their taste in music. Tibetans inside Tibet are comfortable with Chinese pop, while Tibetans in India prefer Bollywood. When Dadon, Tibet's biggest pop star at the time, defected from Lhasa to India in 1995, she was shattered to find that there was no audience for her music. She was virtually unknown, and the exiles accused her of singing Chinese-style songs. Even when the two communities meet in the West, there is often little interaction between them. The exiles in India sometimes see themselves as the 'true' representatives of Tibetanness, and the Tibetans inside as merely passive, oppressed victims—a patronizing attitude that does not go down well in Tibet. The largest exile organization in India is the Tibetan Youth Congress, most of whom were born in India. They have thoroughly absorbed India's long—and valiant—tradition of protest, and lead highly vocal demonstrations on the streets of Delhi, Paris and New York. But they have no means of projecting their words into actions inside Tibet itself.

One external influence that has had a significant effect on Tibetans was created by the Chinese authorities themselves. Their insistence on imposing their own selection as tenth Panchen Lama succeeded in antagonizing all the monasteries, even those which had previously supported the government. The Party then declared a patriotic education campaign, demanding that the monks and lamas denounce the Dalai Lama. The result was to drive into exile some of the most senior lamas, including the Karmapa and Argya Rinpoche from Kumbum (Ta'er) Monastery, who had often acted as moderate voices and Party mediators in the past. The pro-independence demonstrations in the 1980s did not spread much beyond Lhasa because most lamas were ambivalent and used their influence to restrain their followers. In 2008, almost all areas where protests occurred were in places where the senior lamas had left Tibet. There is a constant flow of devotees from Qinghai and Sichuan to the new monasteries these lamas have established in India; but most of their funds come from Chinese supporters of Tibetan Buddhism in Hong Kong, Taiwan, Malaysia and Singapore. If the Chinese authorities want to point to a plot, it would have to be a Kuomintang conspiracy, not a Western one.

But the main outside influence on Tibetans is the Tibetan-language broadcasting on Voice of America since 1991, and Radio Free Asia since 1996. Again, it is not a question of clandestine organization; these services simply provide a source of news and ideas in a society where people are starved of alternatives. Because there is no independent news media, and people are automatically very suspicious of what they hear or read in government sources, they tend to turn to Voice of America and Radio Free Asia for their information. The two stations report on all the Dalai Lama's trips abroad, and on the activities of the exiles in India, giving Tibetans quite international and politicized coverage; the stations are very popular in Tibet, which helps to create a certain climate of opinion there. The Chinese government tries to jam the signal, but people somehow manage to listen to them.

What is the current state of repression in the Tibet Autonomous Region?

At the moment the situation is very bad. Because of the number of people involved in the demonstrations, and because they cut across all classes, the government cannot target one particular group, such as the monasteries; it seems that they have to target everybody. The authorities are trying to exert control at every level of the community, in a way that reminds many people of the Cultural Revolution. It is not only those who have been detained that are subject to punishment—the government is holding meetings in primary and secondary schools, in colleges, government offices, where everyone has to write self-criticisms; so do Tibetan students at university in China. The Tibetan population as a whole is bearing the brunt of this campaign.

How would you characterize the recent wave of Chinese nationalist sentiment, in response to the Tibetan protests—would you say it marks a watershed in the mentality of the PRC?

This is very interesting. The Chinese nationalism currently exhibited on the internet and abroad is essentially a middle-class phenomenon. It is strongly expressed by those who are the main beneficiaries of China's economic success, and who are most conscious of the country's global standing. They are also more exposed to what is happening outside. They feel that, for them, the reforms are going in the right direction; they are afraid of anything that will hamper China's economic advance. But there is a great divide between coastal and inland areas in China. You do not find nationalism of this kind in the poorer provinces— in Gansu, Qinghai or other areas—where people have not benefited from the current policies. Then again, the terrible earthquake in Wenchuan on May 12 shattered the confidence in the Chinese state that many people had been expressing only weeks before. Simple questions are being raised about why school buildings collapsed but luxury hotels and private firms did not. There is much more discussion, new questions are being asked about China.

There is a debate among China scholars as to whether the upsurge of patriotic fervour that accompanied the Tibetan protests was engendered by the government, or whether it arose spontaneously from society. There are strong arguments on the side of those who claim it was engineered and manipulated by the government, since the state has evidently been involved. For example, any differing views posted in internet forums were almost immediately deleted, and people expressing them in chat rooms were shut out. Others argue that this nationalism arose not from within the PRC, but from outside, among Chinese overseas students, and travelled into China from there. Certainly, many of those studying in Europe or North America are much more mindful of recent changes in the PRC, and have clearly benefited from the reforms. They feel that the criticisms made are not accurate, and that Tibet has in some sense been used as a stick with which to beat China. They ask why protests in Tibet have got so much attention in the international media when similar protests happen every day in China, without being highlighted. There is some truth in this; but still, the geographical scale of the Tibetan protests is unprecedented.

I should also say that there is intense diversity within China— it is not as homogeneous as it might appear. Over three hundred intellectuals signed a petition circulated by Wang Lixiong criticizing the government's response to the unrest in Tibet and appealing for dialogue.[2] There were similar articles appearing in a range of publications. A group of Chinese lawyers announced that they would go to defend the Tibetan detainees; these people are risking their livelihood—the government is threatening not to renew their licences. This is not what the media highlights, of course. Many of these dissenting voices were not heard amid the patriotic fervour.

Have there been any attacks on Tibetans in Beijing or elsewhere?

The Chinese authorities have actually taken great precautions to make sure this does not happen, because they are worried that there will be major repercussions. There are about 5,000 Tibetans in Beijing, and according to my own relatives there, there have been no attacks at all.

How do you see Tibet–China relations developing, over the next months and in the longer term?

In the immediate future, the Chinese leadership faces two problems. One is related to the Olympic Games, and to international as well as Chinese opinion. Beijing cannot be seen within its own country to be weakening under the pressure of international criticisms—to be forced into compromise because of protesting Tibetans. So the government needs to present an image of unity and strength, both internally and to the world at large. The second problem concerns President Hu Jintao and his followers. Hu came to national prominence as Party Secretary in Tibet, and is credited with ending the 80s unrest as well as successfully integrating Tibet and the whole western region

2 See appendix.

with the rest of China. Tibet is intimately connected with Hu's leadership—and therefore the leadership of the CCP. A number of people in high positions made their names through their work in Tibet. Almost all the top figures in the Party today were Hu's underlings during his tenure there: Guo Jinlong, the present mayor of Beijing, was his undersecretary, and Hu Chunhua, the last head of the Communist Youth League—an important office, held at some stage by almost all Chinese presidents—and now acting governor of Hebei province, was also a former secretary of Hu's in Tibet. Now these people's successes are being criticized, and Hu Jintao's credibility as a capable leader is being put into question. Within the Party, discussions are taking place as to whether Hu will save himself by dismissing some of those he promoted, or whether his entire entourage will come under attack. Meanwhile Wen Jiabao, the Premier, has made a number of speeches seemingly making a concerted approach to the Dalai Lama. But everything now hinges on the Olympics. Until then the government is paralysed—if they take any action before the Games it will bring doubts and uncertainty, and I think they will wait until they are over before making any major changes.

In the longer term, one has to understand that one of the Communist Party's strongest claims to legitimacy today is that it unified China territorially and made it strong. This has great power among the Chinese population. The Party therefore cannot afford to make any concessions on sovereignty with regard to Tibet, since any compromise would weaken the Party's legitimizing appeal. For this reason, I do not foresee the Party making any major policy changes after the Olympics.

If Tibetans could articulate them freely, what would their essential demands be?

One of the biggest grievances is that the Chinese authorities equate any expression of Tibetan identity with separatism. The government seems to think that if it allows any kind of cultural autonomy, it will escalate into demands for secession. This is something the government has to relax. In Tibet, everything from newspapers and magazines to music distribution is kept firmly under control, whereas all over China there are increasing numbers of independent publishing houses. The joke in Tibet is that the Dalai Lama wants 'one country, two systems', but what people there want is 'one country, one system'—they want the more liberal policies that prevail in China also to apply in Tibet.

May–June 2008

6

Independence after the March Incident

Wang Lixiong

This chapter was inspired by the watershed events of March 2008 popularly known as the 'March Incident'.[1] I had not seriously considered the possibility of Tibetan independence prior to this time. But the incident served as a turning point for me, making me realize that Tibetan independence has recently emerged as a real issue among the Tibetan people, after being little more than a fantasy for so long. This change was brought on by none other than the 'anti-separatist' institutions within the Chinese government's bureaucratic system. From the perspective of Chinese Communist Party (CCP) ideology, China was a victim of Western imperialism from the mid-nineteenth to mid-twentieth century, and as a result, the Chinese tend to remember the humiliations they suffered while rarely considering their own nation to be an imperial power. But despite having been beaten and humiliated by other world powers, China's vast territorial expansion from the seventeenth to the eighteenth century created the territorial heritage that is now modern China. This now includes Tibet.

Today, Tibet makes up one-fourth of China's geographical territory and is hugely important in the politics of its empire.

---

1   This chapter was translated by Lingxi Kong and Tianle Chang.

Within its power structure, there are thirteen institutions at the provincial and ministerial level that are directly concerned with Tibet, including: the government of the Tibet Autonomous Region; the government of Qinghai Province; the government of Gansu Province; the government of Sichuan Province; the government of Yunnan Province; the CPC Tibet Work Coordination Group; the United Front Work Department; the Ministry of Public Safety; the Ministry of State Security; the People's Liberation Army; the Chinese People's Armed Police Force; the State Council Information Office; and the State Council's Religious Affairs Bureau. Each of these institutions includes a division that deals specifically with Tibet, as well as a large number of bureaucrats who have based their entire career on the issue of Tibet. In addition to this are eleven institutions (again, at the provincial or ministerial level or higher) that don't deal directly with Tibet but oversee 'anti-separatist' responsibilities and have 'anti-separatist' divisions and personnel. These are: the Central Commission of Politics and Law, the CPC Xinjiang Work Coordination Group; the government of the Xinjiang Autonomous Region; the Xinjiang Production and Construction Corps; the Inner Mongolia Autonomous Region; the Ministry of Foreign Affairs; the State Ethnic Affairs Commission; the State Council's Taiwan Affairs Office; the Hong Kong and Macao Affairs Office; the Liaison Office in Hong Kong; and the Liaison Office in Macao. So in total, there are twenty-four provincial or ministerial-level institutions within China's bureaucratic system that perform 'anti-separatist' roles, which represents a huge group with a considerable amount of power, personnel and resources. These institutions, acting in league, led the decision-making process that resulted in the March Incident, which would not have happened in Mao and Deng's reign. Instead, decisions back then were made by the highest authority, which were then executed by the bureaucracy, regardless of the task—whether to 'achieve a united front', suppress an insurgency or to enforce martial law. But in the Tibet incident, the highest authorities took no action at all. Everything was executed solely by the ever-growing bureaucracy.

This pattern in decision-making should not simply be regarded as an effect of the devolution of power-from-above. In fact, in the same month that the incident took place, Premier Wen Jiabao, while attending the Greater Mekong Subregion Summit Meeting in Laos, called on the Dalai Lama to use his influence to calm the situation in Tibet. This was previously unheard of and was thought of worldwide as evidence of a new way of thinking among the highest authorities (the CCP had never before acknowledged that the Dalai Lama has any influence among Tibetans). But this was not followed by any action, nor did the 'anti-separatist' institutions change the way they handled the situation. So it is clear from this that the highest authorities need play no role in the decision-making process on the issue of Tibet. Even if the highest authorities had decided on any course of action, it would not necessarily have been put into effect if it did not accord with the purpose or intent of the bureaucratic institutions. In fact, this may have constituted an implicit rule for future decision-making processes.

Top-down processes of decision-making, emanating from the highest levels of authority, can result in absurd actions and brutality, yet they sometimes also result in decisions that are prudent, visionary and capable of producing real breakthroughs. The two extremes are really not so far apart and are often both present in the transient thoughts of the ruler. But when highly bureaucratic institutions dominate the decision-making process, dramatic breakthroughs are unlikely to be achieved in a given situation. Bureaucracies are inherently rigid, inflexible and dogmatic, but most importantly, they tend toward expansion and are interest-driven such that all decisions produced have to accord with their self-interest. When their self-interest conflicts with the public interest, bureaucracy invariably becomes a destructive force, deserting not only the public interest but also the higher authorities it was meant to serve. Through their anti-separatist actions, the bureaucratic anti-separatist institutions are pushing China inevitably toward fracture or even split. It is through this lens that the March Incident must be understood.

Street protests that exhibit a similar degree of violence as the March Incident occur frequently throughout mainland China, and the tactics used to handle these incidents are usually imprecise and crude. But had these same tactics been used to deal with the March Incident—news blockades, deflating the situation through passive means, not stimulating further conflicts, cracking down on the more extreme groups while providing comfort to others, and finding scapegoats at the lower levels of the bureaucracy to appease any anger—the chain reaction that we saw spread throughout the Tibetan region would likely not have occurred.

But the bureaucrats dealing with Tibet did not wish to take such passive stances. First, the international community consistently has its eye on Tibet, and any mishandling of incidents would likely provoke heavy discussion and criticism. Second, turmoil in Tibet would embarrass President Hu Jintao, who had once been in charge of Tibet (he was the General Secretary of the CPC Tibet Committee from 1988 to 1992), and as a result all levels of bureaucracy were afraid they would be found responsible. Third, since authorities have announced on various occasions that Tibet is currently enjoying a golden age in its history, any incident would undermine their words and put them in a difficult rhetorical position.

The current dynamics of Chinese politics are such that if a few individuals or even a department are held responsible for any serious incident, it is seen as acceptable to find a scapegoat to deflate the situation. Tensions between different bureaucratic institutions would not thereby result or escalate. But no single administration can take responsibility for the turmoil in Tibet, since after decades of huge spending and efforts at development and maintaining stability, the large-scale protests have essentially announced China's policy failures in Tibet. China's Tibet policy was codesigned and executed by so many different institutions and agencies that admitting failure in this instance is tantamount to announcing the collective failure of all the aforementioned institutions and anti-separatist agencies. No one can be excused, for the career prospects of many bureaucrats are at stake. So anti-separatist bureaucrats around China must organize themselves into a power bloc, acting in concert and helping bureaucrats in Tibet to shake off responsibility for this policy failure.

The most convenient way to exonerate oneself in this case is to interpret the burden of failure as resulting from the carefully planned and organized efforts at sedition and separatism of the Dalai clique. Because no matter what excuses are readily available, the bureaucrats have to bear responsibility for the failure if it came from within the borders; only by shifting the blame to the outside can the bureaucrats be totally absolved. The TAR administration announced to Xinhua News on March 14, the day of the incident, that there was sufficient evidence to demonstrate that the incident was 'organized, premeditated and carefully planned' by the Dalai clique. This announcement was immediately adopted as the official statement of all the institutions and anti-separatist agencies dealing with Tibet. But to date, they have been unable to present this 'sufficient evidence', nor do they seem concerned about whether they ever can. Their goal is to guide public opinion from the beginning, which they successfully achieved: this untruthful statement became their rhetorical model, possessing an unquestionable certainty that guided and forced the rest of society (including the highest authorities) to follow suit.

The starting point determines the course. This official statement, shifting the blame off the bureaucrats, became the framework upon which ensuing actions were modeled, as well as shaping the course of the events. For example, on March 14, there was a four-hour period when the army occupied the area peripheral to the protests and took no action in the central area, allowing the degree of violence to escalate. Many people were confused by this strange phenomenon. Among the various interpretations, I tend to believe that this practice of non-interference was deliberately meant to agitate the protesters. On the one hand, it took time to set up video equipment in the protest area; on the other hand, they must have known that uncontrolled violence would naturally grow, contributing to the validity of the forthcoming crackdown and giving journalists a better chance to record more dramatic scenes of violence. If the army had taken control over the situation right from the beginning, the scale of the incident would have been much more limited. But although it might have resulted in a better situation generally—less violence and fewer people killed—it would have been unfavourable for the bureaucrats: suppressing violence, even if on a small scale, would have invited waves of international criticism, which would not please their bosses in Beijing. It would make it difficult for the bureaucrats to wash their hands of the blood, potentially irritating Beijing enough to charge them for improper handling. So they had preferred to take no action, allowing violence to increase to such a degree that it could be properly labeled as 'organized, premeditated and carefully planned'; so that when they actually began to suppress the riots, the outside world, alongside Beijing, would have nothing to hold against them.

These are characteristics that are typical of bureaucracy. For every agency, the decision-making process at its very core tends toward the maximization of its personal benefit. Bureaucrats pay no heed to the actual causes, instead actively allowing things to shift toward the extreme in guarding their own interests, no matter how serious the outcome might be.

The construction of racial oppositions

After the March Incident, the bureaucrats had to prove that the crackdown was necessary and valid to the highest authorities in Beijing, the Chinese people and the international community. They not only took immediate action, using all forms of media to broadcast their official statement on repeat, but also blocked off the area in which the incident had occurred, cutting off all modes of communication so that no counter-evidence could be obtained and public opinion could be tightly controlled. When similar incidents break out in the rest of China, media coverage is usually scarce, if not entirely non-existent, with video images broadcast on television being even more rare. The case of the March Incident was remarkably unusual in that TV news reports were sent throughout the country and even around the world within several hours, showing images of Tibetan violence against the Chinese. They did not mention or analyze the causes behind the incident, only showing images of Tibetan attacks and attributing them to the organizational efforts of separatists outside of Tibet, and this in turn directed nationalistic hatred toward the Tibetans.

This ethnic opposition is the root cause behind the incident and may ultimately lead to separation; it should be avoided by all means. Unfortunately, it is the anti-separatist bureaucratic institutions that are generating it. They knew how serious the consequences of this might be, but they nonetheless mobilized this opposition for their own political gain: so long as the nationalistic sentiments of the Han Chinese were bubbling, manifesting in a bitter hatred of their enemy, the bureaucrats were both able to remain out of the spotlight and thereby avoid inquiries and investigation, as well as to channel those nationalistic sentiments toward bringing the highest authorities in line with their own political trajectory. Any suspicions regarding their handling of the incident or suggestions about reducing these tensions would be lost under surging waves of extreme nationalism. Only absolutely unquestionable statements find resonance under these circumstances. It magnifies and amplifies the lies of the anti-separatist bureaucrats, meanwhile absorbing all voices and actions into its rhetoric.

Such propaganda efforts do not deflate these situations but instead fan the flames. The protests that occurred in the 1980s were only geographically limited to Lhasa, but this time extended over the whole Tibetan region. An important factor was television, which was a rare commodity in the 1980s but was now available everywhere. While the images of violence were accepted by most Han Chinese as justification for the crackdown, they achieved the opposite effect among Tibetans. Graphic scenes on television triggered an explosion of accumulated discontent all over the Tibetan region. Tibetans not only empathized with what was happening in Lhasa, but some were misled by the images, thinking they should be acting in the same way to express their own discontent. In some areas, violence against other ethnic groups was carried out after the violent scenes in Lhasa were shown on TV. The fact that protests seemed to break out simultaneously in different areas was taken by the bureaucrats as evidence that they were 'organized, premeditated and carefully planned'. In fact, there was no need for such organization, premeditation or planning. Showing Tibetans what people in Lhasa were doing was tantamount to encouraging them take to the streets as well. The marvelous thing was that this order to mobilize was sent out by the bureaucrats themselves.

But at the same time, the incident was represented as the senseless slaughter of Han Chinese by Tibetans, due to the prejudiced choice of materials used as propaganda to stir up extreme sentiments. It carved out a racial chasm between Han Chinese and Tibetans. Any admiration and love for Tibetan culture among Han Chinese people, which has been a common phenomenon in recent years, was transformed into fear and hatred of all Tibetans in general, who were now seen as an ungrateful people. The internet was inundated by abusive and vitriolic comments, in a display of extreme nationalism. Tibetans experienced discrimination and unfairness everywhere—at the airport, hotels and at checkpoints. Tibetan children were bullied by Han Chinese classmates. Out of spite toward the official propaganda, Tibetans resisted all forms of official rhetoric and responded with hatred to the Han Chinese. It might be said that the racial opposition between the Han Chinese and Tibetans was formed after the March Incident, by which the two sides became divided by blood. In typical fashion, Tibetan children cheered whenever China lost a gold medal during the Olympic Games in Beijing, where they had previously cheered for the Chinese teams. This shift among the behaviour of children indicates something about the long-term direction the issue of Tibet is headed toward.

Before the March Incident, the conditions for independence were all in place—a single ethnicity, religion and culture; clarity of national boundaries and history; high degree of recognition from the international community—except for the most important one: the lack of driving force among local Tibetans to seek for this achievement. Although the 'issue of Tibet' has existed for decades, it has been concentrated in the political, historical or cultural spheres. Those involved in the conflicts and debates were mostly from the government, the upper class, the intelligentsia and the international community. Even the 1959 uprising and the escape of the Dalai Lama were regarded by Mao as the effects of class struggle, not ethnic opposition. The protests of the 1980s did not make a huge impact on Sino-Tibetan relations, since they were localized in Lhasa, without reaching into the other Tibetan areas. Common people of both ethnicities lived more or less harmoniously, even intimately. Since there appeared to be no active movement for independence among Tibetans, it didn't really matter how many of the objective conditions had been met, and it was precisely because of this that I had not considered the prospects for Tibetan independence.

But the March Incident has sharply divided the Han Chinese from the Tibetans. Once ethnic relations take on the form of racial opposition, the nature of the issue has changed. The conflicts among the upper class and elites were easy to resolve through policy changes, institutional modifications or by dealing with individual cases. But conflicts in which people are treated differently depending on blood and race involve everyone, impacting every detail of daily interaction between people on opposite sides. Any individual in any interaction can initiate action that will cause greater conflict, and all conflicts can result in further conflicts, thereby accumulating racial hatred between the two peoples (an eye for eye, a tooth for a tooth) and pushing them further apart, past the point of no return. Within this scenario, the weaker side—the oppressed and discriminated—will naturally yearn for independence. Once Tibetans in the Tibetan region begin generally to envision this as their ultimate goal, all the conditions for independence will have been met. With this important change, Tibetan independence will have emerged as a concrete issue. Though its actualization will depend on timing and objective conditions, at least for Tibetans themselves, the conditions have now all been met. This represents a turning point in the Tibet issue. If supporters of a 'free Tibet' want to express their gratitude to anyone, the most deserving are the anti-separatist bureaucratic institutions that have successfully transformed Sino-Tibetan relations into the form of racial opposition.

Self-fulfilling prophecies

As I've mentioned, the incident has been defined since the beginning as 'organized, premeditated, and carefully planned by the Dalai clique', and since the authorities regard national unity as the paramount principle, their method of handling it was to initiate a crackdown in a resolute and unconditional way. National unity is the principle that government and bureaucrats will not violate, as well as being the guiding ideology for the Armed Police that carry out crackdown operations. After the incident, authorities at all levels in the Tibetan areas and the Armed Police overreacted, initiating large-scale arrests, violent suppressions, cruel interrogations, temple blockades and the persecution of monks, which provoked widespread discontent and motivated more of the Tibetan people to get involved and to resist. This is another major reason that the incident escalated to such a large degree.

Having been inculcated under Party ideology and propaganda, all the Han Chinese soldiers brought to Tibet to carry out crackdown operations saw Tibetans as separatist enemies, and so they unleashed their hatred and violence on the Tibetans, which further provoked unnecessary conflicts. For example, when Han Chinese soldiers found pictures of the Dalai Lama, the 'head of the separatist clique', they would either force Tibetans to destroy them or do it themselves. This was unacceptable to Tibetans who see the Dalai Lama as the supreme leader. When elderly Tibetans were beaten in the attempt to protect these photos, their children, relatives and fellow villagers would get very angry, so that more and more people gradually became involved. These conflicts escalated to become serious incidents, sometimes resulting in shootings and casualties. It was henceforth described as 'premeditated and carefully planned' then followed by massive suppression. Similar events occurred all over the Tibetan region, though often without any political content. People were simply provoked by the government to resist.

After the June Fourth student movement of 1989, the Party announced that destabilizing factors had to be resolved at the grassroots level and nipped in the bud, which became the basic mode of thinking of the bureaucracy, and represents the highest guiding principle of bureaucrats. They believed they could do what they pleased using power and might. In areas dominated by ethnic minorities, their policy was to go on the offensive, dealing with those who stepped out of line and to act preemptively. Later on, the policy shifted toward attacking and pursuing even those 'enemies' who hadn't stepped out of line, which occurred during the March Incident. Many activities that had nothing to do with politics became targeted, such as holidays, horse-racing and religious ceremonies—traditional customs that have existed since ancient times. But the bureaucrats—and especially the soldiers brought from outside—knew nothing of these culture and traditions, believing that 'all non-Han people were rebellious'. Any gathering could result in serious accidents, so that the most reliable preemptive action they could take was to forbid all gatherings and cease all non-governmental activities. Even if they were not entirely banned, large numbers of troops were deployed, surrounding the area in question and threatening them with the presence of heavy weapons. The reactions should have been expected: 'How come you can host the Olympic Games but we cannot even hold our horse races?' Impatient Tibetans engaged in vicious arguments with the cruel and insolent soldiers who saw them as potential enemies. To the authorities, this only validated their belief that gatherings would lead to incidents, and so they increased their efforts to limit these activities, not knowing that these incidents were caused precisely by their own self-fulfilling prophecies. Preemptively 'nipping these problems in the bud' is not a good strategy even from the perspective of the ruler, since many of these 'buds' are not actually destabilizing elements.

The monks in Tibet are rational and peaceful. Had the authorities listened carefully and interacted in a positive way with them when they were expressing their discontent through non-violent means, the stability of the Tibetan region might even have been strengthened in the long run. But instead they view the monks as parasites, acting as the Dalai's roots in Tibet, the midwives of Tibetan independence and troublemakers and instigators—all negative traits. So whenever they are challenged by the monks, the authorities, as if preprogrammed, respond with violence. During the March Incident, the violence was a direct result of the fact that soldiers had been continuously beating the monks, who were acting non-violently, for days.

This is precisely what caused the Lhasa incident in 1987. How surprising that the authorities have learned no lessons from the past! If they knew just a little about Tibetan culture they would know that, unlike the disgust and contempt with which the bureaucrats view them, the monks enjoy very high social status and respect among Tibetans. They are one of the three core elements of Tibetan Buddhism; they are traditional scholars of Tibetan culture; and they are guides and protectors of the spiritual world. Tibetans could hardly tolerate seeing them abused and humiliated. The abuse and violence that armed soldiers rained upon the monks was bound to end in chaos. Only because the imperial bureaucrats were blinded by power were they not able to foresee that outcome.

The authorities never reflected on what happened, acting in ways that actually exacerbated the situation. The monks became the main targets in all areas; many great temples were searched by the Armed Police, which was seen as a great offense. Besides the arrest of many of the participants in the protests, many were confined and deprived of their liberties; some temples were closed indefinitely; monks without registered residence were deported; all temples were ordered to engage in 'patriotic education' in which monks were forced to openly denounce the Dalai Lama. Many monks fled from the temples in order to avoid this punishment, for this denunciation was required of each individual monk. Some temples were completely emptied. Before the March Incident, many monks were apolitical, devoting themselves to spiritual practice and accepting China's rule, only concerning themselves with policy issues. But one result of the March Incident was that the monks began to think about Tibet's political future, and those who supported Tibetan independence began to increase.

The actions of the authorities essentially antagonized the monks, pushing them to take the opposing position, and this is tantamount to having created their toughest adversary. Because the monks have no family ties, they are resolute, single-minded, uncompromising and unafraid to challenge the authorities, which is why they have always been on the frontlines during past incidents. Meanwhile, the respect they hold and their far-reaching influence in Tibetan society means that their discontent and appeals for independence will be widely heard. It will surely have a broad impact on the Tibetan people at large.

The scramble for evidence of organization and pre-meditation—another popular method among the bureaucrats—resulted in a large number of arrests, confessions acquired through torture and cases with no grounds, in turn creating widespread discontent and disillusionment among Tibetans. Yet even after accusations that they were persecuting the Tibetan people, the bureaucrats still couldn't produce convincing evidence to justify their actions. For Tibetans, the charges that the media brought against the Dalai Lama were entirely false. Even in areas where protests did not break out, these charges provoked disgust and aversion, intensifying hatred and inciting further conflicts. Many Tibetans began to think about separatism as the better way forward. In this way, anti-separatist efforts have actually bred a separatist consciousness among Tibetans. The Tibetan word for and concept of Tibetan independence was not previously well known among Tibetans, but after years of anti-separatist education, all Tibetans—old and young—are now familiar with it. During the March Incident, 'Tibetan independence' became a slogan among monks, city dwellers, herdsmen and primary school students alike.

The fear of separatism among anti-separatist institutions is a self-fulfilling prophecy. By treating Tibetans as enemies, they eventually became enemies; by working against Tibetan separatism, they ensured that Tibetans would eventually want to secede. Different commentators have expressed different views on the nature of protests that broke out throughout the Tibetan regions. The main point of disagreement is whether they constituted a political movement for independence, or whether they simply expressed discontent toward specific policies or economic disadvantage. For me, the March Incident may not have been defined by the explicit demand for independence— there were many contributing factors, including the widening divergence of living standards, the influence of the international community, herd mentality, discontent regarding the economy and migration issues, while at the same time official propaganda and suppression added fuel to the flames. But the outcome of the March Incident is that the desire for independence has now been planted in the minds of Tibetans. If similar incidents break out in the future, the movement will be a spontaneous one. Tibetan independence will then be the universal demand among Tibetans, serving as the driving force and guiding principle.

Chinese and Western hostilities

Despite generally good feelings between the Chinese people and those from Western countries today (Westerners are generally well-liked in China and portrayed in the media in a favourable light; both governments receive much criticism from the other side, but this same criticism is not directed toward the Chinese or Western people) the Western world has been greatly antagonized by the Chinese people over the issue of Tibet. They have launched a war against the Western media and passionate diatribes against the people of the West. This shift in attitude is the result of a successful campaign waged by the bureaucrats over the media. But this act of inciting public anger to control public opinion will certainly arouse the suspicions of and criticism from the international community.

On March 14, the day of the incident, the authorities restricted the movements of foreigners to achieve an information blockade, and not long after, forced all foreigners out of Tibet. For a long time, they were not allowed to visit the Tibetan areas, and checkpoints were set up on the roads. Video and photographic evidence was considered the most sensitive, and the Armed Police violated human rights in order to prevent this material from getting out. Foreigners were prevented from taking photos, while Tibetans using cellphone cameras were arrested and cruelly persecuted. Even Han Chinese individuals caught taking sensitive photos were interrogated, their equipment confiscated and their photos deleted. The Western media had trouble accessing first-hand material due to the strictly enforced information censorship, and could only use indirect sources for reporting purposes. These accounts were riddled with errors, which drew heavy criticism and damaged the image of the Western media in Chinese eyes. This was the first time that the Chinese propaganda machine emerged victorious in a battle with the Western media, and the bureaucrats were extremely pleased.

But the Western media was unconvinced. The intimidation and abuses of the Chinese government and people only further aroused the suspicions of the Western media, pushing them to the opposite side of the battle line. Although the Western media would begin to report on the issue with greater care, research and balance, they will also now view the Chinese people as violent and fanatical, alongside the Chinese totalitarian regime. This collective media campaign against China will surely occur again when a similar situation arises in the future. The perspectives and attitudes of the Western people are largely guided by the media. Having been insulted and thereby antagonized, they are bound to portray China in a more negative light. The Western people are likely to follow suit.

But the bureaucratic institutions are not concerned about the opinions of Westerners. In fact, they cited the hostility of the Chinese people toward Western society in this instance as evidence of the government's popularity. Later, when Westerners tried to boycott the Olympic Torch relay, the bureaucrats had those images broadcast repeatedly, further inciting the hatred of the Chinese people toward the Western society. Totalitarian regimes are adept in the craft of creating mass movements and mobilizing the masses. During big incidents like this, the freeze on information prevents the Chinese people from thinking critically and independently, making them easy to manipulate. Although the people hardly agree with the official line on many issues, the majority have accepted the principle of national unity as fundamental and inviolable, and have accepted the separatist/anti-separatist dichotomy in assessing the issue of Tibet—a place far from their daily lives. When the media—universally under government control and therefore speaking in a unified voice—reprimanded Western societies for their hostility toward China and their feverish support of a 'free Tibet', it was not difficult to incite the enmity of the Chinese people. Not only did the March Incident force the Han Chinese and Tibetans into a relation of racial opposition, but it also separated Chinese and Western societies into two opposing camps.

Indeed, the amount of support among the Chinese people for their government was unprecedented. On the internet and in Western districts in China, Chinese patriots and Westerners were fist-to-fist. CNN is censored in China, but the Chinese people vehemently criticized CNN; in China there is no freedom to protest on streets, but overseas compatriots gathered in scenes reminiscent of the Cultural Revolution—some of these performances were encouraged and organized by the Chinese government and consulates abroad. The Chinese people, now seen as hating the West, may be conflated with their government, as they were not before.

The opposing camps no longer relate to one another in reasonable ways. Both apeal to over-simplified criteria in their debates—like soccer hooligans attempting to humiliate the opposing side—without appealing to legitimate reasons and without any conception of right or wrong. Once the Chinese people are portrayed uniformly as supporters of their government, and thereby thought of as uniformly possessing the mentality of colonizers, the Western world is bound to support the liberation of Tibet from Chinese rule, regardless of how China's political system might change. The promise of Chinese dissidents—that Tibet will be free once China democratizes—will cease to find support, since institutional change is not enough to change the people's mentalities. This will make it much more difficult for China in dealing with the issue of Tibet in the future.

The CCP is no longer a revolutionary party that strictly follows its founding ideologies; rather, it has become a pragmatic and opportunistic power bloc. In theory, it would make sense for it to avoid direct confrontation with the West, simply out of self-interest. But its development and progression is connected to its inner logic. Bureaucracies are such that, even if all act in rational ways, the general outcome might be highly irrational and fail to serve the general interest of the group. The evolution of rational parts into an irrational whole, like the Nash Equilibrium, is of vital importance in determining the course of affairs. In the following analysis, I will show how China's logical fallacy in dealing with the March Incident was a result of the rational calculations of the anti-separatist bureaucratic institutions.

'Anti-separatism' as a profession

The most important function of an imperial state is to keep the empire's territory intact. As a result, the anti-separatism institutions established for this purpose hold a privileged position in the state. Phuntsog Wangyal, founder of the Tibetan Communist Party and formerly a high official in the CCP, described the bureaucrats that populate these institutions as utilizing this perceived necessity of 'anti-separatism' to make a living, establish their careers and make their fortune. This is because the more that separatism is a problem, the more power and resources these institutions and bureaucrats are awarded by the empire. At a fundamental level, this has created the instinctive hope among these bureaucrats that separatism will exist permanently as an issue. At both the institutional and personal levels, it is in their interest for the nationality issue to remain unresolved, yet they also deliberately exacerbate existing conflicts and overstate the dangers of separatism. They cast incidents in the most serious light possible; exaggerate situations and make them appear much more acute than they really are; and they create issues when there are none. In order to emphasize their political accomplishments, they sometimes take excessively hardline approaches in dealing with these events, escalating conflicts to a higher level. When mistakes are made, they refuse to admit responsibility, shifting it instead onto others or using bigger mistakes to conceal smaller ones.

This flawed management style is sometimes attributed to the stupidity of executive officials. This is certainly inaccurate, as officials are not lacking in intelligence. They may be aware that their behaviour will harm society, but they still carry on in this way because their aim is not to resolve the underlying issues but to benefit personally from their management. Take the Chinese diplomats stationed in foreign countries, many of whom are educated in the West and spend much time living abroad. When they organize patriotic demonstrations of overseas Chinese residents and students, they know that these events will repulse the people and the media of the host country, thereby hurting China's image abroad. But their careers in the bureaucracy don't depend on the host country's favour or disgust. Instead, it depends on satisfying China's leaders and their institutions. Chinese leaders feel pride when they see images of their national flag and patriotic Chinese out in Western countries in full force, and the diplomats are then more likely to be promoted. This is their motivation. As far as damaging the country goes, this is not their responsbility and they will not be required to shoulder any blame. So they have nothing to worry about.

I discussed earlier how the bureaucratic institutions concerned with Tibet have placed all blame on the Dalai clique, since this is the best way for them to avoid responsibility. But this doesn't apply to the Ministry of Public Safety, the Ministry of State Security and the Armed Police. Their functions are to prevent sabotage by 'hostile' or overseas forces, and because the March Incident—'organized, premeditated, and carefully planned by the Dalai clique'—was successful, these institutions should have to take full responsibility. Why do they allow this a narrative of sabotage to circulate, one that casts them in a bad light? At the same time, this also shows the complexity of the bureaucratic institutions: the most basic instinct of the individual official is to shift responsibility, but a more skillful approach is to turn crisis into opportunity. The agencies concerned with security did not therefore blame themselves, instead claiming that they were crippled by 'external factors' such as lack of resources, insufficient budget, excessive restrictions on their power and mild policies. When they violently shut down the Tibetan protests, they were immediately seen as heroes in the 'struggle against the enemy'. Not only were they free from blame—they were actively praised. At the same time, it demonstrates to the public once again that ruthless crackdowns are the only efficient method available. Having shut down the protests, they reflect on the previous approaches they took—lack of resources, excessive restrictions on power, mild policies—and draw lessons about their effectiveness. In this way, they are able to request more resources and power from higher authorities— to implement their hardline policies and raise their own status. Such tactics are certainly effective—for enhancing the careers of the bureaucrats. By taking advantage of their information monopoly to overstate the brutality of events and the dangers of separatism, they can easily frighten the highest authorities within the empire. The imperial rulers in turn are always willing to pay the necessary price to maintain the integrity of territory.

The events that occurred in Tibet in spring 2008 are likely to interrupt the process of liberalization in the Chinese state. Reform efforts already underway that were meant to ease police measures may also now be aborted. This is particularly true in regions with large populations of ethnic minorities: milder policies implemented before are now being revoked, while oppressive powers that were beginning to be dissipated are now being consolidated once more. In the name of anti-separatism and counter-terrorism, China's minority regions will inevitably be governed under authoritarian police states. This is in large part a result of 'anti-separatism' becoming the professional pursuit of bureaucratic institutions. For despite the larger system in which they find themselves, bureaucrats will always pursue their own interests—which should surprise no one. The bureaucratic-authoritarian system enables clever bureaucrats to harm the nation and regime for their own professional enhancement, which is why it contains the seeds of its own collapse.

'The Democratic Character of Bureaucratic Cliques'

It may seem strange that, although decisions in authoritarian regimes are made from the top down, the high authorities turn a blind eye when their subordinates behave in damaging ways in pursuit of their personal or institutional interests. Why do they not intervene? Even if dictators were shielded by false information in other historical cases, I do not think this is the case here. Instead, the nature of China's power structure is such that the high authorities have no way to override the situations created by their subordinates, even if they know better. This is because, in an authoritarian-bureaucratic system, the decisions of leaders can only be implemented through the bureaucratic institutions. Because of this, although the highest authorities can exercise absolute authority with regard to external players, they lack this actual power internally. They are only able to dictate policy and exercise their authority over these institutions when it doesn't harm their interests. Otherwise the bureaucrats will band together and employ tactics such as delay, distortion and non-responsiveness to strip their leaders of their power in the process of policy implementation. This process by which the authority of authoritarian powers is diminished is what I call the 'democratic character of bureaucratic cliques'.

The democratic character of bureaucratic cliques is a pervasive feature in both ancient dynasties and contemporary authoritarian political regimes. It is not an explicit feature of the system or its mechanisms, instead materializing through the hidden rules of officialdom and evolving into an active mechanism through individual competition between bureaucrats—as if through natural selection. Bureaucrats compete with one another on individual issues, but together belong to the same collectivity. As careerists, they are highly sensitive to the loss and gain of personal advantage; adept at identifying and moving on opportunities; and highly capable of covering for one another—which makes for a low-cost, low-risk mechanism. To exercise their power, authoritarian leaders have to satisfy the conditions of this democratic character of bureaucratic cliques, which means complying with (or at least not harming) the interests of the bureaucratic institutions. Only in this way are bureaucratic institutions useful for the authorities—otherwise they may appear to concede to the higher powers but then act in underhanded ways.

Of course, there have been authoritarian leaders throughout history who take uncompromising stances toward their bureaucratic institutions, which often requires exceptionally strong authority and extreme measures, such as purges. But these are short-term and unsustainable measures. For long-term stability, loyal and efficient bureaucratic institutions are necessary, which cannot be bred through terror and threats. But once this is achieved, the bureaucratic system can essentially run itself. Authoritarian leaders who only seek personal power could simply sit atop the carriage as the bureaucrats—willingly—pull it along.

Despite the extraordinary level of authority Mao Zedong commanded over the CCP bureaucracy, he was unable to publish an article in Beijing, the city in which he then lived, on the eve of initiating a movement that would affect the interests of the bureaucratic institutions. This clearly demonstrates how powerful the bureaucratic institutions really are. Mao eventually chose to bypass the bureaucratic institutions and call for a grassroots rebellion, thus destroying his obstacle. But what became known as the Cultural Revolution eventually failed, despite being an unprecedented event that initially appeared to hold so much promise. The Cultural Revolution could destroy the old bureaucracy, but a new one had to be built to implement Mao's power. Even he could not live without the bureaucratic institutions. Yet whoever populates the bureaucracy—whether it is old or new—it will eventually become the leading power bloc, and the democratic character of bureaucratic cliques will prevail as before. In the end, Mao had no choice but to simply threaten the return of the Cultural Revolution every seven or eight years, degrading his movement from revolutionary status to the cleansing of the bureaucracy from time to time.

The memory of these events is deeply engraved upon a bureaucracy that suffered enormously during that era. Henceforth, the sentiment has been that no dictators should be allowed to destroy the bureaucratic institutions. In the post-Mao era, CCP campaigns for party-building and developing democracy within the CCP are indeed strengthening this democratic character of bureaucratic cliques and shielding the institutions from the whims of the authorities. The essence of this delegation of power— the main component of China's reform—is power-sharing among the bureaucratic institutions. The CCP has to date established a comprehensive system of internal restrictions, while the bureaucratic institutions have achieved the capacity to guard against official purges and block any line struggle that might lead to internal Party division. Today, the highest authorities of the CCP are weaker than at any other time in its history. The power transfer has also been effectively preprogrammed, and the fundamental cause behind all this is the democratic character of bureaucratic cliques.

This is an essential change. In the era of 'ideology-above-all', power struggles at the highest level were carried out in the form of line struggle. Bureaucrats could only choose representatives along different factional lines and then rise and fall with their chosen line in a passive way. But when the CCP transformed from being ideologically-driven to being merely a power bloc, the bureaucratic institutions—who implement the power of the regime and who benefited most from the shift—became its core. With the decline of ideology, power struggles within the party seem ill-founded and lacking in legitimacy. As the democratic character of bureaucratic cliques grows, inner-Party struggles that harm group interests will be boycotted by a unified collective of bureaucrats. The CCP has thus become less divided and more pragmatic. The top leaders are no longer dictators that lord over the bureaucratic institutions but are instead their coordinators and spokespersons. At the same time, the leaders can only enhance their own power by winning the support of the bureaucracy and maximizing their interests.

The bureaucrats understand the machinery of state and can operate it skillfully, more or less possessing the ability to constrain the power of the top leaders, control the appointment of officials and decide on the direction of policies. As long as they retain these capacities, they are not only able to avoid purges or 'cultural revolutions' within the Party, but can also fend off actions they find unfavourable and increase their advantage as much as possible. So to view the CCP's promotion of inner-party democracy as a step toward the democratization of China in general is completely mistaken. 'Inner-party democracy' is just another name for the centuries-old democratic character of bureaucratic cliques. It has nothing to do with popular democracy.

The Tibet issue at an impasse

It should be clear through the examination of the democratic character of bureaucratic cliques and its central role in the CCP why China's current Tibet policy is not likely to improve. I mentioned at the beginning that Tibet is governed by thirteen agencies that are at least at the provincial or ministerial level, alongside twenty-four anti-separatism departments at similar levels. The tactics they employ—deceiving those above, bullying those below, responding to policies from above with countermeasures from below, delaying unfavourable actions indefinitely—have been so effective that if even one agency refuses to implement a certain policy, there is not much the leaders can do—especially when the twenty-four departments are in alliance.

Compared to Mao Zedong and Deng Xiaoping, the current CCP leaders enjoy much less authority. They not only lack expertise, a celebrated history of achievement and charisma, but they are all also bureaucrats, having been part of the bureaucracy for years and knowing the rules of officialdom all too well. Having been promoted, rung by rung, to the top positions, how could they not know the power of bureaucratic institutions? Yet because of this, they are not leaders by nature but top bureaucrats who are not inclined to look beyond. They seek simply to remain in power, never daring to step outside of their designated jurisdictions, so that we can hardly expect them to show the same level of resolve and inclination toward change as Mao and Deng. The top CCP leaders did not act in response to the March Incident until long after it had broke out. Everything was handled by the anti-separatism agencies. This is a unique feature of the event. Those twenty-four departments took control of all the necessary elements of power, including legislation, military force and propaganda. They formed a complete, unbroken chain in decision-making, implementation and coordination. Even without leadership from their leaders, they were together able to coordinate and operate on their own.

The CCP has also fallen into a trap of their own making. Its metamorphosis from a revolutionary party into merely a power bloc has left it with sovereignty as its only remaining substantial ideology—a sovereignty preserved through nationalism and making up the core of the CCP's power. The state has spared no effort in indoctrinating the people and continuously rewriting history, so that most Chinese now believe that China's imperial territory has belonged to China since ancient times. Given this narrative, bureaucrats simply occupy a politically correct position and therefore easily win public support. Yet it also means that they would find it difficult to alter their position or public opinion. The anti-separatism law that was enacted can be seen as both a shield and a weapon: it protects bureaucrats, yet none would dare express dissent when an attack could be launched against them at any time. The alliance of the twenty-four anti-separatist institutions is extremely powerful—in addition to manifesting the only substantial ideology of the Party. Mobilizing their 'inner-party democracy', they are even capable of launching coups against leaders who disagree with them—all in the name of protecting national sovereignty, which also presents an easy avenue for winning support from both the public and members of the Party. So in the face of such a threat, China's current leaders—who see power as everything—always tend toward the official leftist stance in order to avoid attack from their political opponents and the public, never adopting new ideas that might threaten their status. Even if they know with full certainty that maintaining the status quo will guarantee a bigger crisis in the future, they will simply postpone the crisis for as long as possible. With the shift from lifetime appointments to rotating positions of power, China's political system seems to be headed in a progressive direction. But in fact it has also caused more damage: those in power strive to ensure that everything is satisfactory during their term, preferring to defer trouble to future terms instead. When the crisis breaks out, it will appear to be unconnected to earlier leaders.

In my view, when the international community urges Chinese leaders to meet with the Dalai Lama; when the Dalai Lama wishes to communicate directly with Chinese leaders without using intermediaries; and when members of the Tibetan elite write letters of petition to the top leaders of the CCP, they do not really understand the determining factors within this situation. How to resolve the issue of Tibet is not something that the leaders of the CCP have the power to decide on their own. Certainly on some specific occasions, CCP leaders are able to deal with this issue in particular ways—but only in strategic ways that don't affect the substance of the issue. The tremendous influence and pervasiveness of anti-separatism forces within China's power structure should clearly indicate to us that CCP leaders, no matter how open-minded, are unable to resolve the Tibet question. In fact, that is little more than an impractical dream. So long as the bureaucratic institutions reign supreme, Tibet will be pushed gradually further along the road to independence.

2008

7

Echoes of the Past:
China's Response to Tibetan Unrest

Tsering Shakya

In January 2009, in response to the widespread protests that engulfed the Tibetan plateau between March and April 2008, the Chinese government proclaimed for the first time that a festival called 'Serf Liberation Day' was to be celebrated in Tibet. The decision was carefully crafted as a piece of legislation originating from the regional National People's Congress in Lhasa, a body that represents China's promise of autonomy to Tibetans. But in fact, it merely functions as a conduit for transmitting Party directives rather than expressing local views. The announcement was made by the Tibetan members of this Congress's standing committee, as if it were their initiative; their ventriloquized voices were intended to stand for the heartfelt sentiments of the Tibetan people. It is indeed possible that such an initiative may have come from one group of Tibetans: those senior Party apparatchiks who likely faced internal criticism last year for their failure to produce a loyal populace. The senior Tibetan Party leaders certainly failed in this regard, and in an authoritarian regime, when a client administration fails, it has few means with which to absolve itself—other than performance. Accordingly, authoritarian regimes tend to love public spectacles, engineered to perfection, in which the people perform ceremonial displays of contentment—most evident in North Korea. But the local reality behind these displays may be quite different from the external message they communicate. When a North Korean refugee once told me that he liked taking part in these performances, I thought it was because he appreciated their aesthetic merit. But in fact, the reason he liked performing was because the participants were fed during rehearsals and on the day of the performance.

For local Tibetan officials, 'Serf Liberation Day' will thus be their way of delivering public mass compliance to the leadership in Beijing—one in which former serfs will tearfully recount the evils of the past while locals march in the hundreds past the leaders' podium, dressed in colourful costumes and dancing in unison to express their contentment. This event will allow Tibetan officials to produce the performances required to retain their posts; then once the needs of the local leaders have been fulfilled, the local people can be allowed to maintain their livelihoods. As Joseph Conrad pointed out in describing the native predicament under European imperialism in Africa a century ago, the local subject learns to savour the 'exalted trust' of the colonial master.

There is a certain irony to this, since China experienced something similar under the Japanese occupation. During that time, Chinese collaborators like the now-hated Wang Jinwei—an official in the early 1940s now known to most Chinese as a *Hanjian*, or 'traitor to the Han nationality'—were forced to coerce the people on behalf of their rulers. Even today, the Party needs such local intermediaries to provide a semblance of native acquiescence in its dealings with the non-Chinese population, and reportedly, they regularly hold meetings with these officials where, for hours, they are alternately praised and admonished by officials from Beijing.

These people are not accused of treachery, since they too have little choice, but are mocked in Tibetan slang as *go nyi pa*, or 'two-headed men', because of the different things they say to different people. They are sometimes seen as immensely skilful, because many of them have retained their local leadership positions for decades longer than any of their Chinese counterparts—no other leaders from the Cultural Revolution era were allowed to remain in power after the purge of ultra-leftists in 1976. But in fact, the Party could not function without them in the minority nationality areas. Even liberal leader Hu Yaobang once stated openly that the local functionaries who had carried out the Cultural Revolution in Tibet could not be removed from office, apparently because there were so few other local figures who could be relied upon to produce compliance.

Handling culture

This longevity has not been without its semi-comical dimensions, particularly in the cultural sphere, where the Party has maintained a roster of acceptable Tibetan pop stars, whose songs they consider exemplary. But the list has never changed: the official diva of the Tibetan song is Tseten Dolma, who has officially been the most loved of all Tibetan singers since the 1950s. Musical tastes may have changed, but Tseten Dolma is still championed as the number one singer and appears regularly at every political event, even though many people despise her music. For the Party and the Chinese nation, it is not her voice that is enchanting so much as the symbolism constructed around her life: the fairy-tale saga of a poor serf girl who was liberated by the People's Liberation Army (PLA) and achieved national recognition through her voice. She represents a vindication of class struggle and an authentic symbol of native approval for the state.

But the difficulty with elaborate displays of loyalty, such as Serf Liberation Day, is that local interpretations of the same events are always impossible to control. As a child growing up in Lhasa, I remember when the epic Chinese film *The Serf* (directed by Li Jun and released in 1963) was first shown in Tibet. The film depicted the harrowing life of a 'serf' called Jampa, who parents were killed by the evil landlord and who was used as a human horse for his master's child until freed from bondage by the arrival of the PLA. This film is still seen in China as a powerful depiction of the Tibetan social system and was meant, at the time, to arouse indignation amongst the people against class oppression by the Tibetan elite. When it was shown in Lhasa, nobody watched it with quite those same sentiments, especially because many members of the local audience knew the actors and had already watched the crew and director shoot the film. Most had heard stories that the actors were just following instructions and were not allowed to correct many of the film's inaccuracies, so it was thought of by most locals as an elaborate work of fiction. Of course, this didn't affect any displays of sentiment: much as with similar films today, everyone in Tibet was supposed to watch the film and cry, and in those days if you did not cry, you risked being accused of harbouring sympathy for the feudal landlords. So my mother and her friends would put tiger balm under their eyes to make them water: weeping was required. In one famous scene, the hero, Jampa, is shown being beaten by monks for stealing food that had been left as a shrine offering in a temple. He had been driven by hunger to act in this way. But for locals, this was seen not as a moment of class oppression but instead as karmic reward due to a sacrilegious thief. The film became known locally as *Jampa Torma Kuma* or 'Jampa, The Offering Thief': even today, hardly any Tibetan person uses the actual title, *The Serf*, when referring to the film in Tibetan. The risk for China's officials is that Serf Liberation Day will face a similar fate in popular memory once the public spectacle is over.

Statements such as the one the Party was making in this famous scene require a cultural shift as well as a political one to be understood as they were meant—one where the local gods are denigrated and traditions are branded as redundant, even if they remain exotic. Sometimes the directives that marginalize local practices do not originate from the Party Central Committee, who may be unconscious of them. But often it isn't the major political impositions from Beijing that anger people. Instead, it is mostly the fine details of administrative insensitivity that indicate a lack of concern for the local situation on the part of the ruled, as well as the deep lack of knowledge concerning those they rule—a feature that is surprising in China, given that Chinese nationalism is founded upon the sense of national humiliation suffered under Western and Japanese domination. In Tibet, road signs have been painted on stones bearing mantric inscriptions; window frames are built from ancient printing blocks; and monasteries have been rebuilt but stripped of their monk-teachers. These stand as the markers of conquest on the Tibetan landscape and reminders of its distant, alien rulers. Each time they announce the length of new roads they've constructed, the number of new airports opened or any other material improvements they've initiated, the government risks reminding people of the absence of construction in the cultural sphere. The Chinese government understands that cultural and religious respect are politically sensitive issues—this is evident from the care that is taken not to denigrate the religion of the Uyghurs, the Muslim people also seeking independence in northwest China. Yet this same care is never taken when it comes to abusing Tibetan Buddhism and its leader, and the statistical relationship between miles of roads built and the inner life and views of local people is never calculated.

Persuading the homeland audience

The fundamental problem in Tibet has been the inability of the Chinese government to establish good governance and appoint cadres who are attuned to the people. The government has set as its primary goal the life-or-death battle again separatism and the 'Dalai clique', and because of this, local politicians are required to repeat the appropriate slogans and demonstrate their anti-separatist zeal. But this does not generate good policy. It simply encourages the rise of competent cadres, since these are the only criteria needed for survival and promotion. This is not just a recent problem: ever since the anti-rightist campaign of the late-1950s, or even earlier in eastern Tibet, local Tibetan officials who could have achieved genuine accommodation between the Tibetan and Han Chinese people have been edged out of position. This too is a feature typical of colonial administrations, where legitimacy is created through public endorsement by local intermediaries and maintained through mass displays of native compliance. The denial of indigenous agency lies at the heart of this project, though it is typically presented as the opposite: the populace is portrayed as welcoming a foreign model of modernity.

Other political calculations are relatively clear. One is the priority of convincing a home audience of the validity of their actions—in this case, the Han Chinese—rather than the subjected people in the occupied area. Occupation is explained at home, whether the issue is Western imperialism, Israeli nationalism or Chinese policies in Tibet. The ritualized displays of power, ceremony and state symbolism are meant primarily to convince domestic constituencies of the legitimacy of their rule, rather than convincing the conquered people. Sometimes this is blatant, as in the articles that appear frequently in the Chinese press describing the equally frequent exhibitions on Tibet throughout China and the world—meant to demonstrate the evils of Tibetan life before the Chinese arrived in the 1950s. Those articles often feature a Chinese interviewee discussing how persuasive the exhibits were, rather than having a Tibetan confirm their authenticity. During the height of the protests in 2008, the government hastily launched a gory exhibition of historical Tibet in Beijing, and a Chinese visitor was quoted in *China Daily*, an official Party paper, as saying: 'I feel in the exhibition the barbarianism and darkness that permeated in old Tibet, and have a better understanding how the backward system of mixing politics and religion thwarted Tibet's development and progress.'[1] That the metropolitan centre needs to be persuaded of the merits of the colonizing mission indicates the uncertainty and anxiety underlying the entire colonizing project.

But this need to appease one's home audience can be marred by complications. After protests broke out in Tibet in March 2008, Chinese state television broadcast footage of Tibetans lashing out against innocent Chinese civilians in Lhasa and reported the death of shop workers. The same images and reports were broadcast repeatedly, arousing public wrath in

1   Xinhua, 'Tibet Exhibition Draws Appreciation from Visitors', *China Daily*, 5 May 2008. Available at *www.chinadaily.com.cn*.

China and among Chinese around the world against Tibetans. But the wave of support this created for the Chinese government and its subsequent crackdown also inflamed and validated ethnic antagonisms in China, further widening the gap between the Chinese and Tibetans. It also undid decades of rhetoric in China about the unity of nationalities and the harmony of society. Ethnic Chinese were also divided between aggressive nationalist and progressive elements: a group of leading Chinese intellectuals drafted a petition criticizing Beijing's response to the March protest, and the first point they urged on the government was to desist from one-sided propaganda. Zhang Boshu of the Philosophy Institute at the Chinese Academy of Social Sciences in Beijing wrote: 'Although the authorities are not willing to admit it', the problems in Tibet 'were created by the Chinese Communist Party itself as the ruler of China.'[2] These critics, however, risked being declared unpatriotic. A group of Chinese lawyers who publicly offered to provide legal defence for the Tibetans were arrested, visited by security officials and warned that their licenses would be revoked if they represented the Tibetans.

At the same time that the broadcasted images were exacerbating ethnic animosity within China, the authorities were also claiming that the unrest was the work of outside forces: the Dalai Lama, the CIA, CNN, the West in general or other institutions. To respond by deflecting blame is a strategy common to besieged administrations everywhere, from McCarthyism in 1950s America to anti-Islamic rhetoric in current times. At the most basic level, it is a way for the government to avoid answering questions about its own policies, and sometimes unites its core domestic constituents

2   Zhang Boshu, 'The Way to Resolve The Tibet Issue', *China Digital Times*, [22–28 April 2008] 8 May 2008. Available at *chinadigitaltimes.net*.

in nationalist anger against an outside enemy. But it also contains a more complex process: denying the other party—the 'natives'—of the capacity for reason, instead assuming them to be inherently violent in character. Like the knife-wielding, face-painted American Indians bent on destroying an armed garrison of Yankee soldiers in a cowboy film, the protester or the rebel has no mentality, no credible cause for protest. The spectators are not asked to consider why the natives are restless; instead, their violence is presumed to be inherent. The is as true in history as it is in fiction: the Boxer Rebellion of 1900, which is often cited as the first popular uprising against Western imperialism in China, was portrayed by the Western powers at the time as a racist programme by the cruel, heathen masses, from whom Western citizens had to be protected. This then justified the attack by the Western powers on China. In 2008, Chinese residents in Tibet were quoted as saying that they applauded the government-enforced patrolling of streets by armed police day and night, expressing a sentiment similar to what the Western press had reported of Westerners living in Beijing in 1901—order had been restored and life had returned to normal. But for whom? Today, citizens of Lhasa live under surveillance; their houses are searched; and every text produced, every piece of music recorded or downloaded via cellphone is liable to be examined for its ideological content. Every cadre has to attend countless meetings, is humiliated into recounting their life histories and forced to declare loyalty to the Party and the motherland. The central question is not raised: why are the sons and daughters of the 'liberated slaves' rising against the 'liberator'? 'Foreign instigation' and the 'inherent ethnic propensity for violence' have been the only answers provided.

The naturalization of native violence

This naturalisation of the Other's wild and primitive emotions also occurred in the West. In fact, Western imperialism depended on the deployment of words like 'heathen', 'barbarian' and 'savage' to describe the people of the lands they conquered. American conquest today avoids such language, even if the language of defending 'freedom' and 'democracy' has similar implications: that local peoples are incapable of maintaining their own projects of self-fulfilment. When China repeatedly describes Tibetans as 'slaves' or 'serfs', it authorizes the external management of their lives, ensures that ordinary Chinese citizens will view their government's actions as necessary acts of kindness, and reduces the Tibetan people to a primitive state.

Jiang Dasan, a retired PLA pilot who was stationed in the Qinghai region of eastern Tibet in the 1950s, recently recounted a tale on his blog that illustrates this view. He writes of an incident he witnessed after the generals stationed in the area realized that the initial attempt to win over local Tibetans through 'education' had failed, and so decided to invite Tibetan leaders to observe a bombing display by their air force. Upon seeing the fire power of the PLA air force, 'they really believed the PLA was "Heaven's Army". A few people couldn't take it and fainted, some urinated in their pants, and others shouted slogans at the top of their voice: "Long live the Communist Party! Long live Chairman Mao!"'[3] This account echoes those that have appeared in Western colonial literature describing the natives falling to their knees in submission, awestruck by the white man's techno-magical power. In this way, they are

---

3 Jiang Dasan, 'The Suppression of a Rebellion in Tibet', available at *chinadigitaltimes.net*.

reified as emotionally-driven simpletons without the capacity for reflection.

The principal explanation offered by the Chinese government for its response to the 2008 protests has been the unacceptable degree of violence perpetrated by the Tibetans. In an incident in Lhasa on March 14, a number of civilians—the official reports say nineteen—were killed, with twelve of those in fires set by rioters in Chinese shops (though no mention has been made in China of any Tibetans killed or injured by security forces). It's not clear if the arsonists had any idea that there were people hiding in the upper floors or backrooms of the shops, or that they were unable to escape. Even so, this incident cannot be compared to the religious or ethnic pogroms that have occurred in recent memory, as the Chinese media has claimed, such as the murder of hundreds of Muslims by Hindu zealots in Gujarat in 2002, or the ethnic cleansing that took place in Serbia, where crimes were meticulously planned weeks and months ahead, weapons imported from abroad and actions supported by hate propaganda. The 'Lhasa incident' was, like riots against migrants that occur in cities throughout the world, a crime of the urban dispossessed and a failure in the local political process, but it was handled by the Chinese media in a similar fashion to the way British sociologist Paul Gilroy described the aftermath of September 11: 'The deaths are prized according to where they occur and [ethnic marking] of the bodies involved'.[4] The deaths of Chinese shop workers were broadcast repeatedly on Chinese national television and overseas Chinese language stations, with little or no mention of the Tibetan shop workers who died in the same fires. When much larger riots broke out three months later in Wengan, Guizhou and inland China, even

4   Paul Gilroy, 'Raise Your Eyes', *open Democracy*, 11 September 2002. Available at *www.opendemocracy.net*.

Chinese bloggers wondered why the protestors in Lhasa had been demonized on national television as criminals, while in Wengan the local leadership was sacked, an investigation team sent to review local policies, and news of the incident scarcely reported in the official media at all.

As with all struggles of the powerless, the actual voices of Tibetans inside China are relatively unimportant and rarely broadcast; instead it is argued that they must be effects of other forces, whether these are foreign powers, natural disasters or ethnic characteristics. This argument has served the Chinese government well and aroused Chinese nationalistic sentiments. The Chinese community has in large part heeded their government's call to defend the motherland against the West. Today, every pro-Tibetan or human rights protest is answered with hundreds of Chinese counter-protests. Among Tibetan exiles, there have been similar persecution campaigns as well—just as a Chinese student at Duke University, Grace Wang, was attacked by her fellow countrymen as a traitor and vilified even in Chinese state-owned media for giving a hearing to Tibetans on campus, so have exiled Tibetans carried out their own vilification campaign against a young exiled Tibetan student at Harvard, who had spoken on American television in complex terms about the nuances of the current situation, without demonizing the Chinese as oppressors. Tibetan nationalists didn't want to hear the complexity of her arguments and launched a vicious attack on her and her family. Both cases demonstrated the thin dividing line between the two perspectives, both driven by prejudice and blind nationalism, and both exhibiting a crude anger in their choice of language.

Within China, the climate of opinion has changed as well. I received an email from a friend in Beijing saying that Tibetans were being fired from their jobs and that Chinese clientele were boycotting Tibetan restaurants in the city. Tibetan religious leaders and people are vilified daily in the Chinese media as backward and ungrateful. Many young Chinese abroad and those who escaped the aftermath of 1989 have joined in to support their government's actions and condemn the Tibetan protesters as looters and hooligans—the same words used to describe the student protesters of 1989. On blogs and at rallies, one can hear student leaders defaming the Dalai Lama and Buddhism in racist tones, for which they might have been charged under hate crime laws if the statements were about any other religion or religious leader. The Chinese media and cyberspace are filled with calls to 'kill' Tibetans, and such language is scarcely below the surface with officials as well. The Tibetan-language edition of *Tibet Daily*, the official Party paper in Tibet, frequently prints the words of Zhang Qingli, the Chinese official who is the Party Secretary and highest leader in Tibet. Zhang regularly uses extreme language and once told a German reporter: 'Those who do not love their country are not qualified to be human beings'.[5] I can only say that dehumanizing the opponent is a tactic used by all tyrants in legitimizing their own crimes.

The idea of the 'backward' Tibetan is deeply entrenched in the official state discourse on Tibet, as well as in the popular image of Tibetans amongst the Chinese. A Chinese student at Oxford University once said that what she found most interesting about Oxford was that there were Tibetan students at such an illustrious university. But this image of Tibetans as 'backward' has not prevailed throughout Chinese history. It is a relatively recent invention, and in fact, for the most part of

5 'Interview with Tibet's Communist Party Chief', *Spiegel Online*, 16 August 2006.

the past few centuries, the Chinese have been learning from the Tibetans, particularly in the areas of philosophy and religion. It was not uncommon for Tibetan monasteries to accommodate several dozen Chinese students, and this is increasingly the case today as well. The designation of Tibetans as 'backward' was precipitated by the conquest of Tibet, and is part of recasting the conquered people as an uncivilized people awaiting the gift of civilization from their conquerors.

Fifty years of this civilizing mission has left Tibetans and other minority groups with what social anthropologist Stevan Harrell calls a 'stigmatized identity'. Within China, it is a requirement for Tibetans to acknowledge their backwardness and praise the benevolent ruler in their speeches and writings; almost every published text opens with such invocations. Such ritual supplication is seen to legitimize the relationship. People become accustomed to performing their assigned roles in society, internalizing the logic that has made these roles appear natural and inescapable. As the social scientist Emily Yeh has shown, many Tibetans have come to believe the widely held claims that they are more idle than their Chinese counterparts, as if it were a feature of their genetic makeup—but every colonized people is persuaded of the deficiency of its own capacities in similar ways. And as we have seen, when the rhetoric no longer works, the actors protest, sometimes resorting to violence and shocking the rulers when they find that the docile and indolent natives have begun to speak, like a fish that has suddenly begun to utter words in front of ichthyologists.

The economic plea

The other theme common in Chinese reporting on Tibet is the amount of central government investment in the region. Over the past three decades, the Chinese government has injected huge sums of money in Tibet, much of it in infrastructure and construction. The investments in railroads, power stations and highways are evident in towns across the plateau. Yet these reports are not meant as factual descriptions of the construction, instead implying the generosity of the state or the Chinese people, the taxpayers. But it's not clear why a Tibetan would see a reason to be grateful to China, any more than a Chinese would feel grateful to the Japanese for building the railway in Manchuria or for industrializing the northeast region of their country. Gratitude is not a fact of economics but an effect of memory, and what Tibetans choose to remember and celebrate is an index of their own understanding of their history. In speaking about Nagorno-Karabakh, Galina Starovoitova, the murdred Russian politician and human right activist, criticized what she called 'the vulgarized economic arguments, like send some sausages to Karabakh and it will calm [the situation].' She then goes on to say that without a fundamental political solution of the issue, they proved ineffective.'[6]

The Tibetan unrest is a product of the paradox of modern China in which the attempt is made to create a nation out of an empire and construct the present from a past that they've rejected. In this process the government wants the people to passively accept its programme of modernization and its framing of Tibetan subjects as grateful natives. Hu Jintao's notion of a harmonious society is tantamount to a call for passivity on the part of the citizens. The economic and radical social changes are accepted as a facet of modern Tibet, yet the people do not acquiesce—they do not have a voice or a say in this transformation of their lives.

6   Galina Starovoitova, Interview transcribed by Ada Skonechnaya and Taina Tsypkina, Moscow: 1990.

Most commentators have argued that the underlying cause of recent protests in Tibet is economic disparity and the marginalization of Tibetans. The paradigm of economic development is the main discourse of modern China, where the core issues are growth, efficiency, productivity and consumption—and the benefits these can bring. Certainly, material well-being is crucial for any society. Vincent Tucker wrote: 'Without consideration of culture, which essentially has to do with people's control over their destinies, their ability to name the world in a way which reflects their particular experience, development is simply a global process of social engineering whereby the economically and militarily more powerful control, dominate, and shape the lives of others for their purposes'.[7] This is precisely what is happening in Tibet. For the Tibetans, the imposition of this economic paradigm has aroused resistance. The resistance is about the right to have a voice in the process. As long as their voice and dignity is denied, the reasons why people take to the streets will remain. China can and will be able to control the land through its ever-increasing might, but resentment among the people will be hard to erase. Removing the Dalai Lama's pictures and banning songs will not erase the reasons why people put up the photographs in the first place.

The Chinese government, riding a wave of nationalist fervour that it has fuelled with traditional colonial themes and images, will shift increasingly towards a hard-line agenda of control and rushed development as means of eliminating Tibetan opposition, thereby further alienating the Tibetan population. This scenario is already taking shape as the government moves to silence dissent and to demonize its

7   Vincent Tucker, 'Introduction: A Cultural Perspective on Development', in *Cultural Perspectives on Development*, London 1997, p. 4.

critics. The hardliners in the Party have advocated a military solution to the conflict and opposed any political settlement that is based on the devolution of power or a cultural analysis of the Tibetan situation.   Until the underlying issues of perception and language are resolved, until China listens to local voices and local memories are understood, it is unlikely that any progress will occur.

February–March 2009

Appendix

Twelve Suggestions for Dealing with the Tibetan Situation, by Some Chinese Intellectuals

Wang Lixiong and over 300 others

1. At present the one-sided propaganda of the official Chinese media is having the effect of stirring up inter-ethnic animosity and aggravating an already tense situation. This is extremely detrimental to the long-term goal of safeguarding national unity. We call for such propaganda to be stopped.[1]

2. We support the Dalai Lama's appeal for peace, and hope that the ethnic conflict can be dealt with according to the principles of goodwill, peace, and non-violence. We condemn any violent act against innocent people, strongly urge the Chinese government to stop the violent suppression, and appeal to the Tibetan people likewise not to engage in violent activities.

3. The Chinese government claims that 'there is sufficient evidence to prove this incident was organized, premeditated,

---

1   This petition was released by several leading Chinese intellectuals and writers on 22 March 2008 in response to Beijing's handling of protests that began in Lhasa on March 10 and eventually spread throughout the Tibetan region.

and meticulously orchestrated by the Dalai clique'. We hope that the government will show proof of this. In order to change the international community's negative view and distrustful attitude, we also suggest that the government invite the United Nations' Commission on Human Rights to carry out an independent investigation of the evidence, the course of the incident, the number of casualties, etc.

4. In our opinion, such Cultural Revolution-like language as 'the Dalai Lama is a jackal in Buddhist monk's robes and an evil spirit with a human face and the heart of a beast' used by the Chinese Communist Party leadership in the Tibet Autonomous Region is of no help in easing the situation, nor is it beneficial to the Chinese government's image. As the Chinese government is committed to integrating into the international community, we maintain that it should display a style of governing that conforms to the standards of modern civilization.

5. We take note of the fact that on the very day when violence first broke out in Lhasa (March 14), the government authorities in Tibet were already announcing that 'we possess ample evidence that the violence has been organized, plotted in advance, and meticulously orchestrated by the Dalai clique'. If so, then government authorities knew in advance that rioting was going to occur and yet did nothing to prevent it or to stop it from spreading. There should be a rigorous inquiry into the possibility of official involvement and malfeasance.

6. If, in the end, it cannot be shown that the events were organized, plotted in advance, and meticulously orchestrated [by the Dalai Lama] but emerges instead that they were a government-instigated 'popular revolt', then the officials who were responsible for instigating this

'revolt' and for sending false and deceptive reports about it to the central government and to the citizens of the country should be held to account. There should be conscientious reflection, and the learning of lessons, so that such things never happen again.

7. We strongly demand that the authorities not subject every Tibetan to political investigation or revenge. The trials of those who have been arrested must be carried out according to judicial procedures that are open, just, and transparent so as to ensure that all parties are satisfied.

8. We urge the Chinese government to allow credible national and international media to go into Tibetan areas to conduct independent interviews and news reports. In our view, the current news blockade cannot gain credit with the Chinese people or the international community, and is harmful to the credibility of the Chinese government. If the government sticks to true accounts of the events, it need not fear challenges. Only by adopting an open attitude can we turn around the international community's distrust of our government.

9. We appeal to the Chinese people and overseas Chinese to be calm and tolerant, and to reflect deeply on what is happening. Adopting a posture of aggressive nationalism will only invite antipathy from the international community and harm China's international image.

10. The disturbances in Tibet in the 1980s were limited to Lhasa, whereas this time they have spread to many Tibetan areas. This deterioration indicates that there are serious mistakes in the work that has been done with regard to Tibet. The relevant government departments must conscientiously reflect upon this matter, examine their failures, and fundamentally change the failed nationality policies.

11. In order to prevent similar incidents from happening in future, the government must abide by the freedom of religious belief and the freedom of speech explicitly enshrined in the Chinese Constitution, thereby allowing the Tibetan people fully to express their grievances and hopes, and permitting citizens of all nationalities freely to criticize and make suggestions regarding the government's nationality policies.

12. We hold that we must eliminate animosity and bring about national reconciliation, not continue to increase divisions between nationalities. A country that wishes to avoid the partition of its territory must first avoid divisions among its nationalities. Therefore, we appeal to the leaders of our country to hold direct dialogue with the Dalai Lama. We hope that the Chinese and Tibetan people will do away with the misunderstandings between them, develop their interactions with each other, and achieve unity. Government departments as much as popular organizations and religious figures should make great efforts toward this goal.

Wang Lixiong (Beijing, writer)
Liu Xiaobo (Beijing, freelance writer)
Zhang Zuhua (Beijing, scholar of constitutionalism)
Sha Yexin (Shanghai, writer, Chinese Muslim)
Yu Haocheng (Beijing, jurist)
Ding Zilin (Beijing, professor)
Jiang Peikun (Beijing, professor)
Yu Jie (Beijing, writer)
Sun Wenguang (Shangdong, professor)
Ran Yunfei (Sichuan, editor, Tujia nationality)
Pu Zhiqiang (Beijing, lawyer)

Teng Biao (Beijing, lawyer and scholar)
Liao Yiwu (Sichuan, writer)
Wang Qisheng (Beijing, scholar)
Zhang Xianling (Beijing, engineer)
Xu Jue (Beijing, research fellow)
Li Jun (Gansu, photographer)
Gao Yu (Beijing, journalist)
Wang Debang (Beijing, freelance writer)
Zhao Dagong (Shenzhen, freelance writer)
Jiang Danwen (Shanghai, writer)
Liu Yi (Gansu, painter)
Xu Hui (Beijing, writer)
Wang Tiancheng (Beijing, scholar)
Wen Kejian (Hangzhou, writer)
Li Hai (Beijing, freelance writer)
Tian Yongde (Inner Mongolia, rights activist)
Zan Aizong (Hangzhou, journalist)
Liu Yiming (Hubei, freelance writer)
Liu Di (Beijing)
and 338 others

Acknowledgements

This book originated in Wang Lixiong's essay, 'Reflections on Tibet', and Tsering Shakya's subsequent response and critique, 'Blood in the Snows', which both appeared in *New Left Review*. For this, the authors would first of all like to thank *NLR*'s editor at the time, Perry Anderson. That these writings are now accessible to English-language readers cannot be separated from the work of the translators and editors that were involved: Susan Chen, Xiaoyuan Liu, Lingxi Kong and Tianle Chang, who translated the chapters by Wang Lixiong; and Susan Watkins and David Shulman, who copy-edited or proofread at various stages. They would also like to thank the staff at Verso Books and Audrea Lim, their outstanding editor for this book, who has brought it much life and to whom they extend their sincere gratitude.

In addition, Tsering Shakya would like to thank Catriona Bass, Dechen Pemba, Robbie Barnett, Victoria Hui, Micheale Davies and David Hayes for their helpful comments all along the way.

Wang Lixiong would especially like to thank Woeser, who he writes of in one of the chapters and who later became his wife, for her part in changing his views on Tibet over the years. It was she who introduced him to Tibet's emotional world, inaccessible through research alone.